ART MAKING LIFE

ART MAKING LIFE
STUDIES IN HENRY JAMES

Sergio Perosa

Nick Jordan, in long
friendship,

Ugo

New York, Hanukkah, 2016

Welcome Rain Publishers
NEW YORK

*for former students
who became colleagues*

Contents

Foreword

I was first exposed to Henry James in the mid-1950s, when Carlo Izzo lectured on his novellas in the Foscari palace, overlooking the Grand Canal. I caught the virus. Since then I have been working and publishing on him: critical studies, editions, prefaces to half a dozen of his novels and collections, translations, essays and articles on various aspects of his fiction; some thirty titles altogether till now, and growing.

I gather here the essays which were originally published in English in the last twenty years in academic magazines, literary journals, proceedings of conferences, and collective volumes, most of them now hardly available. I left them stand (or fall) as they were, but corrected misprints, removed a few inaccuracies, brought up to date some annotations, with a modicum exchange between them and the texts. Some typographical features are those of the original essays: no strict uniformity has been enforced; occasional shifts from English to American spelling are due to the texts from which I'm drawing or quoting. I have inserted a few sentences here and there to clarify meaning, or to take into account recent scholarly and critical views. Some overlappings have emerged, but I left them, too, trimming them in just one or two cases: repetitions may prove useful, especially in different perspectives, and reveal what I then took and still take to be James's central concerns.

The book focuses on two or three main issues: his unfinished autobiography, his 'international theme' and views of Europe, and in particular Italy, his short fiction, his relations with other writers. It is meant to be read in, not necessarily through, jumping as dictated by the interest or whim of the moment. I feel that critical books should be readable and should be read in pleasure, not in cultural obligation or strain. Frequent and extensive quotations help in that direction: I still believe they work better than hefty explanations. I trust James would have nodded in approval.

This book was originally published in a limited edition as *Studies in Henry James* on the occasion of my eightieth birthday in the 'Collana del Dipartimento di Studi Linguistici e Culturali Comparati', Università Ca' Foscari Venezia, by Libreria Editrice Cafoscarina, 2013. Permission to publish it in this series is gratefully acknowledged.

S.P.

PART ONE

1 *The Fostered Imagination:*
A Small Boy and Others

> We will not anticipate the past!...
> Our retrospection will be all to the future.
>
> Mrs. Malaprop in Sheridan's *The Rivals*, IV, 2

1

A Small Boy and Others, which was to become the first volume of an "Autobiography" left unfinished at Henry James's death in the middle of the third volume, appeared after a long gestation in 1913. The following year, W. B. Yeats completed his *Reveries over Childhood and Youth.* Despite the profound differences between the American expatriate and the Anglo-Irish poet (who was also, however, somewhat of an 'expatriate' in London), there are striking resemblances and parallelisms in the two works.

Both lack a pre-ordained plan or narrative scheme, and follow the random, fragmentary and inconsequential upsurge of memories, images, recollections. Yeats declares it at the outset, and divides his comparatively short book into compressed, isolated, and discontinuous sections. For James, '[t]o knock at the door of the past was in a word to see it open for me quite wide', freeing, as from Aladdin's lamp, a flow of images, figures, places, and recollections that flooded the mind, the scene, and the pages themselves. In the next volume, *Notes of a Son and Brother*, he was to write of an auscultation of the past, and that he had to pull from its jaws the plum of memory. But in *A Small Boy and Others,* doctoral or surgical images of hardness and strain are totally out of place, images offer themselves easily and profusely,[1] so that eventually we have 'a tale of assimilations small and fine'.

Yeats moves from childhood scenes to minute, and sometimes confused, family details and cross-genealogies, descriptions of relatives (uncles and aunts, but mostly his grandparents) who would determine his future in a complex web of influences, and to his earliest artistic and literary discoveries. James proceeds in a similar way: he, too, betrays loneliness and fears, a precocious sense of instability, the joy and partially the pain of the complete freedom he is allowed to enjoy. Both move from place to place, from one country to another.

Both their fathers—an artist, in the case of Yeats, an unconventional thinker and philosopher in that of James—make sure that their sons are given complete freedom from religious bonds, institutions, and regular schools, from work and expectations of bourgeois success. Neither is occupied in getting on, in 'improving books' or habits: their only application is in imagination and sensibility. They are unfitted for most 'average' occupations, practical aims and ideals, for any 'profession' in the common sense of the word. Yeats's father detests merchants and shopkeepers; James's is at the head of a family that for two generations have been guiltless of a stroke of business (pp. 49-50, 56-58). 'My father—Yeats writes—had brought me up never when at school to think of the future or of any practical results'.[2] Both children have to suffer

---

[1]   'I feel that at such rate I remember too much'; 'I lose myself, of a truth, under the whole pressure of the spring of memory', *Henry James's Autobiography*, ed. Frederick W. Dupee, London, Allen, New York, Criterion Books, 1956, pp. 54, 131 (henceforth page references in the text). See also James's letter to his nephew: 'I get on, distinctly, with my work—the only trouble is that the whole retrospect & all my material come to me, flow vividly in, in *too great* abundance ... the only thing is to *let* everything, even *make every*thing, come & flow, let my whole consciousness & memory play in the past as it will', 23-26 December 1911, quoted in Michael Millgate, *Testamentary Acts. Browning, Tennyson, James, Hardy*, Oxford, Clarendon Press, 1992, p. 92.

[2]   W. B. Yeats, *Autobiographies,* London, Macmillan, 1966, p. 55 (page references henceforth in the text).

among friends on this account; both are cut off from actual performance and cut out for perplexity.

They are encouraged to develop their minds, to educate their 'senses', to cultivate and foster their imagination: in the 'free play of the mind', indeed in the riot or revel of 'the visiting mind' (as James wrote, p. 16), they can fulfill the aspiration *to be*, rather than *do*. The frequent moves to which they are subjected—Yeats from Sligo to Dublin and then to London, i.e. from a country-seat to a provincial, then to a cosmopolitan capital, James from Albany, the starting point of the family, to New York, to Brighton, Newport, and finally to Europe—are a means to those ends. Sounds, odors, colors, phantasmagorias of different sensations and images, mark their childhood imagination. Yeats forms and exalts himself in the exercise of a 'wandering mind', eager for flights, excuses and evasions from reality; more than once, James insists on his processes of gaping, dawdling, dodging, removing himself from the hubbub of life, standing aside, being an onlooker. One writes of *reveries*, the other of *flâneries*, of an insisted-upon and sought-for detachment: James *riots and revels*, as we saw, in the 'visiting mind'; 'What was *I* thus, within and essentially, what had I ever been and could I ever be but a man of imagination at the active pitch?' (p. 455).

For both of them, contemplation, day-dreaming, the stimulation and cultivation of sensibility, artistic and otherwise, an existence 'floating in the midst of the actual', opening itself to reality, as it were, rather than creating or dominating it, substitutes for direct involvement in life, for practical purposes or engagements. What matters is their reactions to places, peoples, books: their field of action is the sphere of the ineffectual, of the indirect or 'second application' (as James calls it in his *Prefaces*). In this perspective, their endless peregrinations and moves result in a liberation from provincialism (Irish, in one case, American, in the other), and from family ties, mild and loose as they may be: both play crucial games with the interrelation and interpenetration of inner and outer worlds, which prove essential to the nature and future role of the artist.

There are of course differences between Yeats's physical activism
and James's detachment from the world; between the outdoor sports,
riding and sailing, loves and visions, in which the former revels, and
which the latter denies himself; between the romantic enthusiasms of
the poet and the sober skepticism of the future novelist of manners. In
Yeats, everything leads to a poetic calling or vocation; in James, it is
the literary imagination that is fostered. Yet in both cases there is a programmed urge—self-induced as well as encouraged by their environment—towards an artistic vocation. Both *A Small Boy and Others* and
Reveries over Childhood and Youth are texts that embody the discovery
and the history of a developing imagination, of an artistic consciousness
in fieri. James speaks explicitly of reconstituting 'the history of my fostered imagination', of recording 'the imaginative faculty under cultivation' (p. 65 and 454, just as in the Preface to *The Portrait of a Lady* he
had considered the possibility of writing 'the history of the growth of
one's imagination'); he registers a process of growth that reflects self-
discovery and the discovery of the world of art.

Both their Autobiographies, then, can be properly read and considered
as peculiar expositions of the imaginative growth of a literary genius,
seen and presented—according to the autobiographical mode—from the
height of achieved success, with no pre-conceived wish to codify, orga-
nize, *explain*, but rather following the easy, erratic, discontinuous, sometimes deceitful, and in all cases peremptory upsurge of images and memoirs. James's way of proceeding, in particular, is Proustian:[3] the flow of

---

[3]   *Du côté de chez Swann* was published in 1914: James may have known it, Yeats
      certainly did. An article in the *TLS* of December 4, 1914, compared it with *A Small
      Boy and Others* (see Adeleine Tintner, 'Autobiography is Fiction: The "Usurping
      Consciousness" as Hero in James's Memoirs', in *Twentieth Century Literature*, 23
      (1977), p. 239-60, p. 252 in particular, who examines some possible analogies). In
      order to find a nineteenth-century prototype of a discontinuous, desultory, 'jumping'
      autobiography, one may resort to De Quincey's *Confessions of an English Opium
      Eater* (1822 edition), in particular to the 'Preliminary Confessions' of Part I. In De
      Quincey, however, the upsurge and the superimposition of memoirs and sensations,
      are not so much due to literary, psychological or existential motivations, as to the

recollections is released under the pressure of the spring of memory, which is unpredictable, unstoppable, uncontrollable. As in the beginning of *Du côté de chez Swann*, what matters is the first contact of an adolescent with the world—the happiest and most fruitful moment of an initially sketchy re-appropriation of the past. What both writers added to their first volumes of reminiscences—*Notes of a Son and Brother* in the case of James, 'The Trembling of the Veil', 'Dramatis Personae', *et al.*, in the case of Yeats, which only later on did contribute to form their 'Autobiographies'—does not seem to me to be up to their previous standards. And it is perhaps no mere chance or coincidence that *A Small Boy and Others* ends with a lapse of consciousness at Boulogne, while Yeats in the final section of *Reveries over Childhood and Youth* would write: 'when I think of all the books I have read, and of the wise words I have heard spoken, and of the anxiety I have given to parents and grandparents, and of the hopes that I have had, all life weighed in the scales of my own life seems to me a preparation for *something that never happened*' (p.68, my italics).

The later 'I', trying to link and mingle itself with the lost 'I' of the past in order to recapture it, jumps over the abyss of time and seems to cancel the temporal distance; but spanning the abyss of time makes one dizzy, jeopardizes one's balance, induces a sort of mental void which is a counterpoint to the plenitude which is attained though memory.[4]

---

mental dérèglement of the senses and the mind induced by laudanum. The distinction is of paramount importance, although Georges Poulet (*Mesure de l'instant*, quoted in Alide Cagidemetrio, *Fictions of the Past,* Amherst, Massachusetts U. P., 1992, p. 80) remarks that it was De Quincey's romantic sensibility that fostered new concepts of a time totality in simultaneous experience of past memories and present perceptions.—Roy Pascal, too, in his *Design and Truth in Autobiography*, Cambridge, Harvard U. P., 1960, had dealt with some parallelisms between James's *A Small Boy and Others* and Yeats's *Reveries over Childhood and Youth.*

[4]   We may note here that De Quincey's *Confessions,* too, end on a generalized loss of consciousness, on his abandoning himself to the startling, upward and downward spirals, and on a torpor of the mind. A characteristic shared by these Autobiographies (including their prototype, Wordsworth's *The Prelude,* which was aimed at re-

All this—the striking parallelisms with Yeats's *Reveries over Child-hood and Youth*, the joy and the disorientation of a partial, fragmentary, and suspended recapture of the past—is all the more remarkable in that James (to stay with him now) started from totally different premises and with remarkably different purposes. His 'Autobiography' was not only born against his expectations and his avowed aversion to self-revelation; it grew out of a revealing dislocation of a different intention, or indeed commitment: to write a memory of, or a testimonial to, his brother William, the world-famous philosopher who had died in 1910.

2

After the death of William, to whom he had been linked by a long, loving relation, more than one literary misunderstanding, and some rivalry, James had promised his sister-in-law Alice to write a 'Family book' based on William's letters, papers, and activities—according to a well-established nineteenth-century pattern. But these were difficult times for him: the poor financial returns of the New York Edition of his Novels and Tales, on which he had lavished endless efforts and tiring care, brought with it bouts of depression, possibly a nervous breakdown. He was in poor health, suffering from shingles, and had some difficulties in writing. When in the fall of 1911 he set down to write the 'Family book', according to the testimony of his typist, Theodora Bosanquet, he let himself go to the flow of memories: 'let my whole conscience and memory play on the past', he enjoined himself—he could trim, reduce, and eliminate later.[5]

---

tracing 'the growth of a poet's mind') is a continuous redrafting and re-elaboration of the material, their textual, compositional, and to some extent mental or psychological, instability.

[5]   See Theodora Bosanquet, *Henry James at Work,* The Hogarth Essays, 1924, rpt. Freeport, NY, Books for Libraries, 1970; Millgate, pp. 92-3 (also for what follows). Millgate and Carol Holly, *Intensely Family. The Inheritance of Family Shame and*

This indulgence in the flow of memories entails and determines a gradual removal of William from the scene (James rationalized in a letter to his nephew that 'This whole record of early childhood simply *grew* so as one came to write it that one could but let it take its way'). The titles he had tentatively chosen (*Earliest Memories: Egotistic* and *Earliest Memories: Altruistic*) reflected this dichotomy only partially; what is undeniable is that young Henry took pride of place: 'I daresay I did instinctively regard [the book] at last as all *my* truth, to do what I would wish', he wrote in a letter.[6] Countless pages have been devoted to accounting for this removal of William from the scene, on his marginalization. Henry claimed or pretended that, first, he had to recreate a family atmosphere or ambience, and, secondly, that in order to use William's letters and papers, he had to provide a harmonious frame. But it has been variously observed that James's was a total appropriation of the scene, as well as of the past; in the later volumes, too, William appears rather marginally, and Henry's 'usurping consciousness' (the definition is from the Preface to *The Awkward Age*) settles itself at the center of things and acts in the first person mainly for its own, private, egotistical purposes. We have then the tale of the first steps in the education of an artist—Henry, of course, not William—with all the qualifying traits of an *auto*biography.

As I intimated, James had often declared an opposition to biography, autobiography, and the personal mode or utterance. On at least two occasions he had burned his personal papers (most notably in 1909 he had made a 'gigantic bonfire' of them); as Shakespeare had done, he threw a curse on anyone (the 'post-mortem exploiter') daring or attempting to write his life; in the Preface to *The Ambassadors* he had condemned 'the terrible *fluidity* of self-revelation'; in a polemical exchange of let-

---

the *Autobiographies of Henry James*, Madison, Wisconsin U. P., 1995, emphasize James's poor mental and physical conditions while writing them.

6   *The Letters of Henry James*, ed. Percy Lubbock, New York, Scribner's, 1920, 2 vols., II, pp. 346-47. It is noteworthy that Lubbock presented James's letters from 1869, the year when his Autobiography came to an end.

ters with H. G. Wells he had insisted on the requirement not to speak
directly of one self and dismissed 'the accurst autobiographic form'.[7]

Yet an autobiographical impulse is detectable in his *Notebooks* (notably in the 'American Journals' of 1881-83 and 1904-05), and is more
and more at work as James approaches his last years, in 'The Turning Point of my Life' (1900-01, *Complete Notebooks,* pp. 437-38, see
note 8), for instance. On previous occasions, too, he had shown a similar
tendency to appropriate somebody else's rightful material for his own,
personal uses. When just a few years before he had unwittingly accepted
to write a biography of the expatriate sculptor William Wetmore Story
according to the customary 'Life and Letters' form, he ended up by
pushing him aside, and by making up for the allegedly scanty material
at hand with 'my own little personal memories, inferences, evocations
and imaginations'. Writing about a historical personage, he felt free (or
compelled) not only to *invent* a book, but to give way to 'free imaginings', so that eventually he ended up—as his friend Henry Adams
remarked—by writing 'the history of [their own, rather than Story's]
generation', '—pure autobiography—': Story's expatriation and artistic
fate were used, that is, to define a personal adventure—the question of
expatriation itself, the gain and loss of being an expatriate.

In that book, the crucial question was one's relationship with Europe
and expatriation. James's splendid reportage on the forsaken mother-
country, which he revisited after a twenty-year absence, *The American
Scene* (1907), was centered on his 'poet's quarrel' with it—a rather autobiographical coming to terms with his life and his existential choice.
It has been noted that the *Notebook* entries in which James registered
his first impact with childhood places already betrayed that elegiac and
painful, enigmatic and revealing, accretion of personal remembrances
that was to characterize his Autobiography in a few years, including a
sense of displacement and vertigo. These earlier texts were already a

---

[7]   For more details and more statements to this effect, see Holly, pp. 90-93, and, for
        what follows, Millgate, pp. 76-77, in particular.

journey in search of a national and personal past: 'Everything sinks in; nothing is lost', he wrote in the *Notebooks*, so that he could plunge '[his] hand, [his] arm, *in*, deep and far, and up to the shoulder—into the heavy bag of remembrance—of suggestion—of imagination—of art', much in the same way as in the Autobiography. And, again, it has been widely remarked that James's well-known Prefaces to the New York Edition of his work (1907-09) are also a reconstruction of the very personal story of an artist. (Theodora Bosanquet, his amanuensis, remembered that they were dictated 'in the tone of personal reminiscence', and James himself, in the Preface to *The Golden Bowl*, summed up the experience as 'this infinitely interesting and amusing *act* of re-appropriation'). Even in his latest essays, and in particular in his essay on Shakespeare's *The Tempest*, Millgate has detected a strong autobiographical flavor.[8]

In order to write his 'Family book' James plunged into an uncertain past, and so his act of voluntary surrender to the flow of memories and associations turned *A Small Boy and Others* into a typical childhood autobiography, whose development reveals the growth of an artist's imagination. The 'I' of 1911-13 evokes or recreates the 'I' of the boy in the past and, according to the autobiographical code, he achieves a second, therapeutic result. The very act of revisiting the past allows him to overcome his psychological, physical and mental difficulties, 'the heritage of woe of the last three years'. *A Small Boy and Others* restores James's ability as a writer: the text that went to form his Autobiography can indeed be seen as his last literary masterpiece, in a period when he faced almost a writer's block in dealing with his fictional material, as for instance in *The Ivory Tower* and *The Sense of the Past*, two novels which were left unfinished. (Incidentally, *A Small Boy and Others* and *Notes of a Son and Brother* elicited a far greater response and success

---

[8]   *The Complete Notebooks,* eds Leon Edel and Lyall H. Powers, New York, Oxford U. P., 1987, p. 237, and p. 242; Millgate, pp. 89-90. See also Daniel Stempel, 'Biography as Dramatic Monologue: Henry James, W. W. Story, and the Alternative Vision', *New England Quarterly*, 62 (1989), pp. 224-47; William Hoffa, 'The Final Preface: Henry James's Autobiography', *Sewanee Review*, 77 (1969), pp. 277-93.

in the press and in the market than his preceding works, on which he lavished painstaking efforts.)

That, moreover, the conscience of the narrating 'I' expands itself profusely on that of the narrated 'I', and that the protagonist in the past is made to re-appropriate voraciously every childhood experience, be it egotistical or altruistic, bears testimony to the fact that a typical autobiographical principle is at work here, in a book in which the old Master lets himself go without restraint to a self-reconstruction and a self-definition. That the 'I' of 1911-13 superimposes itself on the 'I' in the past, and that this in turn is presented as a budding artist in terms of the writer writing about him, provides further evidence of an autobiographical code which by definition entails a joining together of past and present.

Freud has reminded us in *Beyond the Pleasure Principle* that the individual is 'obliged to *repeat* repressed material as a contemporary experience instead of…remembering it as something belonging to the past', and this, even outside the Freudian context, proved a liberating experience for James, on the personal as well as the artistic level.[9] Or, as Mrs. Malaprop puts it in Sheridan's play *The Rivals*, in one of her notorious malapropisms, which is however perfectly to the point here: 'our retrospection will be all to the future'.

Even in the very texture of James's book one can easily detect the 'I' of today (1911-13) observing, scrutinizing, scanning and projecting the 'I' of the past, and creating thereby not only a double perspective, but a *double exposure*: in general, the image of the child is vividly and precisely conveyed in his acts, sensations, urges, discoveries, but in some cases it is obscured, muddled, confused, blurred, and only gradually is it revealed and focused as a recognizable entity. The act of writ-

---

[9]   See Cagidemetrio, p. 182: the solution of an upsetting past is in remembering, 'since remembering both frees the individuals, and connects them to the past'. See also Ross Posnock, *Trial of Curiosity. Henry James, William James, and the Challenge of Modernity*, New York, Oxford U. P., 1991, ch. 7 ('James foregrounds both the "strain of holding the I together", and the suspension of that obligation', p. 185).

ing combines vision and subsequent recognition, far-away glimmerings and gained awareness. No wonder that the boy must take in, or take into himself, engulf and introvert, the Other (including his brother William) and that this conjuror over the abyss of time must indulge in what is primarily a self-narration—the autobiography of the childhood education of an artist.

3

James's narration can be defined as the history of a 'generation', both in an individual and personal sense (being born or generated as a child and as an artist), and in the general sense of a period that is defined by temporal, environmental, social and community bonds. He can be said to evoke his past according to a compositional pattern of 'accretions', substituting to cause-and-effect sequentiality the casualness of free associations, which only in time will acquire representational value, much in the way of De Quincey's *Confessions* (or indeed of Proust). The past recovered as a palimpsest of impressions and experiences is 'alive' and 'in action' because it is mainly pursued or reflected on psychological states that make it coexist with the experience of remembering. To an 'objective' representation of the past James substitutes—or intermingles—a representation of the 'I' in the process of taking in, absorbing, the past, perceiving the process of its manifestation, so as to recreate it for the purposes of an autobiographical discourse.

The past is recaptured through the consciousness of the present, as one of its constituent parts, while it is the *cono d'ombra* (the cone of darkness, or of light) projected by the present that allows for its manifestations and epiphanies. In the 1905 *Notebook* entries James had written of the 'heavy bag of remembrance' in which to plunge deep and far, but where one could meet 'the ineffable … cold Medusa-like face of life, of all the life *lived*', and had given vent to a sense of joy mixed with misgivings. There he had recognized the *dis*continuity of the process of remembering, the fleeting, at times tormenting nature of his material. *Basta, basta,* was his final invocation.[10]

In *A Small Boy and Others* the past is pursued and recaptured through a single procedure: letting oneself go to the flow of images, impressions and experiences in the past—a 'letting go' that James had resisted throughout his life and artistic career, though with some occasional lapses in wishing the contrary.[11] The 'letting go' is at first a partial or temporary renunciation of 'composition'—that composition that he had cherished and pursued as the chief aim of all his works—and a surrender to the flow or multiplication of aspects, to the 'swarm' of impressions and recollections that crowd the mind and the scene. Pursuing and following memories and associations is the primary structure of the book, also because, as we know, James dictated his text to the typist as a *continuum.* This succession and overlapping of images, aspects, recollections, constitutes the material and the texture of his autobiographical act. To sort them out or to catalogue them critically would be to go against the very essence of the mnemonic, narrative, and literary procedure that he finally adopted with such a sense of final relief, despite his previous misgivings.

---

[10] *Complete Notebooks,* pp. 237-40. This aspect—reinforced by the sense of freedom and detachment enjoyed by the protagonist (see below)—is what radically distinguishes *A Small Boy and Others* from James Joyce's *A Portrait of the Artist as a Young Man*: a text one could be tempted to pair off with Henry James's text, but which is motivated and sustained by an absolute finality and ultimate direction (with the only possible exception of the very beginning). Joyce's discourse develops through a series of rigorous and well-defined psychological, existential, and above all *intellectual* acquisitions.

[11] See, for instance, his *Notebook* entry for July 13, 1891: 'The upshot of all such reflections is that I have only to let myself *go*! So I have said to myself all my life … Yet I have never fully done it … it seems the formula of my salvation, of what remains to me of a future … The way to do it—to affirm one's self *sur la fin* … Go on, my boy, and strike hard; have a long and rich St. Martin's Summer' etc. (*Complete Notebooks*, pp. 57-58).

Yet some tentative disentangling may prove useful (especially in view of my concluding remarks), such as a primary distinction to be made between what has to do with the small boy and what pertains to the 'others', though one must keep in mind that the two really intersect, converge and overlap a great deal.

The small boy is caught and presented (sometimes even in the third person, as if he were someone else) as always 'open' to experiences and receptive as a sponge: from the beginning he indulges in *flâneries*, hanging back, dawdling, dodging, gaping; everything is a spectacle to him. Yet from the beginning his basic activity is to 'take in', absorb, assimilate, and understand (according to the very first meaning of the term), but also to take in, in the sense of internalize, 'incorporate' and digest. It is a process of surrender to exterior suggestions which becomes a form of inner absorption, of appropriation and possession, both of his world and the conscience of 'others', of seizing power, as a necessary postulate for his process of growth. Revisiting the past is a form of conquest, of appropriation, not only by memory but by the voracious and imperious self: he converts to his own uses unintended things.[12] In either sense, the process is dynamic, strongly motivated, on a system of relations that are instead weak, dangling, loose: the *free* flow of images, the *flâneries,* his dawdling and gaping, his standing aside or hanging back.

The small boy's relations within his relatives is equally open and loose: family relations offer a wide network, but a psychological disconnection obtains within. He is a *hotel* child, with no real home: the house in Albany is for vacations, those in New York are transient abodes, in a suspended condition. One school follows another, but the boy lives

---

[12] 'All but inexpressible—he writes—the part played, in the young mind naturally even though perversely, even though inordinately, arranged as a stage for the procession and exhibition of appearances, by matters all of a usual cast, contacts and impressions not arriving at the dignity of shocks, but happening to be to the taste, as one may say, of the little intelligence, happening to be such as the fond fancy could assimilate' (*Complete Notebooks,* p. 105).

for and by himself: there is no real commitment or obligation. Getting to Europe is in order to 'get such a better sensuous education than they are likely to get here' (as Henry James, Sr., had written in a letter to R. W. Emerson, which Henry, Jr., slightly emends in the book: 'such a sensuous education as they can't get here'). No one in the family, as we saw, has anything to do with business. There is no political sense until the Civil War, the public scene is a blank; the social void of New York itself, when New York was no more than a village, allows for freedom and romance: James speaks of 'felicities of destitution'. It is a past with strangely Arcadian and ambiguously Edenic connotations; according to a stereotype of the American tradition, it leads to introspection, to the revel of the visiting mind. Broadway appears as an alley of Eden, the 'vacant lot' north of the town remains so through the years, goats and pigs show up round the corner.

The very resources of a still young American world appear loose and disconnected in that context, contemplation and observation take the place of active life. Cut off from activity and direct participation, the small boy is led to imagining, to the 'free play of the mind', to 'assimilations small and fine', to a 'fostered imagination'. He lives introspectively, within himself, that is, despite the immense freedom he enjoys. James himself marvels at the few points in which he seems to have touched constituted reality, which in recollection takes on dusty or hazy colorations. His pre-ordained and predictable detachment determines, then and now, an 'inward perversity' that turns to its own use purposeless and vain things. Thus a subtly indirect, purely individual, and, as we shall see in a moment, artistic vision predominates: actuality is 'transformed' or 'converted' by the inner life.

This is indeed the vision that prepares for the Jamesian artist, for the exercise of sensibility and artistic expression, ultimately of writing. *A Small Boy and Others* becomes the narration of a self that predisposes itself to artistic endeavor: but this is where the *outer* swarm of images and impressions, the spectacle of the world, actuality, the 'others', who surround and condition the individual, become of paramount importance. The mind of the child is the pivot for absorbing and revealing history and society, objects, places, and people: hence the sprouting, indeed the breakthrough, of the artist.

4

For the small boy, relatives are the first manifestations of the world: different ethnic genealogies, definite but rather confused relatives, a sense of belonging but also of instability and uncertainty—early deaths, broken lives, unfulfilled promises: 'we wholesomely breathed inconsistency and ate and drank contradictions' (p. 124). Old New York appears as a village in the wilderness—at once bucolic and squalid: this is why, perhaps, James maintains that 'To look back at all is to meet the apparitional and to find in its ghostly face the silent stare of an appeal. When I fix it, the hovering shade, whether of person or place, it fixes me back and seems the less lost' (p. 54). He is rescuing the past on which people and places are waiting to be 'less lost': New York is still an eighteenth-century town, Broadway, Washington Square, 14th Street, are both a peaceful neighborhood and a confusion of coaches, a homely ground and the sparkling theater of the world. James proves a writer of New York, not New England. For once, we have him adhering almost passionately to his American past thanks to a kind of Proustian way of remembering: a sound or a smell, an image or an impression, release the flow of recollections—and, as with Proust, we only have to read and re-live them with him.

In New York the small boy has the first glimpse of 'art'—Shakespeare and *Uncle Tom's Cabin,* artificer and artifact,—and indirectly of history: the revolution in Paris, the Mexican War, fugitive slaves. Art, however, is in popular theaters, illustrated books (both classic and contemporary); in imposing living figures, such as Emerson, Poe, Irving—Dickens, above all, as a primary impression, that might have led, later on, to an anxiety of influence.[13] From writers, illustrators, and painters (an endless string of them appears in the book), young Henry got his precious and precocious 'sense of Europe', first experienced through intermediaries from abroad—*Punch*, actors, governesses, even the mountebanks—and then directly on the European soil itself.

History and Art gradually become two final goals and climaxes: the outbreak of the Civil War is evoked towards the end of the book, while the discovery of (indeed, the 'passage to') Style is enacted at the Paris Louvre. For Art, the most meaningful interference—possibly emphasized by the narrating 'I', by elderly James deeply rooted as he was by then in England—is represented and provided precisely by the sense and the attraction of Europe. A great deal of the inner dynamics of *A Small Boy and Others* seems to lie in the dialectical tension between the adhesion to the lost world of early America (rescued and recovered through memory), and the birth *in it* of the desire for Europe.

That from the very beginning James contrasts the American 'natural' state with the 'formal' state of Europe, that he finds the smell of London in books and the odor of Italy in the pictures he is shown, that he drinks the venom of Europe in the names themselves, and sees his detached condition at home as a push to expatriation, may be construed as a reflection of later (1911-13) convictions on early indecisions. James's apprehension of Paris from the hotel balcony seems modeled on Lambert Strether's in *The Ambassadors*; and it has been noted that the *romance of travel* which is so present in *A Small Boy and Others* contrasts markedly with the feelings of dissatisfaction and unease, even partial refusal, that are found in his letters home during his early travels. Yet the recollections of New York widen in the book to include the first leanings

---

[13]   See also *Complete Notebooks*, p. 238, where in 1905 James writes of the *emotion* left with him by Dickens and of '*l'imitation première* (the divine, the unique)' 'in the ghostly old C[ambridge]' of 1864-65. Yet in the same year he published a rather critical review of *Our Mutual Friend*, which put Dickens at a rather safe distance.— Other writers whose presence became meaningful for him at that time were Harriet Beecher Stowe, Thackeray, George Sand and George Eliot.

towards Europe, where the 'draughts of the wine of perception' seem more generous, in retrospect, and where the bridges seem to lead to more things than at home. (Incidentally, a curious aspect is that France, Switzerland, England, are presented as essentially rural in the book, still leading a pastoral life, as in the forest of Arden, whereas New York, despite its primitive conditions, retains more urban characteristics.)

In this embryo of an international contrast, aesthetic evolution finds its completion in the pictures and in Style, where the previously detached perceptions, or rather glimpses, of Art coalesce.[14] From the beginning the small boy has been interested in the 'scene', the 'drama', the 'picture': these are the great metaphors of James's later artistic and fictional renderings. In the theaters (and at home) young Henry has learned that life can be 'made' or 'produced': even in popular books, pictures, and plays he has plucked those 'artistic gems' which would bear fruit when the protagonist makes his leap towards style and art. Retrospectively, this leap is taken abroad and in the very Temple of Art, in the Galerie d'Apollon at the Louvre, which provides the crucial and conclusive adventure of the book.

The episode has been profusely discussed and commented upon, especially by biographers and Jamesian critics of the 1990s. In his later age—probably around 1910, according to Leon Edel's reconstruction—James had experienced a dream adventure, a nightmarish experience or 'immense hallucination' directly connected with the Galerie d'Apollon, which he chose to insert in a crucial position towards the end of *A Small*

---

[14] Here is the *Passage to Style*: 'It was as if they [the pictures] had gathered there into a vast deafening chorus; I shall never forget how…they filled those vast halls with the influence rather of some complicated sound, diffused and reverberant, than of such visibilities as one could directly deal with … They only arched over us in the wonder of their endless golden riot and relief, figured and flourished in perpetual revolution, breaking into great high-hung circles and symmetries of squandered picture … This comes to saying that in those beginnings I felt myself most happily cross that bridge over to Style constituted by the wondrous Galerie d'Apollon' (pp. 195-96). The whole experience has an uncanny connotation in itself, even regardless of the spectral apparition (see below).

Boy and Others, with a dramatic rupture of temporal levels; and yet, the experience is blended into the narrative as if taking place simultaneously with childhood memories. In this episode, he frightens, scares, defeats, and puts to flight a spectral apparition who tried to frighten him, and that he not only keeps at bay, but routs—turning the tables, as it were, on a ghost which retreats into the dreamy perspective of the Galerie. It is a clear example of mixing what happened after with what went before, of an insertion of the future into the past (a procedure not at all unusual in autobiographies).[15]

Many interpretations have been suggested: a fundamental one, in my view, given the setting and the connections, and James's choice to insert the episode at this point, is certainly the artist's victory over the figures besetting his imagination, crowding his soul, haunting his mind. James, that is, chooses to seal the destiny of the small boy under the form of a nightmare and a hallucination wittingly overcome. The discovery of the world surrounding him, of art and history (the outbreak of the Civil War is placed very close to this episode), gives way to the willful self-assertion of a budding artist who triumphs over the anxiety of a spectral world, that for the rest of his life would be his doom and his challenge.

In the final chapter, *A Small Boy and Others* closes on an illness and a loss of conscience in Boulogne, the news of a financial crisis in the U. S., and the assault of the local and social aspects of Europe, of her aesthetic, historical, and cultural fullness, of her abundance of signs and signification. Everything here represents more than it appears; the Victorian presences betray a crucial *combination* of history, literature, and society: it is a global situation and a complexity that the small boy and prospective

---

[15]   However, James had related a similar dream/nightmare experienced in his youth to Ottoline Morrell, in which he had also defied, pursued, and frightened away a monster at the far end of a 'gallery': see *Memoirs of Lady Ottoline Morrell*, ed. Robert Gathorne-Hardy, New York, Knopf, 1964, pp. 139-40, and Holly, pp. 47-48 and passim, for a discussion of the two episodes; Leon Edel, *Henry James: The Untried Years*, Philadelphia, Lippincott, 1963, pp. 74-80, interprets the experience as Henry's fighting the overhanging 'ghost' of his brother William.

artist has to confront. Once the ghosts of the mind have been defeated, a new challenge looms large: the artist will have to exercise all his power and his control over a baffling but *constituted* world.

5

Some further considerations are in order here. Despite James's initial, and indeed protracted, 'letting go', his surrender to the flow of images, impressions, and recollections, they were held together by the golden thread of the youthful education of a prospective artist. And towards the end of the book, James begins to 'compose' his narration in such a way as to discountenance the 'letting go', the 'no plotted thing at all', and to set into relief the pivotal moment of his 'education': his passage to Europe, his separation from his family, the struggle with the nightmare that represents the price to be paid for any artistic achievement.

Both in the text and extra-textually, James reveals that he is aware of the 'visionary liberties' he constantly took either with chronology, or by omitting, transposing, and conflating episodes: 'I couldn't do without the *scene*', he writes (p. 434; or, as he put it in the *Autobiography*, 'the picture was after all in essence one's aim'). Elsewhere he was to speak of strategies of compensation and transposition; in *Notes of a Son and Brother* he would take liberties with the very text of his brother's (and father's) letters, and with some facts; in *The Middle Years* he admitted 'sincerities of emphasis and "composition"; perversities, idiosyncrasies, incalculabilities' (p. 558). The free-flowing memories were *shaped* by an autonomous force and an artistic will; they were subjected to a dramatizing, creative process.[16]

---

[16] On the 'compositional' character of the narration, the distortions of people, the liberties taken with chronology, the significant transposition or conflation of episodes, see in particular Paul John Eakin, 'Henry James and the Autobiographical Act', in *Prospects*, 8 (1983), pp. 211-60, rpt. in his *Fictions in Autobiography,* Princeton, Princeton U. P., 1985, pp. 56-125, and Donna Przybylowicz, *Desire and Repression.*

When dealing with creativity in an autobiographical work, James applies a creative impulse to it. The relation, the interplay, and the constant interaction, between the flow of memories and artistic composition is a constituting element of James's autobiography, both in its material and its form. This entails a tension and a strain, that are typical of autobiographical works, but that in James's specific case acquire at times (as we have seen before) a 'ghostly', 'apparitional' tone. Despite the sweetness of memories and the distance of age, a relation with the past opens strained and estranged perspectives. To conjoin past and present, self and outer reality, memory and desire, involves risks: as in Proust, time recaptured can turn into a *danse macabre*. If this does not happen in James, it is because the authority of artistic control that was adumbrated in the Galerie d'Apollon, and achieved through decades of rigorous application, allows for that fusion of observer and observed reality, flee-flowing images and compositional aim, the wide-open doors of memory and the closing circle of recollections, without which James would not be James, and his autobiography would not be an autobiography.

The bridge spanning the abyss of the past (which was evoked at the outset), is as it were suspended in the void: looking at America 'as Europe would do' (James's own admission) involves some risks. Around those years James gave at least two narrative proofs of the spectral nature of one's encounter with, or recourse to, the past: "The Jolly Corner", his 'ghost story' of 1908, in which the expatriate protagonist

---

The Dialectic of Self and Other in the Late Works of Henry James, University of Alabama Press, 1986 (in her view, James's discourse is more important than his history, and qualifies itself as fictitious narrative: 'autobiographical works examine the act of perception, the functioning of a mind deconstructing, modifying and re-recreating new realms of being that are detached from palpaple reality; here the narrator's and the character's voices blend indistinguishably', p. 302). Eakin quotes a letter by James to T. S. Perry where he admits: 'I kind of *need,* for my small context, that July 1st '63 *should* have been a Sunday', and that he always thought of the 'Gettisburgh Sunday', i. e. that the battle took place on a Sunday; 'What really happened', he maintains, 'is what the self perceived' (p. 251).

meets the *alter ego* he might have become had he stayed at home—and it is a nightmarish apparition; and the unfinished novel *The Sense of the Past*, where the protagonist's longed-for plunge into the past acquires hallucinatory and nightmarish connotations of constriction, imprisonment, and a desperate wish to escape from it. Looking backwards can turn people into statues of salt; what can be discovered in the past may have the effect of a Medusa-like face.[17]

This particular aspect is just touched upon in *A Small Boy and Others*, where James's typical pilgrimage, personal as well as fictional, is reversed, in that he 'intrudes' into an American past from an English present (not vice versa), and his quest is not so much for 'what might have been'—as is the case of the two texts just cited—, but rather for what was and had to be. 'With the passage of time America had taken on for him the romantic "otherness" once possessed by Europe', F. O. Matthiessen observed; in his own book, James finds and declares himself 'furiously American', while quite a few letters of this period ring the same note. As for 'what might have been', by its very nature the autobiographical act directs or subordinates it to the conditions achieved in the present.[18]

With all his gaps and unbalances, in the very discontinuity of memory and evocation, aware as he is that going back into the past is a sort of tight-rope walking, over two spans of time and two worlds, James escapes the terror of the abyss and the Other, precisely because he balanc-

---

[17] On this topic, see, among others, Cushing Strout, 'Henry James's Dream of the Louvre, "The Jolly Corner", and Psychological Interpretation', *Psychohistory Review*, 8, (1979), pp. 47-52.

[18] *The James Family. A Group Biography,* ed. F. O. Matthiessen, New York, Knopf, 1947, p. 308, and in the Autobiography: 'Thus there dawned upon me the grand possibility that, charm for charm, the American, the assumed, the postulated, would, in the particular case of its really acting, count double; whereas the European paid for being less precarious by being also less miraculous' (p. 458).—'What might have been' and what has been 'point to one end / Which is always present', T. S. Eliot postulated in *Four Quartets*, and it might well apply to *A Small Boy and Others*; but then, 'If all time is eternally present / All time is unredeemable'.

es self-narration with the spectacle of outer reality, present vision and former sights, indirect and direct perception, the Palace of Art where he has landed and the House of Life he revisits. This may be taken to represent another aspect of that double exposure in which outward life resolves itself into inward life, and vice versa.

As for the 'composition' question: in the two volumes that were to follow—*Notes of a Son and Brother* and *The Middle Years,* which trace other stages in the education of a young artist, but in a less unified way, because of William entering the scene and the encumbrance of letters, papers, documentary or reflexive parts, that were absent in the first volume—James gives sufficient indications to this effect. Rather extensive quotations are in order here.

At Harvard he discovers that 'What I "wanted to want" to be was, all intimately, just *literary*' (p. 413). He admits that it was a question of testing his capacity to register and represent, for the purposes of the 'personal history, as it were, of an imagination', in which the play of the strong imaginative passion was the center of interest. 'Fed by every contact and every apprehension, and feeding in turn every motion and every act', James's fanciful protagonist or hero could indeed appear as someone else: 'He had been with me all the while, and only too obscurely and intimately—I had not found him in the market as an exhibited or *offered* value. I had in a word to draw him forth from within rather than meet him in the world before me, the more convenient sphere of the objective, and to make him objective, in short, had to turn nothing less than myself inside out' (pp. 454-55). He reveals himself a man of imagination at the highest pitch, endowed with a divining frenzy. 'Seeing further into the figurable world *made* company of persons and places, objects and subjects alike: it gave them all without exception chances to be somehow or other interesting' (p. 492).

'These secrets of the imaginative life', James writes further on, 'were in fact more various than I may dream of trying to tell; they referred to actual concretions of existence as well as to the supposititious; the joy of life indeed, drawbacks and all, was just in the constant quick flick of associations, to and fro, and through a hundred open doors, between the two great chambers (if it be not absurd, or even base, to separate them) of direct and indirect experience' (p. 494). In *The Middle Years* he postulated that 'there were clearly a thousand contacts and sensations, of the strong direct order, that one lost by not so living; exquisitely because of the equal number of immunities and independencies, blest liberties of range for the intellectual adventure, that accrued by the same stroke' (p. 563). Involved in picturing and composition, in reflections, conclusions, comparisons, that man of imagination, indeed that artist, is made to enjoy an intensity that could give the illusion of the *other intensity*—the intensity of active life—, while the reverse was not true for those immersed in actual life.

Thus the meaning and the terms of that *fusion* (the term is used and underlined by James) become clear. Consistently with his whole life and confirmed artistic procedure, it is indirect vision, the reflected images of life, perception and consciousness, that by confronting time and reality, objects and the world, the self and others, make them referable, representable, and usable.

Towards the conclusion of *Notes of a Son and Brother,* James asked himself if the reader could not 'accuse [him] of treating an inch of canvas to an acre of embroidery', and his answer was: 'Let the poor canvas figure time and the embroidery figure consciousness—the proportion will perhaps then not strike us as so wrong' (p. 521). It is consciousness that diffuses time and unravels the thread of memory, that generates and legitimates the very substance of the embroidery. If one looks closely, time has been reduced to 'an inch of canvas' because it is the embroidery—i.e. inward consciousness—that allows for this fusion of self and world, subject and object, the small boy whose steps have been retraced and the American (or European) scene that witnessed and brought them about.

In this sense, as we saw at the beginning, the act of writing allows James to lay his ghost at rest (this is the very phrase he uses for his cousin Minnie Temple, whose death marks the end of his youth); it may have reconciled him with the present, and restored his artistic ability. If it is true that time recaptured coincides with the glimmerings and the first assertion of an artistic vocation, the Autobiography as such re-affirms the excellence that has been achieved. That James considered *A Small Boy and Others* 'the most impudent volume that ever saw the light', and regarded it as 'locked fast in the golden cage of the *intraduisible*',[19] should not surprise us. The book is unorthodox, as was noted, in the audacity of its self-representation and its construction of an identity that blurs the boundaries with the Other. But it is neither impudent nor *intraduisible*, I believe, precisely because it is the result of a continuous series of linguistic 'conversions', transpositions, and *translations*: far from being the transcript of a rounded-off self, it remains fluid and dynamic in its representations.

Not the least of its 'fluidities' is that the self is seen and presented not only *in* the world, but *at work*, caught in the act (as James repeatedly wrote), as a character to be evoked and pursued until he is acknowledged for what he has become. In this sense, we might say with Rimbaud, *je est un autre*, until it is recognized as the 'I' of an artist. Once this is attained, we come full circle, and the autobiographical act is achieved. As Michael Sprinker rightly remarked, 'The origin and the end of autobiography converge in the very act of writing, as Proust brilliantly demonstrates at the end of *Le temps rétrouvé*, for no autobiography can take place except within the boundaries of a writing where concepts of subjective self, and author, collapse into the act of producing a text.'[20]

---

[19]   See James's letter to Henry Adams, 26 May 1913, discussed in Robert F. Sayre, *The Examined Self. B. Franklin, Henry Adams, Henry James,* Princeton, Princeton U. P., 1964, p. 190.

[20]   Michael Sprinker, 'The End of Autobiography', in *Autobiography. Essays Theoretical and Critical,* ed. James Olney, Princeton, Princeton U.P., 1972, p. 342.

6

In an almost psychotic reaction to James's autobiographical volumes, an old-time friend and admirer, Henry Adams—who had in turn written an 'objectified', intellectual autobiography in the third person, *The Education of Henry* Adams (1908), which proved however the record of his failed education—accused him of having succumbed to the nostalgia of a limited, lost world. Having freed himself of the past by writing it into an imaginative evocation, James had an easy task in rejoining, in a well-known letter, that it was the latent or recovered pull of the artist that had sustained him: '*Of course* we are lone survivors, of course the past that was our lives is at the bottom of an abyss—if the abyss *has* any bottom; of course too there's no use talking unless one particularly *wants* to. But the purpose, almost, of my printed divagations was to show you that one can strange to say, still want to … I still find my consciousness interesting—under *cultivation* of the interest … You see I still, in presence of life (or of what you deny to be such), have reactions—as many as possible—and the book I sent you is a proof of them.'

And he added, in an unforgettable sentence: 'It's, I suppose, because I am that queer monster the artist, an obstinate finality, an inexhaustible sensibility. Hence the reactions—appearances, memories, many things go on playing upon it with consequences that I note and "enjoy" (grim word!) noting. It all takes doing—and I *do.* I believe I shall do yet again—it is still an act of life.'[21]

---

[21] Henry Adams's letter to James is not extant, but can be reconstructed from his reaction; we know that to Mrs. Cameron he had written: 'Poor Henry James thinks it all real and actually still lives in that dreary, stuffy Newport and Cambridge with papa James and Charles Eliot Norton'. See *Henry James: Letters,* ed. Leon Edel, Cambridge, Harvard U. P., 1974-84, 4 vols., IV, pp. 705-06. —For further Bibliographical indications, I refer to the Introduction to my Italian edition of James's book, *Un bambino e gli altri,* tr. Giuliana Schiavi, Vicenza, Neri Pozza, 1993, pp. xxxvi-xli, and to later contributions cited in the previous Notes.—This essay was completed at the Remarque Institute, New York University, November-December 2000: I am grateful for their hospitality.

A Small Boy and Others bears witness to the birth, growth, and per-
sistence, of that 'queer monster the artist', to the stubborn finality and
the 'act of life' to which he is irrevocably committed.

2   *From Victorianism to the Avant-Garde*

1

Henry James's connection with Victorianism is well-known and well-established: much more interesting is his escape from it into realms that are those of early Modernism and the Avant-garde.

His adherence to Victorianism rests, for our case, on two or three basic counts: the morality of literature (though in a Preface he wrote of 'the perfect dependence of the "moral" sense of a work of art on the amount of felt life concerned in producing it'); sexual reticence and/or repression; a belief in social codes and hierarchies, in the social system of the day. It is true that throughout his life James felt that excessive respectability could be a blight on literature, and on several occasions he wrote against the Anglo-Saxon (specifically Victorian) 'conspiracy of silence' in sexual matters. The exclusion of 'half of life', the acceptance of 'unnatural conditions and insufferable restrictions' for the sake of propriety and innocence, so as not to harm young and female readers, was a hindrance and a diminution for the aspiring artist.[1]

Yet, in spite of all his well-meant utterances, James could never bring

---

[1]   Henry James, *The Art of the Novel*, ed. R. P. Blackmur, New York, Scribner's, 1953, p. 45; *Literary Criticism. European Writers and The Prefaces*, ed. Leon Edel, New York, Library of America, 1984, pp. 955-56, 864 ff. (p. 869 in particular).

himself to suit his fiction to his words, and what he called, with characteristic reticence, the processes involved in 'the great world renewal' (i.e. sex) went practically unheeded in his work: extensive psychological foreplay and dire after effects, yes, but never—to echo Shakespeare again—the 'act of sport' itself. Much as James valued and admired Zola, or, for that matter, D'Annunzio, he was dismayed by their 'monstrous uncleanliness' (which he deemed totally unsuitable to the British climate) and in both writers he detected the leak of a bad smell that cut them off from proper company.[2] Young Virginia Woolf, and others with her, were right in seeing him as a stuffy 'Eminent Victorian'—though he had surprises which were not easy to detect.

James's acceptance of Victorian social norms and systems is shown not only by his biographical choices; it is emphasized by his notorious passage in his 1879 book on Hawthorne. Boston was stuffy, parochial and provincial enough; yet, when James moved permanently to Victorian England in 1876, he did so in order to find an even more socially organized, hierarchical society, with all those 'items of high civilization which were absent from the texture of American life.' You remember:

> No State, in the European sense of the word, and indeed barely a specific national name. No sovereign, no court, no personal loyalty, no aristocracy, no church, no clergy, no army, no diplomatic service, no country gentlemen, no palaces, no castles, nor manors, nor old country-houses, nor thatched cottages nor ivied ruins; no cathedrals, nor abbeys, nor little Norman churches; no great Universities nor public schools—no Oxford, nor Eton, nor Harrow; no literature, no novels, no museums, no pictures, no political society, no sporting class—no Epsom nor Ascot! Some such list as that might be drawn up of the absent things in American life—especially in American life of forty years ago.[3]

---

[2]   See *ibidem*, James's essays on Zola's *Nana* and on Gabriele D'Annunzio, and chapter 7, below.

[3]   Henry James, *Hawthorne*, ed. Tony Tanner, New York, Macmillan, 1967, p. 55; *Literary Criticism. Essays, American and English Writers*, ed. Leon Edel, New York, The Library of America, 1984, pp. 351-52.

If, for once, you read the long list in the positive, rather than the negative order—'A State, a specific national name, a sovereign, a court,
personal loyalty, aristocracy, church, clergy, army, diplomatic service,
country gentlemen, palaces, castles, manors, old country-houses, par-
sonages, thatched cottages, ivied ruins; cathedrals, abbeys, little Norman churches; great Universities, public schools, Oxford, Eton, Har-
row; literature, novels, museums, pictures, political society, sporting
class, Epsom, Ascot!'—you would have James's cherished Victorian
England with a vengeance.

Those items would satisfy the need for a 'system' both on the personal and on the fictional levels. With time, England, too, would disap-
point James: his chosen country would become 'this frumpy old England'. Yet one has to look well behind or inside James's motivation: a
strictly organized, hierarchical society such as Victorian England would
provide those social signs and markers, signals or icons, a prearranged
code of references, that were necessary, if not indispensable, for a novelist of manners, or indeed a realistic novelist, who would eschew the
airy regions of (Hawthornesque) romance and try his hand at 'histoire
morale contemporaine' in the way of his French (rather than English)
confrères. 'Faire concurrence a l'état civil'—in Balzac's beautiful
phrase—, to vie with the census officer and the historian, required precisely that type of stratified, multiform and rigid society that Victorian
England could offer. Hence James's decision to expatriate, which identified him once more with the ideals of Victorian life.[4]

James was to add, however, an all-important twist, which I shall
examine presently and which may represent the first wedge or diversi-
fying aspect in his adherence to Victorian standards and codes. In both
aspect of Victorianism I have hinted at so far—sexual reticence and
realism of manners— James acted in a way similar to Shakespeare in

---

[4]   See, among others, Sergio Perosa, *American Theories of the Novel: 1793-1903*,
New York, New York U.P., pp. 113-117, and Id., *L'Euro-America di Henry James*,
Vicenza, Neri Pozza, 1979.

his adherence to Elizabethan codes: a substantial acceptance was undermined by opposing thrusts, conformity allowed for a stealthy disruption of prevailing attitudes.

Let's jump, for the sake of my argument, to the years around James's death in 1916, when the Master died in state, and early Modernism was being launched by a new generation of writers. James suddenly and unexpectedly appeared to them no longer as the pundit of hated Victorianism, but rather as a close forerunner, indeed a father and early practitioner of Modernism. The verdict came from the most active or representative champions of this historical avant-garde.

As early as 1913, Ford Madox Ford placed James at the center of what he termed the Mainstream of the Novel (together with Conrad, Crane, W. H. Hudson and others). The main reasons were three: James was a cosmopolitan, an expatriate and an experimental writer—three premises with which the avant-garde would identify itself. To summarize a rather lengthy argument, James was for F. M. Ford a founder of the New Form of the Novel because he was a supporter of the principle of selection (and Impressionism), an author who was able to develop, thanks to the 'limited point of view', a 'negative personality'—a term often applied to Flaubert, but also later extolled by T.S. Eliot, which stressed and implied impersonality; James wrote 'intense', rather than extensive or descriptive, fiction based on dramatic scenes; finally, he was a practitioner of nonlinearity (he used the time-shift) and reflexive fiction. Novels such as *The Spoils of Poynton* and *What Maisie Knew* were Ford's cherished examples: James was in command of technique (contrary to accepted Victorian practices), of construction and architecture; he *rendered* and did not narrate (i.e. favored *showing* over *telling*, to use his own terms).[5]

---

[5]   See, among others, Brita Lindberg-Seyersted, *F.M. Ford and his Relationship to Stephen Crane and Henry James,* New Jersey, Humanities Press International, 1987 and Sergio Perosa, 'Henry James e Ford Madox Ford', in *Struttura e strumentazione in F. M. Ford*, eds R. Baccolini and V. Fortunati, Firenze, Alinea, 1994.

In 1918, both T.S. Eliot and Ezra Pound devoted essays to James—in both cases seen and presented as a master of Modernism.[6] Eliot's essay is less inspired or inspiring than Pound's. Eliot, too, stressed the importance of cosmopolitanism and expatriation in James, his reflexive attitude in fiction (he had 'a sense of the sense of the past'), his 'deeper psychologies'. Moreover, Eliot found in his work a quality that may appear as highly proleptic (or anticipatory) of his own conception of the creative process: 'It is in the chemistry of these subtle substances, the curious precipitates and explosive gasses which are suddenly formed by the contact of mind with mind, that James is unequalled'.

Pound was, as usual, more boisterous and aggressive, but equally clear on James's role as a writer who took the U.S. into the literary picture (as he wrote), and as a father figure for the Moderns. James had achieved perfect form but also a technique of fragmentation (that Pound was to use in his *Hugh Selwyn Mauberly*, which he considered a condensation of the James novel); James had extended the *art* of fiction beyond the territory occupied by the French; he was both exact and realistic; he did write 'cobwebby novels', but that 'added opacity' was the mark of a new way of writing.

Pound's long essay unfailingly singled out James's novels and short stories of the 1890s—not those of the 'major phase'—for high praise: *The Other House, The Spoils of Poynton, What Maisie Knew,* with a particular liking for *The Awkward Age* and *The Sacred Fount*—James's intriguing and exasperating non-novel of 1901, his totally 'modern' attempt at abstract or meta-fiction. 'In *The Sacred Fount* he attains form, perfect form, his form ... it seems to me one work that he could afford to sit back, look at, and find completed. I don't in the least imply that he did so', Pound wrote: in choosing that novel—and the unfinished *The Sense of the Past* and *The Ivory Tower*—for high praise, he made

---

6   Both essays appeared in *The Little Review*, 5 (1918); Eliot's is rpt. in *The Question of Henry James*, ed. F.W. Dupee, New York, Holt, 1945, pp. 108-119, Pound's in his *Literary Essays*, ed. T. S. Eliot, London, Faber and Faber, 1954, pp. 295-338.

a fellow proto-modernist of James. 'London possible in 1908 because Browning and H. J., and a few others, HAD smacked the teak-heads with their flails / one by one / driving some sense into 'em',—Pound was to write retrospectively in a letter.[7]

The drift of my essay will be precisely to ascertain in or by which ways James provided the case of a novelist who, after embodying so steadily and for so long the very image of Victorianism, came to be considered (legitimately, I believe) as a father and a *confrère* of Modernist writers, a source of inspiration and a supporting presence.

How was this possible, how did it come about?

I shall try to be selective as well as exhaustive—I hope not exhausting—, relatively simple, but also problematic. I shall offer some possible answers under four headings, but we will be left at the end with an open critical question. The four headings are:

(a) realism and the art of fiction;
(b) the 'analytical' novel;
(c) dramatic scene and point of view;
(d) forms of absence and void.

Since the 1880s, James's brand of realism was different from Victorian realism. His essay of 1884, 'The Art of Fiction', not only stressed the need for realism along the lines of the French, rather than the English school; it emphasized a close correlation between realism and *art*, much in the way, again, of the French, rather than the Victorian trend. James opposed the prevailing conception of the naïf novel, devoid of any theory, consciousness and technique. Fiction was considered as 'serious a branch of literature as any other'—as serious as poetry, painting, historiography. It was not 'make believe' (as for Anthony Trollope); its reason was a faithful representation of life; indeed, in an early formulation (which was later modified after R. L. Stevenson's 'humble remon-

---

[7] *Literary Essays*, p. 327; letter of March 3, 1957, quoted in Patricia Hutchins, *Ezra Pound's Kensington. An Exploration 1885-1913*, Chicago, Regnery, 1965, p. 141.

strance'), it had to 'compete with life'. It aimed at an 'air of reality', at 'solidity of specification', at rendering 'the look of things ... the substance of human life'; at giving an illustrative picture of reality, a broad and truthful canvas of contemporary events. Its selection was to be 'typical, to be inclusive'. The question of morality—so crucial and central for Victorian novelists—was to be subordinated to the need of dealing openly with *any* aspect of life, even with those regarded as taboo in the Victorian age, eschewing the blackmail of the 'young readers'. 'The essence of moral energy—James wrote—is to survey the whole field'.

2

I have noted elsewhere[8] a striking similarity with the proto-naturalistic manifesto of the brothers Goncourt in their Preface to *Germinie Lacerteux* (1864), a novel that James had reviewed. There the Goncourts had vindicated the right and the need to lift the literary ban on the 'low classes', 'the people', who had by now 'droit au roman'. The final part of their preface was a plea for scientific realism, for Truth as well as Art:

> Aujourd'hui que le Roman s'élargit et grandit, qu'il commence a être la grande forme sérieuse, passionée, vivante de l'étude litteraire et de l'enquête sociale, qu'il devient, par l'analyse et par la recherche psychologique, l'Histoire morale contemporaine: aujourd'hui que le Roman s'est imposé les études et les devoirs de la science, il peut en revendiquer les libertés et les franchises. Et qu'il cherche l'Art et la Verité.[9]

This connection is crucial. In 'The Art of Fiction' James expounded and extolled a kind of realism that in its combination of scientific premises

---

[8]   Sergio Perosa, *Henry James and the Experimental Novel*, New York, New York U. P., 1983, pp. 16-17 and Id., *American Theories of the Novel: 1793-1903*, pp. 117-22.

[9]   *Anthologie des préfaces de romans français du XIXe siècle*, eds Herbert S. Gershman and Kernan B. Whitworth, Jr., Paris, Julliard, 1964, p. 223.

and artistic awareness was moving away from Victorian complacencies and can indeed be considered an early form of the avant-garde movement. In the impassioned conclusion of his essay, James openly referred to Zola as the novelist 'to whose solid and serious work no explorer of the capacity of the novel can allude without respect'.

It is true that James never dealt extensively with the lower classes—except in some parts of *The Princess Casamassima* and *The Bostonians* (both of 1886). But, first, the Naturalists themselves, contrary to accepted views, had sustained the need *not* to restrict themselves to low topics and settings. In a later Preface to his *Les frères Zenganno* (1878), Edmond de Goncourt had written:

> Le jour ou l'analyse cruelle que mon ami, M. Zola, et peut-être moi-meme, avons apportée dans la peinture du bas de la société, sera reprise par un écrivain de talent, et employée à la reproduction des hommes et des femmes du monde, dans des milieux d'éducation et de distinction,—ce jour-là seulement, le classicisme et sa queue seront tués.

They, the Goncourts, had begun with the 'canaille' because it was simple and uncomplicated: now the need was felt for some novelist who would depict the *manners* of society people, deal with 'le grand monde ... le monde le plus quintessencié', with its 'éléments délicats et fugaces':

> Cet roman réaliste de l'élégance, ça avait été notre ambition à mon frère et à moi de l'écrire. Le Réalisme, pour user du mot bête, du mot drapeau, n'a pas en effet l'unique mission de décrire ce qui est bas, ce qui est répugnant, ce qui pue; il est venu au monde aussi, lui, pour definir, dans de l'écriture *artiste*, ce qui est élevé, ce qui est joli, ce qui sent bon, et encore pour donner les aspects et les profils des êtres raffinés et des choses riches: mais cela, en une étude appliquée, rigoureuse et non conventionelle et non imaginative de la beauté.[10]

---

[10]   *Ibidem*, pp. 226-7.

It was as if he had James in mind. Ezra Pound, in his essay of 1918, noted immediately that 'all James would seem but a corollary' to these passages, and indeed James's aligning himself with some of the tenets of Naturalism in his novels of the 1880s—*The Princess Casamassima, The Bostonians, The Tragic Muse*—was precisely along those lines. In more than one way, James espoused the cause of what was then regarded as *radical* realism, all the more so in that he duly stressed the need for a personal impression and an *artistic* form. Now, Realism of the French school—the realism of Maupassant, Gautier, Flaubert, as well as the Goncourt brothers and Zola—was an alien and revolutionary proposition in Victorian England. Fiction was still considered basically as entertainment, a low form of literary expression. Stressing its seriousness of purpose as well as its need for architecture, composition, form, painstaking artistic care, was and was felt to be a radical stance. As is not often realized, James's vindication and practice of *that* kind of fiction was a first step in a clearly anti-Victorian move: fiction for him was literature and a work of art.

That it was so is borne out by my second point (or heading). Even James's own and peculiar form of psychological realism—which distinguished him from his French *confrères*, with the possible exception of another expatriate like himself, Ivan Turgenev—came to be considered in the 1880s as a threat and a menace to Victorian norms. I refer to the controversy that arose, on both sides of the Atlantic, after the publication of W. D. Howells' essay 'Henry James jr.' in 1882.

Howells had praised James for his 'artistic impartiality' (a term usually applied to Flaubert), his interest in character over plot, and what he (Howells) termed his 'analytic tendency'—his analysis of motives, psychological moods, states of mind, of the innermost springs of action and consciousness. This, Howells felt, was a more mature type of fiction than that of Dickens and Thackeray (the possible exception being George Eliot), and peculiarly American *(vide* Hawthorne before James). Such a view was of course likely, indeed bound, to cause resentment, suspicion, and opposition in England: James came to be regarded as the exponent of 'a new school of fiction, based upon the principle that the best novelist is he who has no story to tell'. According to Arthur Tilley, for instance, writing in the *London National Review*, this new school eschewed rounded plots and completion (the obvious reference being to *The Portrait of a Lady);* its analysis of character had no real ethical interest (as for instance it had had for George Eliot).[11]

Moreover, over-analytic studies of inner states of mind and motives, the subtleties of psychological investigations, the searchings and prob-ings into the secret recesses of human souls, appeared to be the result of a cold, detached, scientific mentality—the same that operated in Zola's 'scientific' realism. The 'morbid introspection' of American novelists—James being the foremost—seemed a danger equivalent to Naturalism. In both cases there was insufficient respect for the sanctity and privacy of the human heart. James came to be regarded as the champion of a scientific attitude and of analytic probings in fiction that prominent Vic-torian critics—from Tilley to George Saintsbury—saw as a threat to es-tablished norms of decency and literary decorum. Here is Saintsbury:

> The analyst ... is in this worse off than the naturalist pure and simple, that instead of mistaking a partial for a universal method, he takes for a complete method what is not strictly a method at all. The faithful copying of an actual scene or action sometimes results in something that is at least an integral part of a story. *The elaborate dissection of motives and charac-ters can only result in something that stops short of being even a part of a story—that is only preliminary to part of a story* [my italics].[12]

James's type of psychological realism caused at the time as much fear as resentment: by dissecting the inner structures of characters it de-stroyed the illusion that they were real persons; it betrayed an intellec-tual, rather than emotional or sympathetic, attitude; it did not give the

---

[11]   *American Theories of the Novel: 1793-1903*, pp. 105-109.
[12]   'The Present State of the Novel: II', *Fortnightly Review*, n.s. 43 (1888), pp. 116-118.

reader real stories. What we rightly consider James's highest contribution to Victorian (as well as modern) fiction was regarded and dismissed as alien, to say the least. And in this respect, too, he *was* moving away from, and ahead of, his age.

He himself felt, in the 1880s, that his 'analytic' fiction was a step ahead of the French tradition. Maupassant, for instance, in his Preface to *Pierre et Jean*, had considered the analytic fashion of telling a story less profitable than the simple epic (i.e. objective and impersonal) manner, and maintained that psychology should be hidden in a book. James took the matter up in his essay of 1888, 'Guy de Maupassant', and stressed, instead, the difficulty of describing 'an action without glancing at its motive': 'For some people motives, reasons, relations, explanations, are a part of the very surface of the drama', he maintained; a novelist could not skip, as the French or the English had done for so long, the reflective part of men and women—'that reflective part which governs conduct and produces character'.[13]

James's real break with Victorian forms of fiction—if not with its ideologies—took place, however, in his theories and novels of the late 1890s. After the small success of his realistic novels of the 1880s, and the total failure of his theatrical attempts in the early 1890s, when James rededicated himself to fiction-writing he experimented with and developed new technical principles that opened the way to Modernism and truly qualified him as one of its fathers or early practitioners. This is by now a well-known story.

As I have argued elsewhere,[14] in James's Notebook entries of the mid-90s we can trace the contemporary, concomitant and combined rise of two principles that were to break and to explode the Victorian novel from within. One was the breaking-down of the pictorial, illustrative method into the juxtaposition of short, intense, objective 'dramatic scenes'. Pursuing an analogy with the well-made play—rather than the

---

[13]   *Literary Criticism. European Writers*, pp. 529-30 and 547.
[14]   Perosa, *Henry James and the Experimental Novel*, chapter II.

'picture'—James envisaged his stories more and more as tight sequels
of compressed episodes, confrontations of characters, encounters or
clashes of people, which were to follow the objective rules of scenes
in a play—self-evident, relying as much as possible on outer behavior,
on character caught in action, often in almost pure dialogue ('dialogue
which is always action'), avoiding that 'going behind' to 'compass explanations', to analyze motives and feelings, for which James had ac-
quired a solid—though for some 'dubious'—reputation. The principle
of the 'dramatic scene', self-contained and objective, implied a careful juxtaposition and montage of the single episodes and moments—
a structure no longer relying on the big *scènes à faire* of the Victorian
novel, and on their long descriptive, illustrative or 'analytic' prepara-
tions. The structure—I insist—became more and more identified with
juxtaposition, montage and *progression d'effet:* all key-points and key-
terms for later Modernist writers (I refer back here to my opening remarks on F. M. Ford and Pound).

In the Notebook entries and in the novels of the late 1890s, however,
while developing the new technique of the dramatic scene, James was
simultaneously drawn to envisage, and experiment with, a correlated
principle—that of the 'limited point of view', i.e. the use of an 'intelligent observer', a character involved in the story, a narrator from whose
limited point of view those dramatic scenes would be glimpsed, perceived, reconstructed and presented to the reader. The two principles,
far from being opposed, are born and work together in later James: they
are 'two ends of one stick', R. P. Blackmur once remarked, and no one
can tell 'where either end begins'.

In recording the germ and the development of *The Spoils of Poynton*, for instance, James started with a clear view of dramatic scenes
which almost irresistibly required the controlling presence of a central
character, Fleda Vetch, as intelligent observer and center of consciousness, to whose view and feelings the story was to be referred. In laying
out the germ and the development of the almost contemporary novel,
What Maisie Knew, James started instead with the intuition of a young

girl through whose bewildered eyes and feelings the story was to take place as a series of sharp dramatic scenes. I cannot indulge in details here, but the parallelism of the two discoveries is really striking.

As it turned out, in these and some later novels, the observer or center of consciousness allows for the dramatic scenes to be presented in their 'guarded objectivity', while at the same time qualifying the presented occasion with the play of his or her subjective view and participation. If the narrator presents the relevant facts as they happen objectively, he or she provides the 'foreshortened' perspective and the angle of vision, the obliqueness and the ambiguity of a personal, subjective, *involved* view. The novelist could thus achieve his greatest aspiration: to reconcile objectivity of presentation with subjective vision, impersonality with participation (in this sense James could subscribe to Flaubert's idea of the artist 'present in his work like God in Creation, invisible and almighty everywhere felt but nowhere seen').[15]

3

The consequences, for our purposes, are obvious, and far-reaching: the story-line is broken and fragmented, the montage and juxtaposition of scenes become of paramount importance. The structure and the view of the Victorian novel are broken from within: they'll never be as they were before. All the more so in that the reader becomes more and more involved in the process of ascertaining the real consistency of facts and possible meanings, of seeing and evaluating experience. If experience is more and more presented and expressed through the consciousness of the narrators, we, the readers, participate in the process of apprehending elusive and partial truths, are drawn into the play and the labyrinths of perception.

---

[15] See James's essay 'Gustave Flaubert' (1893), rpt. in *Literary Criticism. European Writers*, pp. 295-314 .

As always, this technical experimentation that opened the way to the modern novel—no need to name names here, I trust—involved and implied crucial epistemological, philosophical and ontological revolutions. The very idea—that was Jamesian as well as Victorian— of a novelist who could control, order, indeed fashion and create a unified view of the world, is shattered. From now on the writer can only deal with fragments, broken images, partial portraits, ephemeral aspects and glimpses of an elusive, baffling, uncontrollable reality. Montage and juxtaposition—so cherished and pursued by the Moderns—are a makeshift, the only way to counteract the slipping away of certainties and established rules. 'Things fall apart, the center cannot hold': the writer must do with limited access, circumscribed views, with ambiguities and indeterminacies, if we now want to start using these words.

The world gradually becomes unknowable, ungraspable; reality cannot be apprehended and comprehended; a whole picture is no longer possible. If James opens the way for the Moderns with his new techniques, his fictional substance now verges on forms of elusiveness, ambiguity and dissolution, 'openness' and void. Hence the recognition by F. M. Ford, T. S. Eliot, Ezra Pound, of the crucial importance for *them* and the avant-garde of James's novels of the 1890s—*The Spoils of Poynton, What Maisie Knew, In the Cage, The Sacred Fount.* (Parenthetically, I shall not bring in the novels of the 'major phase', as they seem to me to overcome most of the difficulties which had begun to beset the Victorian novel, by combining, again, picture with scene, the broad canvas and the limited view—though I am aware that there are modernist elements there as well).

It seems to me that a text such as *The Turn of the Screw* offers an example of Victorian modes and feelings, settings and premises (in both senses) being exploded from within, just as *In the Cage* registers a closure, or indeed a foreclosure, of a view of Victorian London as the privileged seat of signs and recognizable references. Signs and references are lost, dispelled, dissipated there, just as in *The Turn of the*

Screw ambiguity suggests emptiness, and the eeriness of its void allows for all sorts of ambivalences and ambiguities.

Ambivalences and ambiguities of that sort already qualify James as a proto-modernist writer. In an intriguing novel of 1901, *The Sacred Fount*—so much praised by Pound—James brings them to their extreme consequences. The Narrator of the story—a not very intelligent observer—must register the impossibility of giving a rational, possibly an artistic order, to the wealth of ambiguous and contradicting signs which are offered by experience. As his motivations seem to imply an artistic urge, but life eludes all his attempts at making sense of it, it seems plausible to see *The Sacred Fount* as a novel on the impossibility of constructing a novel: no exhaustive or conclusive order can be imposed on the contrasting data and suggestions of experience; no artistic reality, objectively true, can be organized or created through the mirror and point of view of the self. The interesting aspect, of course, is that James *did* manage to write a *novel*—if my interpretation is correct—precisely on the impossibility of writing a novel. He wrote, in other words, an early example of the so-called anti-novel—fiction that disclaims the very possibility of composing a fictional view of the world.

If, as Albert Camus argued in his *L'homme revolté*, the nineteenth-century novel (Victorian as well as Jamesian, in our context) aimed at 'rival creation', at creating a *naturam alteram*, another world which competes with *(fait concurrence à)* the actual world, *The Sacred Fount* marks the break-down or the failure of that claim: life is unamenable to artistic order and meaning, the artist can only mirror the confused and confusing flux of experience. Twisting James's own terms, art can no longer *make* life, make interest, make importance;[16] fiction has come to an *impasse*: it can only register states of confusion, indeterminacies, graspings in the void. Reality can only be apprehended marginally and

---

[16] 'It is art that *makes* life' (etc.), James had written in a well-known letter of 1915; see *Henry James and H.G. Wells*, eds Leon Edel and Gordon N. Ray, London, Hart Davies, 1958, p. 267.

tangentially, or askance, in bits and pieces; putting them together is a hopeless endeavor. James is a precursor of that modern sense of bafflement and exclusion, uncertainty, impotence and doubt, that we experience every day in trying to perceive, penetrate, understand reality—all the more so if we are artists.

No wonder Ezra Pound was excited precisely by this novel of James's, which seems to prefigure well-known aspects of early Modernism— Gide as well as Thomas Mann or Kafka—and to break completely with all tenets, claims and beliefs of Victorianism. It is indeed an avant-garde text, not only in its ambiguity, but in its ontological, epistemological and fictional premises, including the fact that the reader is part of the process and the failure, is made to participate in acts of wondering and baffling recognitions, is called upon to share the dubious pleasure of reading riddles—if still possible.

Other texts of this late period deal with failures of communication, with conditions of expressive silence, with emptiness and void assumed as the only ontological and fictional realities. They, too, exemplify and qualify James as an inhabitant of early Modernism and the avant-garde. Doubting, wondering, staring into the void, are conditions not only of knowing and of writing—but of existence itself. I am ready at this point to risk the name of Samuel Beckett.

Take for example two well known short stories: 'The Beast in the Jungle' (1903) and 'The Bench of Desolation' (1910). If before terror and wondering, suspense and waiting, had been mainly internalized, now they become a condition and a form of experience, they are inherent in life. Absence and void are the only true 'figures in the carpet' of these exemplary stories, which are examples of almost unrealistic, symbolic and poetic writing, set in rarefied, abstract and rather indeterminate settings. The lonely, empty figures evoked in 'The Beast in the Jungle' and 'The Bench of Desolation' prefigure the lonely, estranged outsiders of Modernism: Kafka's, Musil's and Beckett's characters, Eliot's Prufrock. I am forcibly reminded of Salvatore Quasimodo's three-line poem: 'Ognuno sta solo sul cuor della terra / trafitto da un raggio di sole: / ed è subito sera'.

The spasmodic waiting of the protagonist of 'The Beast in the Jungle', John Marcher, is for something that will never happen—rather, that did happen, but passed him by, went unrecognized, almost unrecorded. 'Life is what happens while we are engaged in something else', another Italian writer (Raffaele La Capria) has written. By missing what went by him, John Marcher has lost both the illusion that he was marked for something special, and the chance of leading a normal life: hence his desolate weeping and break-down at the end, the feeling that all chances in life are lost; that there are perhaps not even chances or 'rare distinctions' in life—that no beast is ever going to jump at us from any jungle. John Marcher's, as James himself defined it, is a great 'negative adventure'—pre-kafkaesque, allow me to insist; life as such is a negative adventure, a flashing in the void, an existential doom. 'The fate he [John Marcher] had been marked for he had met with a vengeance—he had emptied the cup to the lees; he had been the man of his time, *the* man, to whom nothing on earth was to have happened.'

One senses a metaphysical frisson here. In 'The Bench of Desolation' the protagonist is doomed instead to accept a way of life that is pure deprivation and bootless toil. His occupation, his existential position, is to sit on an emblematic bench staring at the emptiness of the sea. The sea is by definition a mirror of the self, but also elemental formlessness and desolate loneliness; the bench is thus an equivalent of John Marcher's unlit fireplace. The new protagonist, in turn, is defined as the man to whom nothing worth more than twopence could happen. He is, incidentally, given a second chance: but a similar attitude of destitution and desolation qualifies both negative adventures. Life, in both cases, is merely subject to the winds of fate—as flies to wanton boys they are to their gods.

Desolation, emptiness, inner destitution, staring with blank eyes at the sea or at the void are key-figures; these characters stare at missing chances or missing dates, look for what might have been, and was not, for what should have happened, and did not. Words are unspoken, conversations falter by fits and starts, thoughts crowd the mind but are not spelled out; communication relies on glances, glimpses, winks, slight turnings of the heads, small, insignificant gestures. What is left unsaid may turn out to be more important than what is told, silence is more expressive than words, wonder and bewilderment have taken the place of feelings.

I believe that with this later James we have stepped right into early Modernism and the avant-garde. Victorianism—with its stuffiness and overcrowding and oppressive presences—has been left very far behind; it looms in the distance as a forgotten starting point, no longer an option. Yet, a startling critical question remains open, and I wish to touch briefly on that by way of conclusion.

4

I did duly review, for this essay, various books devoted to the genealogy of Modernism, but I was eventually more attracted by a series of volumes dealing with crucial aspects of the fin-de-siècle that were influential in dispelling the atmosphere and uprooting the very foundations of Victorianism, and in sowing the seeds of the modern temper. Let me pile up in haste titles and names: Mario Praz's *Romantic Agony* (which in its original version bears the revealing title *The Flesh, Death and the Devil*); William Gaunt's *The Aesthetic Adventure*, various anthologies of literature of the 1890s, including the two-volume *Strangeness and Beauty: An Anthology of Aesthetic Criticism*, 1840-1910, down to Philippe Julian's *Dreamers of Decadence* and Bram Dijkstra's *Idols of Perversity.*[17]

---

[17] Mario Praz's *La carne, la morte e il diavolo* was originally published in 1930 (English translation, *The Romantic Agony*, Oxford, Oxford U. P., 1933); William Gaunt, *The Aesthetic Adventure,* London, Cape, 1945; *The Eighteen-Nineties. A Literary Exhibition,* London, British Book League, 1973; *Aesthetes and Decadents of the 1890s. An Anthology,* ed. Karl Beckson, New York, Vintage, 1966; *The Yellow Book: Quintessence of the Nineties,* ed. Stanley Weintraub, New York, Doubleday,

The gamut of 'revolutionary', anti-Victorian attitudes, practices and poses, is impressive: aestheticism and *l'art pour l'art*, in the first place, impressionism and symbolism in both painting and poetry, dandyism, a belief in the supremacy of artificiality, 'The Yellow Book', the decadent movement, theories of de-evolution and degeneration, the cult of pessimism, the Celtic Twilight and the Rhymers' Club. In terms of subject-matter and themes: sadism and Satanism, the dream of Byzantium and exoticism, Belles Dames sans Merci and Medusa-like figures, legendary, mythical, macabre and exotic Chimeras, Fairies and Sphinxes, endless Salomés (as well as Liliths, Istars and Lulus), Pierrots and Masks. The great authors are for everybody to choose from: Gautier and Baudelaire, Flaubert (*Salammbô* and *The Temptation of St. Anthony*), Swinburne and D'Annunzio, Pater and Arthur Symons, Huysmans and Wilde, George Moore and Max Beerbohm, Mallarmé and Verlaine, Villiers de l'Isle-Adam and Barbey D'Aurevilly, Beardsley and Whistler, Maeterlinck and Gustave Moreau.

All these built in the 1890s a counter-current to Victorianism that would sweep it away and cancel it for two generations. It was through 'la Décadence' that Victorianism expired.

The interesting aspect, for my purpose, is that Henry James had practically nothing to do with these movements and schools, kept carefully away from them, and yet managed all the same to break and dispel the very roots and essence of Victorianism as it were *from within*, without going in any recognizable way through the experience of Decadentism. If I were to propose a subtitle for this essay, it would probably be: *The*

1964; *Strangeness and Beauty. An Anthology of Aesthetic Criticism, 1840-1910*, eds E. Warner and G. Hough, Cambridge, Cambridge U.P., 1983, 2 vols.; Philippe Julian, *Dreams of Decadence. Symbolist Painters of the Decadence,* Phaidon, 1969; Bram Dijkstra, *Idols of Perversity. Fantasies of Feminine Evil in the Fin-de-Siècle Culture,* New York, Oxford U.P., 1986, John Auchard, *Silence in Henry James. The Heritage of Symbolism and Decadence*, University Park, Pennsylvania State U. P., 1986; Jean Perrot, *Henry James et la Décadence,* Thèse Lettres, Université de Paris IV, 1980, 4 vols. (microedition du texte dactylographié); Nancy Blake, *Henry James: Écriture et absence,* Petit-Roeulx, Cistre, 1985.

By-Passing of the Decadent Imagination. This seems to me to be the peculiar characteristic of James's case in the context of our topic, and it throws light both on his rather special move from Victorianism to the avant-garde, and on one aspect of early Modernism (at least in fiction) which tends to be overlooked, and on which I wish to conclude.

James was very critical, on at least two occasions, of *l'art pour l'art*, criticized the Impressionist painters, was wary of symbolism (in its American and French varieties) and sceptical about Wagner. He stayed away as much as possible from dreams and chimeras of Decadence, the claims of artificiality, exoticism, idols of perversity and Salomés, mystical moods and trances. He was perhaps, only slightly, a dandy and an aesthete; he was, only slightly and vicariously, interested in some celebrated amours of the period. He worked from within the ground rules of Victorianism, and his breaking away from its artistic codes and norms, even in the latest texts I have referred to, was still based on the belief that an 'air of reality' and 'solidity of specification' were of essential importance for the novelist. This is the crucial point: his advocacy of the art of fiction, his 'pictorial' mode and even his 'analytic' ways in the 1880s, his poetics of the limited point of view and the dramatic scene in the 1890s, even his adoption of silent and abstract moods, his reliance on emptiness and absence, grew out of, and were always referred back to, a solid ground of realism, of observed and expressed reality.

It is my final contention that this *combination* of experimental, even revolutionary literary techniques, with a sound apprehension of visible reality, was what appealed to the early masters of Modernism. In F. M. Ford, T. S. Eliot, Ezra Pound—to go back to those I started from—but also, for instance, in Joyce and Proust, the modern temper was out to combine a refined artistic mastery and control, experimental forms and techniques, with a solid grasp—not a dissolution—of recognizable, social, geographical and historical reality. The cases of Joyce's *Ulysses* and of Proust's *À la recherche du temps perdu* are in my view conclusive examples.

James, then—to conclude—provided exactly that model or that possible pattern: new, experimental, avant-garde ways of dealing with and

presenting a comprehensive view of life—the subtleties of consciousness and the vagaries of perception—together with the recognition (as
he had put it in an early dialogue) that 'art without life is a poor affair',
that it is only through reality that even its dissolution can be artistically
recorded and rendered.

3 *Italy in the International Theme*

> The ever hungry artist has only to trust old Italy
> for her to feed him at every single step from her hand.
> The great private palaces that are the massive
> majestic syllables, sentences, periods,
> of the strange message the place addresses to us.
>
> *Italian Hours* (1873)

1

Henry James's best-known motivation for his expatriation to Europe and for his choice of the international theme is in a notorious passage in his 1879 book on Hawthorne: 'the flower of art blooms only where the soil is deep … it takes a great deal of history to produce a little literature … it needs a complex social machinery to set a writer in motion.'[1] The absence of "all these things" in America had led Hawthorne into the airy regions of allegory and romance. But the post-Civil War American novelist, like his European *confrères* Balzac and Maupassant, Flaubert and Turgenev, had to face reality, to confront contemporary *mœurs*, to depict the customs of the age—*faire concurrence à l'état civil*, in Balzac's beautiful phrase. To write novels of manners, or indeed realistic novels, the American writer had therefore to go to Europe, where hierarchical, historical, and social aspects and signs were plentiful, and where, as James put it in a 1913 letter, 'after a fashion part of the work of discrimination and selection and primary clearing of the ground is already done for one … whereas over there in America I seemed to see

---

[1] Henry James, *Hawthorne*, ed. Tony Tanner, London, Macmillan, 1967, p. 23.

myself ... often beginning so 'low down' ... that all one's time went to it and one was spent before arriving at any very charming altitude.'[2]

One went to Europe, however, not to write about Europe as such, but to write about America *within the milieu and from the point of view of Europe.* This is made clear by a passage in James's *Autobiography:* 'To be so disconnected for the time, and in the most insidious manner, was above all what I had come out for ... There were, it appeared, things of interest taking place in America, and I had had, in this absurd manner, to come to England to learn it.'[3] Europe gave saliency by contrast to American features, characteristics, and idiosyncrasies. The 'international theme'—the confrontation of American characters and *mœurs*, morals and manners (or lack of manners) with European characters and *mœurs*, manners and morals (or lack of morals)—was therefore not only a 'burden' for the American writer ('for he *must* deal, more or less, even if only by implication, with Europe; whereas no European is obliged in the least to deal with America,' as James had observed in the *Notebooks*),[4] but a necessary choice and a challenge.

Elsewhere, in a later Preface, with a surprising image, James was to write of the confrontation between America and Europe in terms of two ladies on a dusty stage, propping up each other's 'infirmities':

> It does thus in truth come home to me that, combining and comparing in whatever proportions and by whatever lights, my "America" and its products would doubtless, as a theme, have betrayed gaps and infirmities enough without such a kicking-up of the dramatic dust (mainly in the foreground) as I could set my "Europe" in motion for; just as my Europe would probably have limped across our stage to no great effect of processional state

---

2   *The Letters of Henry James*, ed. Percy Lubbock, New York, Scribners, 1920, II, pp. 297-98.
3   *Henry James: Autobiography*, ed. F.W. Dupee, New York, Criterion, 1956, pp. 558-59.
4   *The Notebooks of Henry James*, eds F.O. Matthiessen and K.B. Murdock, New York, Braziller, 1955, pp. 24, 32-36.

without an ingenuous young America (constantly seen as ingenuous and young) to hold up its legendary train.[5]

Yet the choice of the international theme sustained most of James's fictional career and, as I have argued elsewhere, allowed him to dramatize the complexities of human behaviour on either side of the Atlantic, and as it were in between, through a functional and symbolic use of contrasting settings, characters and *mœurs*.

To put it briefly, for the sake of convenience and by way of introduction, the international theme had three main articulations in James.

First, the 'passionate pilgrim' or the American artist, starved and deprived at home, going to Europe to find historical depth and artistic richness, passion and human warmth, to be inspired and elated—only to find that passion and warmth are there excessive, the colors too strong, the richness too rich, so that he is crushed by the very wealth of the inner and outer inspiration he has sought. (An easy formula could be: *if America does not create, Europe destroys.*)

Second, the businessman or the self-made man, the 'new man', going to Europe to find leisure and the enjoyment of life, enlightenment and entertainment, a pleasurable use for his money, social refinement, possibly even a wife—and being of course defeated and betrayed by the complexities and the callousness of European society, the devious practices and the corruption, the lack of scruples and of morals, lurking under the lustre of European manners. (Here the formula could be: *if Europe has manners, America has morals.*)

Third, the American girl, the flower of the New Continent, the so-called or self-proclaimed 'heiress of all the ages', the free and open heroine of the expanding and unsubdued self, going to Europe to realize and express her freedom and her eagerness to live—only to find her innocence misunderstood, schemed upon, and betrayed, her aspira-

---

[5]   *The Art of the Novel: Critical Prefaces by Henry James*, ed. R. P. Blackmur, New York, Scribners, 1934, pp. 200-201.

tions 'ground in the very mill of the conventional', her imperious self bruised, constrained, and imprisoned by 'the hard carapace of circumstances'. (The formula here: *if you act by conviction, you're crushed by conventions.*)

Readers of James will have immediately identified my obvious references to *Roderick Hudson*, *The American*, *Daisy Miller*, and *The Portrait of a Lady* (in this order, and among others). In this complex game, the role of Europe is often ambivalent and paradoxical: she is glamorous and enticing, but treacherous and corrupting; rich in history and art, in social graces and social ease, but lacking in fundamental decencies and moral values, in honesty and human kindness, in seriousness of purpose. She pays with carelessness and corruption, moral insensitivity, physical as well as psychological violence, for her savoir faire, her historical depth, her artistic refinement. If you imagine a scissor-like movement (it is visualized below, chapter 11, section 1), Europe is up in manners but low in morals, whereas gauche and awkward America, so innocent of the world, is innocent in two ways—of social graces but also of corruption, of sophistication but also of deviousness: if she is down in manners, she is up in morals.

This is not, however, a clear-cut division: the good on one side, the bad on the other, good guy versus villain. The interest of James's contrast lies exactly in its problematic and ambivalent character, in what I have called its scissor-like movement: what you lose on one side, you gain on the other—the higher the level of morals, the lower the refinement of manners (in their all-encompassing sense, which includes art, history, tradition, a knowledge of the world), and vice versa.

In this complex articulation of the international theme, Italy plays a very specific, recognizable, functional, and symbolic role—especially involving the first and third narrative situations or strategies—and her ambivalent and paradoxical quality is beautifully exploited for the fictional purposes of contrast and definition. Italy is the land of beauty and of passion, of art and history, of longing and nostalgia, where the past is visible and visitable at almost every step, where it is indeed an inescapable presence; but Italy also proves again and again to be, in Conrad's terms, the destructive element; her beauty is terrible and devastating, her past a curse and a doom; her art and her social *mœurs* are unsettling, disturbing, often a trap for the unwary Americans.

2

In James's early stories on the international theme, Italy is very much the land of the picturesque, of artistic, historical, and sentimental exaltation. Some of these stories read like disguised Baedekers, barely fictionalized travelogues, and show the influence of both Ruskin and Hawthorne. Italy is predominantly and pre-eminently represented—mainly, however, as a background, a backcloth, a mere setting or a pretext for mildly inconsequential plots. She is the land where the passionate pilgrim can revel or be disquieted, but she is only incidentally connected with the development of narrative motifs.

In 'Travelling Companions' (1870), for instance, most of Italy is 'done'—from Milan to Venice, from Florence to Rome—with extensive descriptive passages that read like tourist guidebooks: the 'enchanting romance of Italy', the beauty of her people as well as of her landscapes, overwhelm a group of American travelers who 'must go in for the beautiful', are enthralled by the genius of the picturesque, are even tempted (as Hawthorne had already warned) by Catholicism. Love at first denied is, after the experience of Italy, accepted: but the story does seem a mere pretext for the description of cherished places.

In 'At Isella' (1871), too, the romance of Italy is made to coincide with romantic love, and the figures of her stark and inspiring past, from Lucrezia Borgia and Bianca Cappello to the heroines of Stendhal, are evoked. Nature is there 'refined and transmuted to Art'; one speaks of the 'symptoms' of Italy as of a mild intoxication, and a lengthy passage spells out the magic and the lure of the place, its 'Platonic' idea, for excessively passionate pilgrims:

> 'I have come on a pilgrimage', I said. 'To understand what I mean, you must have lived, as I have lived, in a land beyond the seas, barren of romance and of grace. This Italy of yours, on whose threshold I stand, is the home of history, of beauty, of the arts—of all that makes life splendid and sweet. Italy, for us dull strangers, is a magic world. We cross ourselves when we pronounce it. We are brought up to think that when we have learned leisure and rest—at some bright hour, when fortunes smiles—we may go forth and cross oceans and mountains and see on Italian soil the primal substance— the Platonic 'idea'—of our consoling dreams and our *richest* fancies.'[6]

It comes as no surprise that the Italian heroine is freed from bondage by an American hand which is ready to favour romance. In the opening pages of *Confidence* (1880), which are set in Siena, we are made to breathe in full 'the charm of the Italian spring', to feel the spell of the 'high picturesque' (including a *contadino* with donkey), and to see "what painters call a subject" in the view. Moving to Dresden in chapter 2, after Siena and Venice, is a letdown for the novel itself.[7]

---

6   *The Complete Tales of Henry James*, ed. Leon Edel, Philadelphia, Lippincott, 1961-64, II, p. 327. In *Italian Hours* we read of 'The way in which the Italian scene ... seems to purify itself to the transcendent and perfect *idea* alone—idea of beauty, of dignity, of comprehensive grace, with all accidents merged, all defects disowned, all experience outlived, and to gather itself up into the mere mute eloquence of what has just incalculably *been*, remains forever the secret and the lesson of the subtlest daughter of History ... when high Natural Elegance proceeds to take such exclusive charge and recklessly assume, as it were, *all* responsibilities'. And: 'Man lives more with Nature in Italy than in New or than in Old England; she does more work for him and gives him more holidays' (*Italian Hours,* New York, Grove Press, 1959, pp. 359, 165 [1873]).

7   At the very beginning of the novel we move from Siena, the 'flawless gift of the Middle Ages to the modern imagination', to an Arcadian scene in the countryside, with a terrace, an empty church, a fresco and an old beggar woman, a wall with a stone bench, 'what the painters call a subject' (p. 13).

Yet such idyllic and impassioned notes—which echo those lavishly provided by James in his travel essays—soon begin to betray signs of undisguised tension. As the heroine of James's earliest novel, *Watch and Ward* (1871), admits while traveling in Europe to assuage a sentimental crisis, 'One grows more in this wonderful Rome than in a year at home'. That growth and that knowledge are, however, soon identified with a sense of danger, of dissipation, of evil: 'I had rather not meet you again in Italy. It perverts our dear old American truths' says a character in 'Travelling Companions'. The experience of Italy, of its past as well as its present, is unsettling, to say the least, for the American devotee.

In 'The Madonna of the Future' (1873), the speaking character gives vent to a paradigmatic lament on Americans as the 'disinherited of art', condemned to be superficial, excluded from the magic circle, lacking the deeper sense; yet the American artist who has gone to Florence— where the ghosts of the past are all over the place—to paint a beautiful Madonna, finds himself in the evening of time and sinks into oblivion. He is bogged down, as well as sustained, by a bourgeois Egeria, and he must recognize that he has been dawdling for twenty years and has become a failure. This is the whimper of the failing artist in Italy, as against the bang we will hear in *Roderick Hudson*.

And what happens if, dissatisfied with the present, one tries to unearth and relive the past? In 'The Last of the Valerii' (1874), still very reminiscent of Hawthorne's *The Marble Faun*, the American heroine marries Count Valerio because 'he's the natural man', 'like a statue of the Decadence'. But when a real statue of Juno is unearthed in the garden, what at first appeared as a Garden of Eden turns into a nightmare. The statue casts a spell, Rome betrays a chilling strain, and the past hovers over the present as a blight. The statue—and the past—must be buried again.[8] In a similar way, in another early tale, 'Adina' (1874), the

---

[8]   While visiting the Forum in Rome James had seen the past 'bodily turned up with the spade and transformed from an immaterial, inaccessible fact of time into a matter of soil and surfaces' (*Italian Hours*, p. 143).

'blonde angel of New England origin' is made to go through a harrow-
ing experience until the topaz belonging to the times of Tiberius, found
in the Campagna, is buried again.[9]

These are rather conventional, even trifling stories, which only show
James's appreciation of Italy as a setting. 'Adina', in particular, reads
very much like a disguised travel guide and an exercise in the picturesque. The germs of the dichotomy as to the double role, function, and
nature of Italy in the international theme are, however, visibly there.
They become more clearly apparent in the novels.

In *Roderick Hudson* (1875) we have a perfect rendering of place,
and the paradigm of Rome's (and Italy's) destructive role. The young
American artist is brought there in order to find the inspiration and the
support he cannot have at home: he finds too much of it. Rome destroys him with its *excess* of beauty and of art, of activity and emotion
(even 'a passive life in Rome ... takes on a very respectable likeness to
activity', ch. 4), and through its double nature: 'if Roman life doesn't
do something substantial to make you happier, it increases tenfold
your liability to moral misery'.[10] 'Passion burns out, inspiration runs
to seed' (ch. 6). If living in Rome 'was an education to the senses and
the imagination', it nevertheless involves a deep sense of depression
and mortality, a premonition of disaster and ruin, which are brought
down on Roderick as much by Christina Light—'nominally an American. But it has taken twenty years of Europe to make her what she is!'
(ch. 5)—as by the place itself.

Rome is 'done' by James in this novel at length and at leisure, and
often in a recognizably romantic way: Villa Ludovisi and the Colos-

---

9   Before the gem is returned 'to the moldering underworld of the Roman past', in the
     Capuchin convent James sets up a perfect scene in *chiaroscuro*, with candles burn-
     ing in the dusk, where the American soul feels the strong attraction of Catholicism
     in a Hawthorne-like way. (*Complete Tales*, III, p. 241 ff.)
10   Similar ideas are expressed in *Italian Hours:* 'if in Rome you may suffer from en-
     nui, at least your ennui has a throbbing soul in it' (p. 205); there 'One has really
     vibrated too much' (p. 214), 'the pulse of life beats fast' (p. 255).

seum, the Church of St. Cecilia, St. Peter's, of course, which (here and elsewhere) James insists on seeing as a great mundane and vociferous social haunt. Yet another typical and revealing theme is the long association of the Palace of the Caesars (ch. 28) with the idea of vanity, decadence, dissipation, and death.[11]

An intoxication with Rome proves a subtle and destructive disease (it infects and unsettles even Roderick's fiancée Mary, from Northampton, Mass.). It can suggest a Hawthornesque (or indeed a Melvillian) idea of *felix culpa*, of a happy fall: "If I had not come to Rome I shouldn't have risen, and if I had not risen I shouldn't have fallen" (ch. 21).[12] But Roderick's agonized cry at the end sums up, and gives out, the real nature of his experience and of its setting: 'take me at least out of this terrible Italy ... where everything mocks and reproaches and torments and eludes me! Take me out of this land of terrible beauty, and put me in the midst of ugliness. Set me down where nature is coarse and flat, and men and manners are vulgar. There must be something awfully ugly in Germany.

---

[11] Although, in St. Peter's, Isabel Archer's 'conception of greatness rose and dizzily rose ... [and] she paid her silent tribute to the seated sublime,' James adds immediately that there was 'something almost profane in the vastness of the place', ministering to material as well as spiritual contemplation (*The Portrait of a Lady*, chapter 27); in 'The Solution' (1889) we read that 'If we treated the great church as a public promenade, or rather as a splendid international *salon*, the fault was not wholly ours' since St. Peter's protected conversation and even gossip harboured 'a faith that has no small pruderies to enforce' (*Complete Tales*, VII, p. 365). In *Italian Hours*, that church is likened to Piccadilly, Broadway, and the Paris boulevards (p. 149). For the Palace of the Caesars, see *Daisy Miller*, chapter 4 ('that beautiful abode of the flowering desolation'). In the *Autobiography* (pp. 153-54), James writes of the visual influence of Thomas Cole's ample canvasses—one of which was the celebrated view of the Palace of the Caesars as the seat of decadence.

[12] This idea is echoed in 'Four Meetings' (1877): 'I should go crazy if I did not go to Europe, and I should certainly go crazy if I did'. For Mary's puzzlement in Rome: 'at home ... things don't speak to us of enjoyment as they do here. Here it is such a mixture ... Beauty stands there ... and penetrates to one's soul and lodges there and keeps saying that man was not made to suffer but to enjoy. This place has undermined my stoicism, but ... I love it!' (*Roderick Hudson*, ch. 22).

Pack me off there!' (ch. 22). This is indeed a devastating conclusion for
a passionate pilgrim. Roderick is then brought to the placidity (not the
ugliness) of Lake Como, a kind of earthly paradise which is presented
as the epitome of the picturesque, where he could live forever: but he is
eventually lost in a precipice of the sublime Alps.[13]

Italy, then, the 'dishevelled nymph', the 'tousled *bonne fille*', rather then the *old coquine* or the *Hausfrau*, has wreaked a kind of vengeance on the aspiring artist: too much is too much.[14] In *Daisy Miller*
the geographical path is reversed—we move from Switzerland down to
Rome—but the result is pretty much the same. True, 'the child of nature
and of freedom' is betrayed more by Europeanized Americans than by
the Italians themselves; yet in Rome, so lovely in the spring, one feels
'the freshness of the year and the ambiguity of the place reaffirm themselves in mysterious interfusion' (ch. 4). The beauty is on the Pincio
and in Villa Borghese, in airy views of the city and its people that seem

---

[13]   For Como as an earthly paradise: 'it was the Italy that we know from the street
       engravings in old keepsakes and annals, from the vignettes on music-sheets and the
       drop-curtains at theaters; an Italy that we can never confess ourselves—in spite of
       our own changes and of Italy's—that we have ceased to believe' (chapter 23), and
       see below, ch. 4. One is reminded, in passing, that a crucial scene of confrontation
       between father and daughter in *Washington Square* (1880) is set in the Alps (chap-
       ter 24).

[14]   See *Letters* (Lubbock), II, p. 80, and in *Italian Hours*, p. 330: 'the sense of a su-
       premely intimate revelation of Italy in undress, so to speak (the state, it seemed,
       in which one would most fondly, most ideally, enjoy her); Italy no longer in win-
       ter starch and sobriety … the brilliant performer, in short, *en famille* … thanks to
       which she is by so much more the easy genius and the good creature as she is by
       so much less the advertised *prima donna*'; and p. 331: 'the tousled *bonne fille* of
       our vacational Tuscany'. James reserves for Italy (and particularly for Venice) his
       only expressions of almost physical love. – In real life, too, Italy could be too much
       for the artist: writing of the American sculptor and writer W. W. Story, who had
       settled in Rome, James noted that 'In Rome, Florence, Siena, there was too much
       … was it not this "too much" that constituted precisely, and most characteristically
       and gracefully, the amusement of the wanton Italy at the expense of her victim?',
       Henry James, *William Wetmore Story and his Friends,* London, Thames and Hud-
       son, 1903, II, p. 226.

to remind us of Boldini's paintings, on the Coelian Hill and the Arch of Constantine, even in St. Peter's. The Colosseum, however, harbours its secret venom—the *malaria*, the bad air, the Roman fever, the real as well as symbolic poison of the place[15]—and in the final scene, which provides a perfect example of *chiaroscuro* used for effect as much as for functional purposes, the unfortunate girl who has sought freedom and affirmation in Europe, with innocence and naïveté, is also destroyed by the ambivalent nature of Italy: 'The historic atmosphere was there, certainly; but the historic atmosphere, scientifically considered, was no better than a villainous miasma' (ch. 4).[16]

In its expanded version, in *The Portrait of a Lady* (1881), Italy appears as a crucial setting after England (in chapter 21); it appears as the land of promise, comforted by endless knowledge, where the love of the beautiful prevails. Isabel pauses in San Remo on the edge of a larger adventure. We all know what beautiful Italy, and her Italianate American, Gilbert Osmond, have in store for her. The double nature of Italy and the type of experience she leads to is suggested mainly by and through her buildings. The Florentine villa, in chapter 22, has a front which is a mask, not the face of the house; it has lids, but not eyes, its windows 'seemed less to offer communication with the world than to defy the world to look in'. It is again a prolepsis, or a premonition. One does acts of mental prostration to Italy; "Rome, as Ralph said, confessed to the psychological moment" (ch. 27); it is an exquisite medium for impressions (ch. 28). Isabel is struck by St. Peter's and pays 'her silent tribute to the seated sublime'. Yet she ends up in Palazzo Rocca-

---

[15] See 'The waning moon is veiled in a thin cloud-curtain; the empty arches of the dusky circle of the Coliseum are cavernous shadows, but the arena is clear and silent; there is a fusion of deep shade and luminous dusk. Of course one has to read lines out of Byron's *Manfred* there' (chapter 4).

[16] Similar ideas are expressed in *Italian Hours*: 'The Roman air is charged with an elixir, the Roman cup seasoned with some insidious drop' (p. 205), or in this passage about the waste of the Casino of Villa Madama [1909]: 'Endless for the didactic observer the moral, abysmal for the story-teller the tale' (p. 208).

nera, 'a kind of domestic fortress ... which smelt of historical deeds, of crime and craft and violence', much in the tradition of the Gothic novel, where her aspiration to freedom and self-possession will be crushed by Osmond's viciousness as much as by the spirit of the place.[17]

As we know, the land of beauty gives way to the place of oppression. Isabel's free and imperious self is crushed by the 'hard carapace of circumstances' she has overlooked. Her 'innocence' of the world and her wish to follow purely her inner convictions lead her to misery and ruin. Yet Italy becomes part of, or has a role in, that process of enslavement. Osmond himself will warn her against the superstition of an excessive love for Rome (ch. 48),[18] and Isabel herself will eventually feel Rome's misery (ch. 40). Gardencourt, the English country house of the first chapters of the novel, stands as the opposite of her Italian edifice with its dark, cold dusk (ch. 54). Italy has turned into a land of oppression, a darkened world, in a physical as well as a psychological sense; and the Italian setting has much to do with Isabel's well-known sentiments during her vigil (ch. 42):

> she had suddenly found the infinite vista of a multiplied life to be a dark, narrow alley with a dead wall at the end. Instead of leading to high places of happiness ... it led rather downward and earthward, into realms of restriction and depression ... It was the house of darkness, the house of

---

[17] In *Italian Hours* James had identified Italy with the 'extraordinary in the romantic' and referred to her Gothic potentialities. The Benedictine convent at Subiaco, 'which clings to certain more or less vertiginous ledges and slopes of a vast precipitous gorge, constitutes, with the whole perfection of its setting, the very ideal of the tradition of that *extraordinary in the romantic* handed down to us, as the most attaching and inviting spell of Italy, by all the old academic literature of travel and art of the Salvator Rosas and Claudes' [1909] (p. 221).

[18] We also read that 'Italy, all the same, has spoiled a great many people ... It made one idle and dilettantish and second-rate'. For Osmond, 'there is nothing tonic in Italian life'.

dumbness, the house of suffocation ... She seemed shut up with an odour
of mould and decay.

This sense of oppression and suffocation is what, tragically and para-
doxically, the beauty and promise of Italy has left her with.

Yet old Rome, which Isabel has taken into her confidence, teaches
her that suffering is the common lot of humanity, that 'in the world of
ruins the ruin of her happiness seemed a less unnatural catastrophe'. 'In
the large Roman record', hers was small; the place where so many had
suffered 'seemed to offer her a companionship in endurance'. At such
moments, in Italy, she could not 'have been more liable to a spiritual
visitation'. Isabel's ride in the Campagna draws her to gaze 'through the
veil of her personal sadness at the splendid sadness of the scene' (ch.
49). This final oxymoron is applicable to her own experience.

3

After *The Portrait of a Lady*, James took a deep breath and turned away
from the international theme. Italy, however, appears in intriguing and
crucial ways in some of his in-between studies. In *Washington Square*
(1880), a purely American novel, in a lonely valley in the Italian Alps
where the heroine has been sent—as usual—to get wise, Catherine
Sloper confronts her father and tells him that she is not going to give
up her dubious lover. She will be steady. In *The Princess Casamassima*
(1886), a purely English novel, the crucial turning point of the young
revolutionary, Hyacinth Robinson, is brought about by his experience
of Paris and Venice in particular. In Venice, as he tells his mentor in his
well-known 'Letter from Venice' (chapter 30), he has had a 'revelation
of the exquisite', a vision of artistic beauty that totally unsettles his
composure and leads him to renege on his pledge to destroy the existing
order of society. Such a 'splendid accumulation of the happier few', so
'precious and beautiful', makes him feel 'capable of fighting for them'.

'The monuments and the treasures of art, the great palaces and properties, the conquests of learning and taste', in spite of being based 'upon
the despotisms, the cruelties, the exclusions, the monopolies and the
rapacities of the past', lead him to swerve from his vow. The beauties
of Italy are a crucial experience for Hyacinth Robinson; nothing can or
will be the same after such knowledge.

Venice is again overwhelmingly present in *The Aspern Papers*
(1888), a tale that could be read, in fact, in the light of the international
theme. Here, too, the city plays a fundamental, indeed, a double role,
with new emphases and a possible twist. We have here the Venice of the
tourist guide and the romantic imagination: St. Mark's as an 'open-air
salon', the ghostly church, the house within the garden in Rio Marin, an
environment and atmosphere which form the perfect shrine for the cus-
todians of the relics of the great American poet (even if the references,
we read, 'would have seemed to carry one back to the rococo Venice of
Casanova'). The Piazzetta and Florian's are forcefully present as tourist
places. Yet the city acquires a strong symbolic connotation: the Grand
Canal, on the occasion of two gondola rides, the lagoon itself way out
to the Lido, become a perfect objective correlative of the windings of
the protagonist's mind, of his doubts and fears.[19] As he wanders about
in the city, we are told, he wonders: a strict connection is established in
perfect Jamesian fashion between the physical and the mental orders:
'floating aimlessly about on the lagoon' is a way to shed, or indeed to
increase, bewilderment. Being lost in the labyrinthine city is, for the
protagonist, the perfect way to be 'lost in wonder' (ch. 9). In the afternoon of that day of reckoning, moreover, in which he has to make his

---

[19]   In *Italian Hours* we are warned that 'Venice isn't in fair weather a place for concen-
       tration of mind' (p. 13); yet in *The Aspern Papers*, in early autumn, the freshness
       of the weather from the sea is conducive to meditation and thought. 'I wanted to
       walk, to move, to shed some of my bewilderment'; we also read of a 'long day of
       confusion, which I spent entirely in wandering about, without going home, until
       late at night; it only comes back to me that there were moments when I pacified my
       conscience and others when I lashed it into pain' (chapter 9).

choice, a prominent feature of the city, the elevated statue of Colleoni, looking 'far over his head', makes him realize that his battles and stratagems are of a very different kind, that he is no man of action, that he is imprisoned in the poor logic of the intellectual and the amateur, that he is living his life vicariously by preying on the ghosts of the past.

Venice, in *The Aspern Papers*, is a city of sociability, 'without streets and vehicles ... the place has the character of an immense collective apartment'; it is a theater of human life. Yet, in spite of its Ruskinian touches, Venice—and by extension, Italy—acquires here a direct bearing on the characters and their experience. It is mildly unsettling, a crucial place for bringing their souls to a crisis. 'So right and left, in Italy—before the great historic complexity at least—penetration fails ... But we exaggerate our gathered values only if we are eminently witless', James was to write in the preface to that tale. The 'gathered values' of Italy (and of Venice in particular, as Venice seems to become more and more one of James's cherished settings)[20] will soon be in full force again.

In stories like 'Georgina's Reasons' (1884) and 'A Modern Warning' (1884), both loosely dealing with international themes, Italy is purely incidental, a matter of simple local reference. In another story, 'The So-

---

[20]   See *The Art of the Novel*, p. 160. James's well-known description of Venice in this tale is worth quoting again: 'Without streets and vehicles, the uproar of wheels, the brutality of horses, and with its little winding ways where people crowd together, where voices sound as in the corridors of a house, where the human step circulates as if it skirted the angles of furniture and shoes never wear out, the place has the character of an immense collective apartment, in which Piazza San Marco is the most ornamental corner and palaces and churches, for the rest, play the part of great divans of repose, tables of entertainment, expanses of decoration. And somehow the splendid common domicile, familiar, domestic and resonant, also resembles a theater in which actors clicking over bridges and, in straggling processions, tripping along fondamentas. As you sit in your gondola the footways that in certain parts edge the canals assume to the eye the importance of a stage, meeting it at the same angle, and the Venetian figures, moving to and fro against the battered scenery of their little houses of comedy, strike you as members of an endless dramatic troupe' (chapter 9).

lution' (1889), the pictorial Rome of the popes and its Campagna, 'before the Italians had arrived and the local color departed', reappear in a purely romantic light: for impoverished and unimaginative Americans, Rome is the capital where the least money 'would go furthest in the way of grandeur'. Frascati is a place for picnics and the Campagna is 'like a haunted sea'. The great church of St. Peter's reappears 'as a public promenade, or rather a splendid international *salon*' which 'protected conversation and even gossip'.

Italy is here a perfect place for pleasant comedy, reverting back to Arcadian innocence, and evokes acts of pure chivalry: but it is mainly background. Two years later, in 'The Pupil' (1891), Venice resurfaces as the topos for the young protagonist's crisis, which is cast in an almost sinister, autumnal light. Thus, romantic Italy becomes once more imbued with tragic potential.[21] The November rain lashing about in a livid lagoon is of course a central element—not merely a background—of the next, great 'international' novel, where the Italian setting is featured in a prominent way: *The Wings of the Dove* (1902), James's swansong on the fictional use of Italy, and of Venice.

4

In *The Wings of the Dove*, the theme is the almost decadent one of 'death in Venice', but the implications and the forces at work are tragic. Quite understandably, Milly Theale's premonition of her fate in Italy is Wagnerian: 'It was the Wagner overture that practically prevailed, up through Italy, where Milly had already been' (Bk. III ch. 5). Her final tone is that of subdued surrender to silence and death.

---

[21]   In *Italian Hours*, Venice is at length and variously described as 'the most beautiful of tombs' (p. 32), providing a 'terrible standard of enjoyment' (p. 20), and representing all Europe (p. 69). Under the weight of her treasures, she is 'insupportably sad'; in contrast, Florence offers 'the sense of saving sanity' (p. 274). The Arcadian side of Italy is stressed in the almost contemporary tale 'The Solution' (1889).

The 'potential heiress of all the ages', the American natural princess, 'looking down on the kingdoms of the earth', 'one of the finest, one of the rarest ... cases of American intensity', hovering, rather than pouncing, on her destiny—'isolated, unmothered, unguarded, but with her other strong marks', rich and free as she is, with her big money that is a poor and treacherous compensation for her failing health, goes to Europe for its 'remedial properties'. And in Europe, desperately wanting to live as she is, she will naturally meet her death and transfiguration. First we have London, where the dangers are admittedly greater than in New York or Boston; Venice only witnesses the final steps of her extinction, but it is far more than an appropriate setting. It is the symphonic ambience and specular image of her fate. Milly is first 'successfully deceived' in England and by English people, but the consummation of her deception, betrayal, and death finds in Venice the proper conditioning and the suitable echo.

Venice is 'done' in the novel because of the city's relation to the heroine and because Milly is in full possession of the place (VII 26): we have the Rialto and the Bridge of Sighs, with a central role assigned to St. Mark's as the 'great social saloon', the 'blue-roofed chamber of amenity' (VIII 27).[22] But when the crisis comes, we all know, 'It was a Venice of evil ... A Venice of cold, lashing rain from a low black sky, of wicked rain raging through narrow passes'; the 'great drawing room, the great drawing room of Europe' is profaned by bad weather, and it is precisely there and in that climate that Milly hears of her betrayal from Lord Mark—so that it comes as no surprise that 'the vice in the air, otherwise, was too much like the breath of fate'. I take it that this phrase is meant to emphasize the perfect coincidence of place and destiny, of locale and story: 'The weather had changed, the rain was ugly, the wind wicked, the sea impossible, *because* of Lord Mark' (IX 30).

---

[22] Yet in the Palazzo Leporelli, Milly Theale also feels 'as in a fortress', 'a painted idol'. We think for a moment of Isabel Archer. And Milly wanders (and wonders) in Venice much as the narrator of *The Aspern Papers* had done.

The rain *is* tears. The wind makes Milly face the wall, and when after three days 'Venice glowed and plashed and called and dived again' (IX 32), the horrible feeling of an unprecedented, cold Venice in the rain is not dispelled. This death in Venice has a cutting edge, has nothing in common with Thomas Mann's. It is a bang, not a whimper, in spite of James's well-rehearsed silences and reticence. One might contend that Venice *after* the lashing rain ('the air was like a clap of hands, and the scattered pinks, yellows, blues, tea-greens, were like a hanging-out of vivid stuffs, a laying down of fine carpets', [IX 32]) prefigures Milly's eventual transfiguration into a dove hovering in the air with protective, outstretched wings: but this would be to forget that her wings are also threatening and doom Kate Croy and Merton Densher, the betrayers, to separation and defeat ('we shall never be again as we were!' as the last line reads). A streak of evil and destruction seems to pertain even here to the beauty of Italy—that beauty which is ominous and terrible. As such it is a double-edged gift of history, or of the gods. Doom is inherent in beauty, the wealth of art and money is chilled by a gust of rain.

One might stress that the pressure of the place is here intense but less pervasive than in *The Portrait of a Lady*, a novel with which *The Wings of the Dove* is often compared, if only to show the path James traveled from his early to his late manner. One would have to ascribe this to James's increasing rarefaction of his backgrounds, and to his belief that in his 'major phase' he was eschewing 'international' notations and connotations.[23] Yet in *The Wings of the Dove* he reverted to a close correlation of theme with setting, and Italy plays there a crucial part in the long series of fictional exploitations I have been describing so far.

Just as, nearing the end of his career, James erected this complex setting for the betrayal and death of an American princess, so too did

---

[23]   *The Art* of *the Novel*, pp. 198-99. In a letter, Edith Wharton had been one of the first to remark on the rarefaction of James's settings in his later novels.

he contemplate the fall of Italian princes. In 'Miss Gunton of Pough-keepsie' (1900), a little-known story revolving around a question of pique, a young and wilful American girl breaks her engagement with a Roman prince ('one of the most ancient of princes'), and happily marries an American. Italy here is very much a shady background. And what about that great majestic structure of James's last years, *The Golden Bowl* (1903)? There is no description of places, no overwhelming presence of functional or symbolic locales in this most rarefied and abstract of his novels: only the frail Murano crystal as a central but elusive symbol. Yet Prince Amerigo is meant and made to embody, though mainly 'by indirection', his Roman past and heritage, history and tradition, Renaissance as well as papal Rome. And this imposing figure, whom the American millionaire Adam Verver sees as a 'great Palladian church' (I 7), and who evokes the image of an outlandish pagoda in his daughter Maggie (II 1), is bought as 'a rarity, an object of beauty, an object of price' (I 1) and exiled in London, in spite of his yearning and nostalgia for the sunny, and even the picturesque, side of Italy.[24]

The quintessence of historical and artistic Italy is here made to pay tribute to the acquisitiveness and tight control of a new American family. I do not wish to stretch the point—which would probably be unfair to both James's total absorption, at this stage, in the problems of consciousness, and to his late American pilgrims to Europe. I offer it only as an aftermath in the long, long story of James's 'international theme', in which the beauty and the enticement of Italy prove a double-edged menace. Her sunny atmosphere harbours mischief; her magnificent past can be a blight; her exuberance proves destructive; her open vistas close like vices on unsuspecting pilgrims. There the weight of tradition lies heavy on the soul, and the pressure of social circumstances crushes the

---

[24]   On Prince Amerigo as an epitome of Italy, and related aspects of *The Golden Bowl*, cf. Carl Maves, *Sensuous Pessimism: Italy in the Work of Henry James,* Bloomington, Indiana U. P., 1973.

hopeful dream of the imperious American self. Knowing Italy, for most
of James's characters, is equal to eating of the Tree of Knowledge, and
this implies turning innocence into experience, an encounter with evil,
often a premonition of death. 'After such knowledge', one is tempted
to say with T.S. Eliot, 'what forgiveness?'—except that all this is done
in James's beautifully paradoxical or chiastic way. Beauty is still there
after disaster has come; the blast of evil is almost a fair price to pay for
its existence.[25]

---

[25] Much as he preferred the pre-1870 'romantic' Italy, James was also aware of the
      'new' Italy after unification, and has revealing aperçus in *Italian Hours*: 'Young
      Italy, preoccupied with its economical and political future, must be heartily tired
      of being admired for its eyelashes and its pose' (p. 111); 'It is in this attitude and
      with these conventional accessories that the world has seen fit to represent young
      Italy, and one doesn't wonder that if the youth has any spirit he should at last begin
      to resent our insufferable aesthetic patronage' (p. 112). He had seen Rome 'in its
      superbest scarlet in 1869' (p. 198) and has nostalgic pages on papal Rome, but he
      also draws a comparison between present and past Italy (p. 248) and wishes 'to try
      at least to read something of the old soul into the new forms' (p. 271). As for my
      reading of the role of Italy in James's novels, I refer to my second epigraph: 'the
      great private palaces that are the massive majestic *syllables, sentences, periods,* of
      the strange message the place addresses to us' (*Italian Hours*, p. 252; my emphasis)
      as providing a crucial key.

4 *Henry James and Northern Italy*

> Our observation in any foreign land is extremely
> superficial, and our remarks are happily not addressed
> to the inhabitants themselves, who would be sure
> to exclaim upon the impudence of the fancy-picture.
>
> *Italian Hours*

1

Henry James had a peculiar way of characterizing countries, by pros-opopeia, or personification—mostly feminine. England was 'a good married matron,' Germany a tidy *Hausfrau*, Amsterdam (and by extension, Holland) 'the portrait of a thrifty farmer's wife.' Switzerland was 'a magnificent man,' while Italy was 'a beautiful dishevelled nymph' (though she could also be, in turns, the 'old *coquine*,' a *prima donna*, sometimes in undress, or a 'tousled *bonne fille*', as we have intimated in the previous chapter). In his 'inexorable Yankeehood,' even at a later stage he could not refrain from quoting Robert Browning's 'Oh Italy, thou woman-land!'.[1]

---

[1]   Leon Edel, *Henry James. The Untried Years,* Philadelphia, Lippincott, 1953, p. 295; *Henry James: Letters,* ed. Leon Edel, Cambridge, The Belknap Press of Harvard U. P., 1974-84, 4 vols, I, p. 137 (henceforth *L* in the text); Henry James, *The American Scene,* in *Collected Travel Writings*: *Great Britain and America* [vol. I]; *The Continent* [vol. II], New York, Library of America, 1993, II, p. 666 ('the Dutch city [Amsterdam] is a complete reversal of the Italian'), II, p. 372 ('after two months of Switzerland the Lombard plain is a rich rest to the eye'), and II, pp. 586-87 for Italy *en famille,* a *prima donna* and a 'tousled *bonne fille*' [henceforth *CTW1* and *CTW2* in the text]). *The Complete Tales of Henry James,* ed. Leon Edel, London, Hart-Davis, 1961-1964, 12 vols. (henceforth *CT* in the text).

Henry James cut through Europe from NW to SE, from Great Britain by way of France, Belgium, Switzerland, sometimes Bavaria, down to Italy, and left almost everything else out of his view. In this partial and highly personal view, countries and places acquire metaphorical values, and James seems to set up a series of contrasts to emphasize or enhance his predilection for artistic Italy at the expense of her neighboring countries. In Switzerland you have 'nature in the rough'; 'an overdose of mountains and valleys, however beautiful and transmuted to art' (*CTW2*, p. 625; *L*, III 391; *CT*, I 307). Germany is not only homely ('wherever the German tone of things prevails, a certain rich and delectable homeliness goes with it,' *CTW2*, p. 632), but plain, indeed ugly: 'Germany is ugly … Munich is a nightmare, Heidelberg a disappointment (in spite of its charming castle) and even Nuremberg not a joy for ever' (*CTW2*, p. 345, echoed in *L*, I 23-32). By contrast, Italy is stereotypically, but also crucially, the land of beauty, the garden of art, the seat of the past and of historical consciousness: not only 'the sweetest impression of life,' but 'quella terra santa' [*sic*], 'that Paradise that makes every other place a purgatory at best.'[2]

So much has been written on this topic, on James's applying of the aesthetic varnish on Italy—though he realized that she might resent what amounted to an 'insufferable aesthetic patronage' (*CTW2*, p. 393)—that I need hardly mention it, except to stress, for our purposes, the series of contrasts, open or implied that he set up in his view and treatment of Italy and her surrounding countries. They involved Nature, History, and above all Art.

---

[2]   *Letters*, III 394, and *CTW2*, p. 511: 'Adorable Italy in which … these so harmoniously-grouped and individually-seasoned fruits of the great garden of history, keep presenting themselves'; James was never in tuning with the Germans: 'I can't do much with the Germans—they are somehow not in my line … They are ugly and mighty—they have (I think) lots of future, but a most intolerable present' (*L*, III 367). His personal and artistic dislike became cultural and political during World War I (*CTW2*, pp. 768-70).

We go to Italy to gaze upon certain of the highest achievements of human power—achievements, moreover, which, from their visible and tangible nature, are particularly well adapted to represent to the imagination the *maximum* of man's creative force. So wide is the interval between the great Italian neighbouring nations, that we find ourselves willing to look upon the former as the ideal and the perfection of human effort

he wrote in an early review of W.D. Howells's *Italian Journeys*.[3]

'The heart grows heavy as one reflects what art might have come to if it had developed exclusively in northern lands,' he pondered; painters in Italy may 'fall short of beauty … The early Germans do not seem to have suspected that such a thing existed' (*CTW2*, pp. 661-62).

In 'blest old Italy,' which was at one point identified with the '*extraordinary in the romantic*' (*CTW2*, p. 490), Henry could 'at least—for the first time—live!', as he wrote in a well-known letter (*L, I* 160). His brother William, instead, idealized the Swiss precisely as a contrasting focal point to Italy, which was for him, at least for a number of years, sunk in decay, covered with grime, too much preoccupied with art. The 'superior morality of the Swiss' was an antidote to the 'moribund latinity' and 'sweet rottenness' of Italy. William saw Germany as the place of the mind, of intellectual stability and pursuit. Whereas Henry was seeking for style, artistic beauty and historical values through the senses, visual impressions and a vibrant consciousness, William favored the qualities of intellectual application, learning and cultural strain that he associated with Germany.[4] This polarity between the two brothers reflected a divergence in outlook and commitment which allowed Henry

---

[3]   1867, in Henry James, *Literary Criticism. Essays in Literature. American and English Writers*, New York, Library of America, 1984, p. 476.

[4]   In a typically nineteenth-century manner, Henry's attitude is that of the idler, the *flâneur*, dawdling and gaping so as to be exposed to sensory and artistic impressions. See his *Autobiography*, ed. F. W. Dupee, New York, Criterion, 1956, *passim*. Germany was not conducive to it. His brother William had (as usual) a quite different view.

to build his majestic view of contrasts not only between Europe and America, but within Europe herself, in essays, letters, novels and tales.

2

If Italy was the land of the sun and breathed 'the spirit of the South,' we know that every South has its North and every North its South; their values are purely relative, interminglings are inescapable. 'Once I am in Italy it is about the same to me to be in one place as in another,' Henry James wrote *(L,* III 145), but it was not really so.

Rome, Florence and Venice were the cities of the Grand Tour and remained for him places of the imagination, epitomes of poetic associations, of artistic and historic accretions: they represented the 'Platonic idea' of Italy (*CT,* I 367). Yet Northern Italy—i.e. the Alpine crescent and the Po valley, with 'that golden chain of historic cities which stretches from Milan to Venice' (*CTW2,* p. 336)—was seen and represented in essays and countless letters as a kind of borderline, a sort of neutral ground where North and South could meet, 'and each imbue itself with the nature of the other' (to paraphrase Nathaniel Hawthorne). It was a region allowing for the propinquity or the coexistence of opposites, which in his fiction often became the seat of crucial rites of passage.

On the autobiographical level, the note is given in his well-known letter: 'the sense of going down into Italy—the delight of seeing the north melt slowly *into* the south ... Down, down—on, on into Italy we went—a rapturous progress' *(L,* I 128). This borderline region is marked at the two extremes, West and East, by two poetic and almost purely ideal *enclaves*: Lake Como, on the one side, often represented as a demi-paradise, an Eden-like combination of natural beauty and suspended peace (see chapter 3, above), and Venice, on the other, at the far end of the Veneto-Austria (as it was once called), as the absolute embodiment of unsurpassed artistic beauty and enchantment, and as the epitome of Europe itself ('Venice which represents all Europe as having at one time or another revelled and rested ... there' [*CTW2,* p. 351]). In-between, the downward movement allows to mediate between the masculinity, the decorum, the sobriety of Northern and Central Europe, and the charm, liveliness and femininity of the South, in a region which is characterized by a mingling of intellectual control and restraint with the claims of art, sentiment, and beauty.

In these mediations and encounters, mountain passes are James's cherished metaphors of felt experience:[5] they open up vistas of loveliness through narrowness and constraint. Mont Cenis, the Simplon, the Old Saint-Gothard, the Splügen appear in this function in so many of his early letters (notably to T. S. Perry [*L,* I 23-26], or the one to Alice about his appropriation of Italy, [*ib.,* pp. 126-30]) and essays, such as 'From Chambery to Milan' and 'The Old Saint-Gothard' (1873). They open up to the beauty of Italian lakes (*CTW2,* pp. 374, 384), which stand this side of the mountains as a sort of initiation *into* a cool and clear 'South.' In the following essay, 'The Splügen' (1874), the movement is reversed; but the implications are the same: Northern Italy is seen as a mediator between North and South, i.e. between detachment and felt life (*CTW2,* pp. 655-56). As you leave it, you enter the Via Mala and end in the anticlimax of Chur, whose stance and whose ornaments 'are both very florid and very frugal' (*ib.,* p. 660).

The first section of 'The Splügen' is on Milan, its Cathedral and, rather surprisingly, its women. This brings us to a second, crucial consideration. The cities of the northern golden chain are usually described and characterized in artistic terms and in their feminine and/or masculine prosopopeias, which are here often combined or made to coexist— whereas we know, for instance, that for Venice only feminine qualifications will do. Genoa is a 'topographical tangle,' the 'crookedest and most incoherent of cities,' where great structures are superimposed on dark alleys and bee-hives teeming with people (*CTW2,* p. 395). Turin is

---

[5] This is before the oncoming novelty of tunnels, by which nature is going to be superseded (*CTW2,* p. 382).

a city of arcades (*CTW2*, pp. 368-69), of rectangular prospects; a 'place less bravely peninsular than Florence or Rome' and 'more in the scenic tradition than New York or Paris' (*CTW2*, p. 389); it has a palatial quality, elevation and extent, grand proportions (*CTW2*, p. 390)—not the magnificent flimsiness and aerial incorporeity of Venice, at the other end of the spectrum.

It is in Milan, however, that the mediation between metaphorical opposites is clearly perceived: 'in its general aspects [we read] still lingers a northern reserve which makes the place rather perhaps the last of the prose capitals than the first of the poetic. The long Austrian occupation perhaps did something to Germanise its physiognomy; though indeed this is an indifferent explanation when one remembers how well, temporarily speaking, Italy held her own in Venetia' (*CTW2*, p. 369). 'If not bristling with the aesthetic impulse,' its Cathedral betrays a peculiar, double nature: it is 'a supreme embodiment of vigorous effort,' of difficulties mastered, resources combined, labor, courage and patience (all hardly 'Italian' qualities: 'And there are people who tell us that art has not to do with morality!', James adds [*CTW2*, p. 370]).

These quotations are from the essay 'From Chambery to Milan.' In the already-quoted 'The Splügen', James had expressed similar views: the great Milan Cathedral, 'a very noble piece of Gothic architecture,' is characterized by 'splendid solidity of form' (*CTW2*, p. 654), by coolness and grandeur combined, which allow for human feelings and participation. Milan women are finally singled out as 'the most sympathetic' in Italy, and contrasted with those south of the Apennines, especially at Rome and Naples, where 'one enters the circle of Oriental tradition,' the realm of Zuleikas and Gulnares (*CTW2*, p. 655). Milan can also boast of 'the most scientific, the most calculating of all the painters,' Leonardo: but his masterpiece, the Cenacolo, is subject to the cruellest irony of fate—the 'anguish of decay.' He built 'his goodly house upon the sand' (*CTW2*, p. 372): this is the danger of mediating between contrasting principles.

In these three aspects of James's Milan I perceive the embodiment of a Northern Italy at the crossroads between stern North and mellow

South, between the solidity of Central Europe and the dissipation of sunny lands. As we move eastward with James in the Po valley, we meet with similar situations.

The charm of Verona, James confesses, is deepened by a subsequent ten-day experience in Germany. 'I rose one morning at Verona, and went to bed at night at Botzen! The statement needs no comment,' he remarks in 'Venice: An Early Impression' (1872), 'and the two places, though but fifty miles apart, are as painfully dissimilar as their names' (*CTW2*, p. 344). Bozen was then in Austria,[6] but it served the purpose of contrasting the ugliness of the German polarity (here James launched on his tirade against Munich and Heidelberg and Nuremberg which I quoted at the beginning), with its southern counterpart. 'If Munich is ugly,' he continued, 'Verona is beautiful enough. You may laugh at my logic, but will probably assent to my meaning' (*CTW2*, p. 345). The meaning, if we assent to it, at least in terms of my reading of James's Northern Italy, is that Verona is solid as a German city and at the same time 'all deliciously Italian'; it is 'blessed by the presence of *manlier* art,' by 'majestic chastity.' The Tombs of the Scaligers represent and embody the 'exquisite refinement and concentration of the Gothic idea' (*CTW2*, p. 346), he wrote. We know that ever since the Renaissance 'Gothic' meant 'German' in opposition to the ideal of Italian composure: the sentence may stand here for what I have been trying to convey so far.

The same, or something similar, is true of Ravenna, to which James devoted an essay written while he was in Switzerland (1873): the 'mortal sunny sadness of the place' (*CTW2*, p. 592) does not detract from its historic dignity. The Corso—as against the Corso in Rome,

---

[6]   Later on, in June 1890, when James went to Oberammergau with the Curtises to see the Passion Play, he was enchanted by the journey and the countryside: 'all these Tyrolean countries are beyond praise—and the several days' drive was magnificent.' But he found the Passion Play 'curious, tedious, touching, intensely respectable and intensely German' (*L*, III 293: here we go again). And for a further view of Verona *vs* Germany, see *L*, I 296-97.

for instance—speaks of seclusion and repose; 'all her monuments and relics are harmoniously rigid' (*CTW2*, p. 594). Although now almost a village in her dreariness, the city dominated by the mausoleum of Galla Placidia ('This is perhaps on the whole the spot in Ravenna where the impression is of most sovereign authority and most thrilling force' [*CTW2*, p. 597]) and by the grave of Dante, speaks the language of a Mediterranean sternness.

This is not the case, as I intimated earlier, of Venice, at the far end of the line or spectrum, which James visited for the first time just a few years after it had been reunited to Italy, which he declared explicitly 'Italianissima,' and which he always saw as the place of absolute and timeless artistic achievement—'the Venice of dreams, more than of any appreciable reality' (*L*, I 134), though frequently in danger of turning into 'the most beautiful of tombs' (*CTW2*, p. 314). So much, again, has been written on his views and representations of Venice,[7] that I will restrict myself to just a few remarks in the next section on the rites of passage James enacted in this double-edged Northern Italy. By 'rites of passage' I mean the divesting of one's former self and identity and the assumption of tempting (or tentative) new ones; the shedding-off of preconceived notions in favor of tantalizing new ones, however temporary.

3

I have used enough oxymora in my last sentences—'sunny sadness,' 'majestic chastity,' 'harmoniously rigid,' 'beautiful tomb': rites of passage between opposites find their appropriate setting precisely in a region where geography and metaphors are steeped in oxymora. Como, we saw, was frequently identified in James's essays and fiction with the valley of Eden ('They spent a couple of days on the Lake of Como ...

---

7   See, among others, Tony Tanner, *Venice Desired*, Oxford, Blackwell, 1992, and *Henry James e Venezia*, ed. Sergio Perosa, Firenze, Olschki, 1987.

They agreed it was the earthly paradise ... It all was consummately picturesque'). Yet 'The Lake of Como has figured largely in novels of "immoral" tendency,' James noted,[8] and he capitalized on these ambivalences.

One of his earliest stories, 'Travelling Companions' (1870), reads like a fictionalized counterpart of his early essays, except that it preceded them. We move with the characters from Milan to Venice by way of Verona and Vicenza (only the final part is set in central and southern Italy), and we have extensive descriptions of the cherished Northern Italian places I have so far touched upon: the descent to Italy, the architectural and artistic sights, etc. The story reads indeed like an extended travelogue, and the metaphorical set-up corresponds exactly to that of the essays. The protagonist comes to Northern Italy after an extended stay in Germany, and is deeply 'German'; in Milan he revels in the 'builded sublime' of its Cathedral, the Cenacolo, and so forth; in Venice, at the other end, he encounters sadness and romance. His love story with a deeply American young woman is kindled and brought to solution by and within those polarities.

As we saw, another early story, 'At Isella' (1871), expresses the ideal, and indeed the 'Platonic idea,' of Italy in impassioned pages (*CT,* I 327); it uses the borderline between Switzerland and Italy for the solution, by a well-meaning American, of the romance of an Italian heroine, who is allowed to flee for safety to Switzerland (the place, as we saw, of brute nature *vs.* the refinement of Italy). The story and its characters are steeped in stereotypes. As for Roderick Hudson, the protagonist of the novel of that name (1876), we saw that he is ruined by destructive Rome, and we heard his cry: 'take me at least out of this terrible Italy ... Take me out of this land of terrible beauty, and put me in the midst of ugliness. Set me down where nature is coarse and flat, and men and manners vulgar. There must be something awfully ugly in Germany.

---

[8]   *Roderick Hudson* [1878], London, Hart-Davis, 1961, p. 353 (henceforth *RH*), and *CTW2,* p. 374.

Pack me off there!' *(RH,* p. 350). He will ironically find his death in the Alps, in what may be termed a rite of passage backwards (i.e. the resumption of a previous self and the return to former values). The Alps are made to witness Catherine Sloper's crucial decision to stick to her untrustworthy lover in *Washington Square* (1881, chapter 24).

Much as it is the place of timelessness and oblivion, Venice in the Veneto-Austria is the setting where decisive rites of passage are enacted for a number of representative Jamesian characters in search of themselves, of fruition in felt life or of annihilation in easeful death. Hyacinth Robinson in *The Princess Casamassima* (1886) is led to his fateful decision to renounce his pledge to anarchism by the 'revelation of the exquisite' in Venice and by the realization that its beautiful monuments and treasures of art, though built on the despotisms, cruelties, monopolies and rapacities of the past, are worth preserving (chapter 30, his well-known and already mentioned 'Letter from Venice').

The 'publishing scoundrel' of *The Aspern Papers* (1888) *is* brought to face his nature, his crucial decision and possible deceptions in a Venice which is as much the Venice of Casanova as it is perceivably Austro-Hungarian. Such is also the case, as we saw, of 'The Pupil' (1891). As for Milly Theale in *The Wings of the Dove* (1902), Venice is the place where she can seek life and love, only to find the consummation of betrayal, disillusion, and one of the typically nineteenth-century 'deaths in Venice'. There seems to be a subtle fictional thread linking the two geographical and metaphorical ends of Northern Italy. Could we say, for short, that just as Como is for the vagaries of 'illicit' love in the midst of Paradise, so Venice is for the depths of conscience and the realization of dissipation and death in the midst of unsurpassed artistic beauty?[9]

---

[9] As in James's later work, 'reality' seems to be absorbed and refined out of existence by language and style, so that geographical connotations are often blurred (on this aspect, see Bonney MacDonald, *Henry James's* Italian Hours. *Revelatory and Resistant Impressions,* Ann Arbor, MI, U.M.I., 1990, pp. 87-99 in particular). James had expressed the impenetrability of Italy in his Preface to *The Aspern Papers:* 'So right and left, in Italy—before the great historic complexity at least—penetration

This is a well-known, much-researched, indeed heavily-ploughed territory. Let me finish with a necessary specification. Rites of passage are at the core or at the root of so many James novels and tales, whether set in Rome, London, Paris, or even America, that singling out Northern Italy for their venue may seem stretched or far-fetched. Unless one keeps in mind what emerged in my earlier, brief survey of essays and letters: this part of Italy is, for James, double-edged, suspended as it were between two geographical or metaphorical countries, the seat of 'passes' (in all senses: mountain passes, moral passes, sexual passes) and ambivalence. There one can rest assured that the solidity of the North is wrecked on the shoals of Southern dissipation, just as the flimsiness and fluidity of this disposition finds adjustment and correction in the clear light of an eminently stable state: where the scirocco mingles with, or is swept away by, the *tramontana*.

---

fails; we scratch at the extensive surface, we meet the perfunctory smile, we hang about in the golden air' (*The Art of the Novel*, New York, Scribners, 1934, p. 160). I had therefore to rely mostly on his earlier works.

PART TWO

5 *Short Fiction:* The Aspern Papers

The Aspern Papers is one of Henry James's most successful and best known *nouvelles,* and it immediately poses a question of definition.

In his critical writings James distinguished the short story from the *nouvelle*, not only in terms of length but of inner form. In 'The Story-Teller at Large: Mr. Henry Harland' (1898) he wrote of the short story as 'a form delightful and difficult ... an easy thing, no doubt, to do a little with', but very difficult if one is 'trying for the more, for the extension of the picture, the full and vivid summary'. And he went on:

> Are there not two quite distinct effects to be produced by this rigour of brevity—the two that best make up for the many left unachieved as requiring a larger canvas? The one with which we are most familiar is that of the detached incident, single and sharp, as clear as a pistol-shot; the other, of rarer performance, is that of the impression, comparatively generalised—simplified, foreshortened, reduced to a particular perspective—of a complexity or a continuity. The former is an adventure comparatively safe, in which you have, for the most part, but to put one foot after the other. It is just the risks of the latter, on the contrary, that make the best of the sport. These are naturally—given the general reduced scale—immense, for nothing is less intelligible than bad foreshortening, which, if it fails to mean everything intended, means less than nothing.

The second possibility already foreshadows a different kind of 'short story' altogether: in the prefaces written for the New York Edition of his works (1907-1909) the distinction is at first tentatively, then conclusively pursued:

> A short story, to my sense and as the term is used in magazines, has to choose between being either an anecdote or a picture and can but play its part strictly according to its kind. I rejoice in the anecdote, but I revel in the picture; though having doubtless at times to note that a given attempt may place itself near the dividing-line. (Preface to vol. VII)
> The anecdote consists, ever, of something that has oddly happened to someone, and the first of its duties is to point directly to the person whom it so distinguishes. He may be you or I or any one else, but a condition of our interest—perhaps the principal one—is that the anecdote shall know him, and shall accordingly speak of him, as its subject.' (Preface to vol. X).

The anecdote is to be followed 'as much as possible from its outer edge in rather than from its centre outward', but it is opposed to the very idea of development: it requires 'chemical reductions and condensations' and implies the 'struggle to keep compression rich' (preface to vol. XIII). When the story is allowed to develop both in comparative length and thematically, however, it becomes a *nouvelle:* 'on the dimensional ground—for length and breadth—our ideal, the beautiful and blest *nouvelle'* (which had accounted for so many triumphs of Turgenev, Balzac, Maupassant, Bourget, and had been poorly followed in the English-speaking countries):

> Shades and differences, varieties and styles, the value above all of the idea happily *developed*, languished, to extinction, under the hard-and-fast rule of the 'from six to eight thousand words'—when, for one's benefit, the rigour was a little relaxed.' (Preface to vol. XII).

'For myself', James added, 'I delighted in the shapely *nouvelle* ... of which the main merit and sign is the effort to do the complicated thing with a strong brevity and lucidity—to arrive, on behalf of the multiplicity, at a certain science of control'. In view of all this, though it appears in James's collections of short stories, *The Aspern Papers* should properly be considered a *nouvelle*, and it is consequently treated as such in this essay.[1]

The story belongs to a period, the 1880s, in which the writer, after having amply explored the international theme—i.e., the differences in morals and manners between Americans and Europeans—turned his attention to the European world, in particular to the problems of conscience and individual behaviour.[2] James began, and for the most part composed, his *nouvelle* while at Villa Brichieri, near Florence, after having spent a few weeks in Venice, at Casa Alvisi, and completed it in the latter city, this time as a guest at Palazzo Barbaro.[3] The story is part of a group of works centered on Italy, which exploit its romantic atmosphere and the richness of its environmental and thematic suggestiveness.

The *nouvelle* is entirely set in Venice and is famous for the masterly way in which it evokes the city. Venice changes from the colors of spring to those of autumn, passing through the sultriness of summer, but it is more than the privileged background of the action. It is also a metaphorical landscape, the topical place for an investigation aimed at revisiting or reviving the past, the symbolic dimension of an obsession that courts drama and ends up in defeat. The very nature of the city, however, gives this obsession not only a sense of death but also something like an ironic tone or at least a partially amused qualification.

---

[1] The *nouvelle* was published in the *Atlantic Monthly* (March-May 1888). Quotations are from Henry James, *Literary Criticism. Essays, American and English Writers*, New York, The Library of America, 1984, p. 285; *The Art of the Novel*, ed. R. P. Blackmur, New York, Scribners, 1934, pp. 139, 181, 233, 240, 220, 231; see also *Theory of Fiction: Henry James*, ed. James E. Miller, Lincoln, Nebraska U. P., 1972, pp. 99-105.

[2] See Sergio Perosa, *Henry James and the Experimental Novel*, Charlottesville, Virginia U. P., 1978.

[3] Leon Edel, *Henry James: The Middle Years*, 1882-1895, Philadelphia, Lippincott, 1962, pp. 213-226.

Furthermore, it is among the most popular of James's stories on account of its narrative style, which is calm and mature, full of echoes and reverberations, fluid and fluent. It is a style capable of a strong dramatic vividness as well as a nostalgic coloring; yet it is veined with hesitations and suspensions, second thoughts and ambivalences in which the perspectives of ambiguity lie hidden or suddenly show themselves.

Finally, it is one of James's paradigmatic works because one finds here, in explicit or in barely noticeable form, side by side or subtly interwoven, many of his central and most crucial themes: the contrast between privacy and the public light to which the artist is exposed; the opposition of art and life; the gap between intellectual passion and human involvement; the urge to learn and to know, which at every step may betray the temptation or the exercise of an underhanded power, a form of violence to others. And one could add the terrible weight or at least the ambiguous presence of the past in our lives, the difficulty in rediscovering or reliving it without disturbing one's correct relationship with the present; the weak resistance of one's conscience to the violence of time; the power of temptation or perversion that money can have; the distortions due to isolation imposed by circumstances or sought in order to turn away from the world; disasters and disturbances caused by a self-centered vision of reality—or perhaps courted when the protagonist is entrusted with both the narration and the qualification of it.

Another crucial Jamesian motive appears in the story and its unfolding: to what extent can one trust the tale or the teller (if the teller is the subject of the experience)? Does not the heuristic obsession itself, the will to know, create its own monsters? In this case, even the most banal facts can be artificially colored with the tones of tragedy and melodrama, can take on hallucinatory dimensions, become lost in the tortuousness of the labyrinthine mind (a motive which is present in *The Aspern Papers* not only tangentially, but centrally, though it is not immediately perceivable).

We are then confronted with a circular movement, since the partially comic element, the ironic-grotesque germ from which James had started, not only reappears at the end of the tale but also unfolds step by step with his exploration of the drama: a drama that is caused by the protagonist's poorly concealed curiosity, by the sphinx-like face that, according to the gothic tradition, the past takes on to 'chill' the living.

James got the germ of his story from a conversation about Count Gamba, a nephew of the Guiccioli, and about the letters of Byron of which that family proved to be 'rather illiberal and dangerous guardians.' Owing to their 'discreditable' character, one of them was perhaps even burned. This germ joined with another anecdote, which concerned not only Byron but also Shelley: Jane Clairmont (or, as she preferred to be called, Claire), once Byron's mistress and the mother of his daughter Allegra, had lived until the age of eighty in Florence, with a niece and in total isolation, jealously guarding the letters she received from the two poets. An ardent Shelley fan, Captain Silsbee succeeded in being taken in by them as a boarder, hoping to lay hands on those letters at her death: the niece, however, a fifty-year-old spinster, had offered him the letters in exchange for marriage. The poor captain (according to the anecdote) *court encore*, was supposedly still running.

As James wrote in the Notebooks:

Certainly there is a little subject there: the picture of the two faded, queer, poor and discredited old English women—living on into a strange generation, in their musty corner of a foreign town—with these illustrious letters their most precious possession. Then the plot of the Shelley fanatic—his watchings and waitings—the way he *couvers* the treasure. The denouement needn't be the one related of poor Silsbee; and at any rate the general situation is in itself a subject and a picture. It strikes me much. The interest would be in some price that the man has to pay—that the old woman—or the survivor—sets upon the papers. His hesitations—his struggle—for he really would give almost anything.[4]

---

[4]   *The Complete Notebooks of Henry James*, eds Leon Edel and Lyall H. Powers, New York, Oxford U. P., 1986, pp. 33-34.

Here are almost all the elements of the story: two women isolated from
the world, tied to the memory of the poet and the old city, the poetry
lover who wants to gain possession of the letters, and their ambiguous
relationship. Added to this is the fundamental idea of the *price* to be paid
for the papers (or in general for the literary passion, for the violation
of privacy and the disturbance of conscience) and of the protagonist's
hesitations, through which he becomes conscious, at least subliminally,
of the moral question involved in his behavior.

For reasons of delicacy, James chose to move the setting to Venice,
a choice that would prove very felicitous and decisive. And just as he
transformed the two women into two American expatriates, he ran a
calculated risk by making the great poet of the past an American bard.
This was historically unlikely, given the period in which the poet would
have lived (the early decades of the nineteenth century),[5] but James
found here a sort of challenge.

As so often with him, he was interested in the atmosphere of total
mystery, of emptiness and absence, with which he could surround his
Jeffrey Aspern. Another characteristic change concerned Juliana, Miss
Bordereau, the custodian of the precious letters: *she* conceives the idea
that in order to have the letters, the fanatical admirer of Aspern should
marry her spinster niece. In this way, as a firm counterpoint to and lit-
mus test of the exaltation of the protagonist's discovery, James inserts
the sordid theme of money and 'exchange' value, since the plot of the
old woman ends up paralleling that of the protagonist.

A final point should be noted. James made his protagonist the narrator of the story, by relating everything—intentions, facts, events, possible motivations and interpretations—to his point of view and to his
word. Thus the *nouvelle* calls for direct participation on the part of the

---

[5]   James himself discussed this 'vicious practice' in his Preface to vol. XII: 'I find his
      [Jeffrey Aspern's] link with reality then just in the tone of the picture wrought round
      him ... The retort to that of course was that such a plea represented no "link" with
      reality—... but only a link, and flimsy enough too, with the deepest depths of the
      artificial' (see *The Art of the Novel*, pp. 166-167, 168).

reader and acquires immediacy. Knowing James, however, and knowing that his narrators should be not blindly and thoroughly trusted—the example of *The Turn of the Screw* is a good case in point—one must maintain throughout a modicum of doubt.

The protagonist, who remains without a name to the end, engages in a regular siege against the *sancta sanctorum* of Miss Bordereau's house in Venice, where he insinuates himself as a boarder by paying an enormous rent. There he moves about rather craftily in order to lay hands on the treasure of the much desired Aspern papers. His is a continuous but decisive movement of *rapprochement.* First, he approaches the palace (modelled on Palazzo Cappello in Rio Marin)[6] in which he then installs himself; next, from the garden, he moves towards the rooms of the old women and gets himself invited in by persistently sending them flowers; then he accosts the poor niece, Miss Tita (the name was rightly changed to Tina for the New York Edition),[7] in whom he tries to arouse not only sympathy but also complicity; he then approaches the old woman and, finally, the room in which he thinks the papers are hidden and preserved. One night, uninvited, he secretly enters that room, and while groping about with his candle, he is suddenly discovered and unmasked by old Miss Bordereau.

There, for the first time, she reveals to him her eyes, now no longer covered as usual by a green 'curtain'. This episode is not only the crowning touch of a gothic vein à la Poe that runs through the story, but also the first of two major dramatic climaxes around which it is masterfully constructed. At that point, the protagonist takes the final step in an escalation by which his literary passion risks both the violation of another's privacy and the violation of that person's very conscience and heart. At that point, this fanatic lover of the poet and his poetry, this passionate student of relics and memories, he who at all costs wants

---

[6]   See Marilla Battilana, *Venezia sfondo e simbolo nella narrativa di Henry James,* Milano: Laboratorio delle arti, 1971, p. 112, and p. 145 for a picture of it; see also Edel, *The Middle Years*, p. 213.

[7]   'Tita' is in Venetian a man's name, not a woman's.

to revive the past and unite it to the present, truly risks reducing himself to what Miss Bordereau reproaches him with being: a 'publishing scoundrel'.

This scene, however, is in the penultimate (the eighth) section: as one moves towards that culminating scene, one realizes that the siege is not unilateral, that, instead, one is dealing with a *reciprocal* ambiguous game of cat and mouse, that Miss Bordereau is also involved in the escalation process. The exorbitant rent that she demands as a ploy to discourage the boarder, and that instead he is willing to pay, betrays his real interest. But it also becomes a means for securing a dowry for her niece. Since the presence of the boarder cannot but revive in her the weak sparks of a life on the verge of being extinguished, the terrible old woman, in her own way as crafty and as rapacious as the intruder, contrives the idea of making his interest in the Aspern papers the bait that she hopes will lead him into the arms of poor Tita and will wed him forever to her house, her memories and to Aspern.

This is why the green screen that Miss Bordereau always wears over her eyes is more than a symbol of her reserve, of the mystery that she is guarding, of the intense past of passion and poetry that she has lived, a barrier against intruders and the world. It is also—somewhat like the pastor's veil in Hawthorne's short story 'The Minister's Black Veil'— a mask, an indication of her mysterious and isolated nature, of the intrigue that she herself has laid out for the intruder. Thus, when she is caught without the veil, in the 'gothic' scene in which the protagonist's wrongdoing and violation are most evident, she can only die. But while she lies dying in Tita's arms, she entrusts her niece with the awkward prosecution of her plan.

The story then moves toward the second, decisive, major climax: Tita, who has saved the papers from destruction but is tied to the memory and the injunction of her aunt, cannot—not even she— divulge them or give them to a stranger. She can offer them, clumsily, only to someone who belongs to the family, a relative; someone who has a right to them. Dismayed, the protagonist wanders out to the Lido and to Malamocco in a gondola—a scene of confusing displacements through the labyrinth of the city, which acts as a counterpoint to a preceding scene in which, always in a gondola, he had accompanied Tita through the Giudecca and on to St. Mark's, revealing to the poor recluse an unexpected perspective of unknown places and active people, reawakening in her the sense of a possible life outside of her palace-prison and the captivity of time and memory.

Then it was the graceful Venice of the cafés, swarming with life, vivid with colors, and opening to the world. Now it is the labyrinth of the lagoon and the canals that mirror the mind revolving around itself. Upon his return, at sunset, the questing protagonist, confused and torn within himself, finds himself in Sts. John and Paul Square. Contemplating the statue of Colleoni, which stands out high up in the square, he recognizes what separates his own type of stratagems and battles from that of the 'condottiere.' On the one side is life and action; on the other—his—reflection and the mere mental or intellectual passion. Not for nothing, at this crucial point, does Venice reveal or confirm itself to him as an enormous and busy theatre:

> And somehow the splendid common domicile, familiar, domestic and resonant, also resembles a theatre, with actors clicking over bridges and, in straggling processions, tripping along fondamentas. As you sit in your gondola the footways that in certain parts edge the canals assume to the eye the importance of a stage, meeting it at the same angle, and the Venetian figures, moving to and fro against the battered scenery of their little houses of comedy, strike you as members of an endless dramatic troupe.[8]

He played his game inside, in a closed-in space, on an entirely inner stage, fascinated not by the spectacle that surrounded him but by the survivors and the ghosts of the past. His, we could say, is a drama of the mind, even to some extent a hallucination. Taught by the spectacle

---

[8]   *The Complete Tales*, ed. Leon Edel, London, Rupert Hart-Davis, 1963, vol. VI, p. 379.

of the city and in reaction to his very own sneaky and pusillanimous
game—or perhaps because he is by now incapable of renouncing the
possible crowning of his intellectual passion—he returns to the house
the following day to declare himself ready for the sacrifice, ready to
offer himself (is it not rather a question of exchanging or bartering himself?). But Miss Tita has understood her own pathetic failure, and having overcome her humiliation, late at night she burns the papers, one by
one. Only a miniature of the poet and the sense of a painful loss remains
for the fan of Aspern.

Even from this brief sketch, the complex role which the city has in
the *nouvelle* is evident. It is not a mere background for the adventure,
but an agent of it, not only the masterfully evoked milieu, but the symbolic extension in which the nature and the dilemmas of the characters
are mirrored. On the one hand, we have a decadent, dying and self-
enclosed world in which the cult of the past and the memory takes root
like ivy in the tumble-down walls, and, on the other hand, the explosion
of life, theatricality and colors capable of offering an antithesis—if not
an antidote—to the prison of the past or of the soul which has turned
in on itself.

In the Preface to the *nouvelle*, written twenty years later for the New
York Edition of his works, James insisted on the challenge that the historical and scenic complexity of Italy flung at him and on the romantic
thrill that Venice gave him. The charm which he confessed himself to
be extremely attracted by was that of a close relationship with the past,
a past directly touched and discovered almost behind the present. It was
the charm 'of a final scene of the rich dim Shelley drama played out in
the very theatre of our "modernity"', of an unexpected continuity that
had drawn itself between then (1820) and now (1880).

It was a question, he wrote, of recovering and of evoking 'a palpable
imaginable *visitable* past', 'fragrant of all, or of almost all, the poetry of
the thing outlived and lost and gone, and yet in which the precious element of closeness, telling so of connexions but tasting so of differences,
remains appreciable'. Yesterday and today were to touch and to remain

in perfect balance on the scales. What better scenario than Italy, and in particular Venice, to take in the 'afternoon light' of the Byronic age (even if Jeffrey Aspern is only weakly sketched as a New York poet)?[9]

Entirely absorbed by the idea of the visitable past, whose continuity with and almost overlapping of the present he was to evoke with so much empathy, James insisted on the tone of amusement and on the light form of the *nouvelle*, on the lack of a true relationship with the real (except for Venice, naturally), and on its ties, rather, with the deepest depths of the artificial. We acknowledge his success in this, including also the comic and the grotesque element that insinuates itself in the most dramatic moments and in the conclusion. But, as already suggested, there is no doubt that the events also touch upon some of James's most characteristic cords and involve crucial motifs of a much wider application.

To what extent does the protagonist's genuine interest in the great poet of the past mask a pernicious curiosity in the lives of others, which ends up in a violation of their privacy? His desire to save the poet's papers for posterity is legitimate and understandable. But in an epoch in which criticism (one should note) was essentially biographical, we can be sure that James ended up viewing the activities of his protagonist with dismay, repugnance and, finally, open condemnation.

In the revised version of the story for the New York Edition,[10] a good share of the changes and additions make his fault, or at least his neglect of the rights and feelings of others, more explicit. In various letters, in the *Notebooks*, and in a whole series of novels and short stories (from *The Bostonians* to *The Reverberator*, from 'The Real Right Thing' to 'Sir Dominick Ferrand' or 'The Papers': but one could also include *The Sacred Fount*), James expressed directly or indirectly his disapproval of journalists, nosy biographers and 'publishing scoundrels'.[11]

---

[9]   *The Art of the Novel*, pp. 163-164.
[10] *The Aspern Papers* is grouped, in vol. XII, with *The Turn of the Screw*, 'The Liar', and 'The Two Faces'.
[11] See Henry James, *Parisian Sketches: Letters to the 'New York Tribune', 1875-*

On the other hand, his protagonist involves in his hypocrisies and swindles (the words are his) not only the survivors of the past, but also the pathetic Tita, in whom he awakens a nearly extinguished desire to live, only to frustrate it. Here the literary obsession ends up causing direct and perhaps irreparable damage to the soul and heart of a defenceless woman. The fact that the protagonist is also the narrator of the story serves, if anything, as some scholars maintain,[12] to disguise the vulgar nature of his interest, the shabby means of which he avails himself in order to satisfy it, the hyperbolic ends he boasts of, his very faults.

Not the least among these is an inability to live, his having substituted his interest in the past for his involvement in the present, intellectual abstraction for feelings, selfishness and self-centeredness for participation, mental fixation for the understanding of others ('In life without art you can find your account' James had written; 'but art without life is a poor affair').[13] In short, he would be, to a good extent, a villain.

It seems to me that—along these lines—one may go beyond James's own position in being too morally strict; there is no need to be too upset with the unfortunate fanatic of Jeffrey Aspern, who is sneaky but is ultimately moved by a genuine interest in his idol. After all, great poets must pay a price, the price demanded by fame: once a public figure, one must face the loss of one's absolute right to privacy. James himself, in the *Notebooks*,[14] did not minimize the responsibility one incurs by destroying literary papers and letters which belong to history.

1876, eds Leon Edel and Ilse Dusoir Lind, London, Hart-Davis, 1958, pp. ix-xxxvi; *The Letters of Henry James*, ed. Percy Lubbock, New York, Scribners, 1920, 2 vols., I, pp. 46-47, II, p. 304; *The Complete Notebooks*, p. 40; and James's final outburst in *The Question of Our Speech,* Boston, Houghton Mifflin, 1905, pp. 43-44 (among others).

12   See, e.g., Charles G. Hoffman, *The Short Novels of Henry James,* New York, Bookman, 1957, pp. 45-47; Laurence Holland, *The Expense of Vision: Essays on the Craft of Henry James,* Princeton, Princeton U. P., 1964, pp. 139-154.

13   'Daniel Deronda: A Conversation' (1876), in *Partial Portraits*, ed. Leon Edel, Ann Arbor, Michigan U. P., 1970, p. 92; *Literary Criticism. English Writers*, p. 992.

14   *The Complete Notebooks*, p. 34 and *passim*.

But the word 'villain', even if it cannot be applied to the protagonist, is suggestive and appropriate in our case. There is a good deal of the 'gothic' or 'dark' element in *The Aspern Papers*, due precisely to its nature, its setting and its development (this is also supported by James's own remarks). In short, if it is not an out and out ghost story, it is something very close to it, and James did couple it with *The Turn of the Screw* in the New York Edition. If nothing else, he flirts with the gothic tradition and its motifs, and surely draws inspiration from Hawthorne and from Poe: even if the mode, of course, is typically Jamesian.

We have already mentioned the gothic flavour of the nocturnal (and central) scene in which the protagonist is surprised and unmasked by Miss Bordereau, by the flash of her naked eyes. In writing about the 'afternoon light' of the epoch he intended to evoke, James specified that it was not yet 'darkened'.[15] To us, instead, it seems that in the way he evoked it, there is indeed a cape of darkness and obscurity, of gloom and (in every sense) blackness cast over it. The Venice we have already described, but also the self-enclosed and walled-up palace, its empty and ghostly rooms, and above all the garden (which recalls the one described in Hawthorne's 'Rappacini's Daughter') are typical elements of the American gothic tradition.

The way in which the protagonist sneaks about that palace in an attempt to revive, recover, and resuscitate the past smacks of an almost necromantic operation, which demands its victim and sows its disasters. Above all, once we have entered the almost bewitched circle (profoundly artificial, James defined it) of the story and the secret rooms of the palace, the figures of Miss Bordereau and Tita (especially, of course, the former) acquire an almost sinister light. They move about in silence and with the muffled step of ghosts, they sink into the darkness of dis-

---

[15] *The Art of the Novel*, pp. 164-165. For the latent Gothicism of the story see Holland, pp. 117-118; on its grotesque, as well as gothic, elements, see Kenneth Graham, *Henry James: The Drama of Fulfilment,* Oxford, Clarendon Press, 1975, pp. 58-78 (chapter 3: 'The Price of Power in *The Aspern Papers*').

tances and seem to emerge from the obscure depths of the past, to live an entirely anachronistic, unreal and invented life.

In short, by going to seek them, by awakening them from their sleep and from their long silence, by arousing in them the glimmer of a painful rebirth, by removing the dust in which they are buried, the protagonist does nothing, when all is said and done, but conjure up ghosts, artificially prolong a state between life and death, seek to enter a past which, as in James's posthumous novel *The Sense of the Past*, ends up acquiring the characteristics of a nightmare or at least vibrating with sinister creakings and omens.

Here Venice and her charm fit perfectly, as do her aura of death and James's ability to subtly and ambiguously examine his characters' consciousnesses, his ability to suggest evil without naming it, and his probing of the dark side of the soul without making it appear. Naturally, James's use of irony is also relevant here and from it stems what I would define as the half-gothic, half-grotesque tone of the tale and that 'fusion of narrative modes' which is so often his distinguishing mark.

6   The Wings of the Dove
and the Coldness of Venice

The Venetian setting of *The Wings of the Dove* partakes of, and is inscribed in, two 19th-century archetypes (which then became stereotypes):

(a) Venice as a particularly suitable seat for plots and conspiracies, deceptions and betrayals;

(b) the 'decline-' or 'death-in-Venice' literary motif, which had a long pedigree in 19th-century literature.

The first motif, which can be traced back to Elizabethan times, is detectable in various 19th-century works of fiction: in the US, for instance, in J. F. Cooper's sensational and 'gothic' novel *The Bravo* (1831); in England, in Wilkie Collins's 'detective' novel *The Haunted Hotel* (1878).

The second motif had its origin in modern Europe, in William Wordsworth's sonnet 'On the Extinction of the Venetian Republic' (1802, published 1807) and in the Romantic poets' 'double vision' (or indeed troubled vision) of Venice. After the Fall of Venice, decline, deterioration, and death were perceived as inherent in her beauty and her splendour; conversely, her beauty appeared as especially attractive when corrupted, decaying or in decline. This romantic, post-Napoleonic perception of 'glory in decay' and 'splendour in rags' opened the way for a view of Venice as a place fostering feelings and yearnings for death, where death is experienced almost as 'a consummation devoutly to be wished'.

Oxymoron is inherent in the definition itself, and seems essential to the very concept, conceit or *concetto*, of 'death in Venice'. I speak of a *concetto*, because death is feared or pursued, cherished and enacted in the decay of splendour, in the excess and corruption of beauty, in the surplus and added value of crumbling art and compromised history—in the ambivalence, that is, of sensual, mental elation, and a lugubrious atmosphere of doom.

The image of Venice as the seat for deception plots went against a well-established, century-old view of the city as 'the eldest child of Liberty', an independent *republic* in times of monarchical or papal predominance all over Europe. A vision of Venice as the paragon of a perfect state already obtained in Elizabethan times, when it was hoped that the *Serenissima* might become a bridgehead for Protestantism in the Catholic South of Europe. In 1570 Roger Ascham had viewed the city as the seat of just laws, wise rulers, and free citizens. In the only republican period of English history, Oliver Cromwell's parliament had looked to Venice as to a model of republican survival; in the 18th century, John Locke and Voltaire, among others, had viewed it as a fundamentally just society.[1]

Other Elizabethan writers, however, including Christopher Marlowe, Ben Jonson (*Volpone, or, the Fox*) and partially Shakespeare (*The Merchant of Venice, Othello*), a 17th-century playwright like Thomas Otway (*Venice Preserved*) and later 'gothic' novelists, dramatized fantasies of Venice as a hedonistic and/or corrupt state of secret police, secret murders and ferocious oppression, a den of iniquity, the perfect place for deceptions, betrayals, plots and conspiracies.

Accordingly, even in early post-Napoleonic times, James Fenimore Cooper had no 'political' delusions about Venice: his novel *The Bravo* (1831), which was set in a stereotypical early 18th-century Venice, was

---

[1]   See Denis Cosgrave, 'The Myth and the Stones of Venice', *Journal of Historical Geography,* VIII, 2 (1987), pp. 145-69, the exhibition catalogue *Venezia da stato a mito*, Venezia, Marsilio, 1997, and Michael L. Ross. *Storied Cities. Literary Imaginings of Florence, Venice, and Rome,* Westport, Greenwood Press, 1994.

intended to illustrate the moral that 'any government in which the power resides in a minority conduces to oppression of the weak and perversion of the good' (the reverse of 'accepted' contemporary opinion about its 'just' government). His Venetian palaces were symbolical of a tyrannical government, while 'bravoes' could exercise their power unhindered. Later in the century, Wilkie Collins's novel *The Haunted Hotel* (1878) set the crucial murder of Lord Montberry, and the ensuing ghostly or macabre apparitions, in an old Venetian palace which had been turned into a hotel: plots and assassinations were at home in the city.

The long pedigree of the second motif—which is of greater relevance for my purposes—started with Wordsworth's sonnet (which mourned 'The Shade / Of that which once was great is passed away'),[2] Byron's 'Ode to Venice' (1818-19), and P. B. Shelley's 'Lines Written among the Euganean Hills' (1818), among others.

In canto IV of *Childe Harold's Pilgrimage* Byron contemplated a 'dying Glory'; on the Bridge of Sighs, in the famous beginning, one has 'A Palace and a prison on each hand'; Venice, a city of shadows and dissolution, 'Sinks, like a sea-weed, unto whence she rose! /... Even in Destruction's depth' (stanza 13). She is 'declined to dust' (stanza 15), enveloped by a cloud of desolation; 'Perchance even dearer in her days of woe, / Than when she was a boast, a marvel, and a show' (stanza 18).[3] Desolation attracted Shelley, too: the daughter of the Ocean, seen from

---

[2]   'Once did She hold the gorgeous east in fee; / And was the safeguard of the west: the worth / Of Venice did not fall below her birth, / Venice, the eldest Child of Liberty./ She was a maiden City, bright and free; / No guile seduced, no force could violate; / And, when she took herself a Mate, / She must espouse the everlasting Sea. / And what if she had seen those glories fade, / Those titles vanish, and that strength decay; / Yet shall some tribute of regret be paid / When her long life hath reached its final day: / Men are we, and must grieve when even the Shade/Of that which once was great is passed away.' (Wordsworth, 'On the Extinction of the Venetian Republic', lines 1-14).

[3]   Canto IV is 'centrally concerned with ruin and decay; or, rather, in the absence of a centre it hovers restlessly and obsessively around ruins and ruination', writes Tony Tanner—though he properly adds that Byron looks for forms of energy to counteract 'this deathward', this tendency to death which pervades Canto IV, and

afar as a glitter of light, turns already into a 'masque of death'; her luminous and golden towers are, in fact, 'Sepulchres, whose human forms, / Like pollution-nourished worms, / To the corpse of greatness cling, / Murdered, and now mouldering' ('Lines Written among the Euganean Hills').

It was the great singer of Venice—John Ruskin—who made a literary and visual myth of her, who sowed the seeds and drew the outlines of what would quickly become the *topos* or conceit of 'death in Venice'. He introduced the eminently literary element of Decadence—with a capital D—into the picture. 'I do not *feel* any romance in Venice. It is simply a heap of ruins', he had written in a letter to his father. He elaborated a totally a-historical and moralized myth about Venice, and portrayed its decadence as a wood-worm worming its way into, and corroding, the beauty of a lost Eden.

In tracing its dissolution, Ruskin deployed the lexicon, the very vocabulary, that would go into the making of so many literary deaths in Venice. Blight, stagnation, darkness, decline, and ruin, mark the end of volume I of *The Stones of Venice*; in volume II, Time and Decay, which in the past were an adornment for the city, threaten her destruction, while images, situations, premonitions, even evocations, of her ultimate death are scattered in Volume III—significantly titled 'The Fall'—which registers a disintegration, whose features would reappear in quite a number of 'deaths in Venice' to follow. Here is a revealing passage:

> Venice had in her childhood sown, in tears, the harvest she was to reap in rejoicing. She now sowed in laughter the seeds of death. Thenceforward, year after year, the nation drank with deeper thirst from the fountains of forbidden pleasure, and dug springs, hitherto unknown, in the dark places of the earth. In the ingenuity of indulgence, in the variety of vanity, Venice surpassed the cities of Christendom as of old she had surpassed them in fortitude and devotion.
>
> . . .

which Hobhouse's notes had stressed (*Venice Desired*, Oxford, Blackwell, 1992, pp. 27, 30).

That ancient curse was upon her, the curse of the Cities of the Plain, 'Pride, fullness of bread, and abundance of idleness'. By the inner burning of her own passions, as fatal as the fiery rain of Gomorrah, she was consumed from her place among the nations; and her ashes are choking the channels of the dead, salt sea. (*Works*, eds E. T. Cook and Alexander Wedderburn, Oxford, George Allen, 1903-12, 39 vols., XI 194-195)

These views of the Fall of Venice provided the seedbed of the many literary deaths in which the 19th century revelled, from Charles Dickens to Wilkie Collins to Maurice Barrès, and which culminated in the early 20th century in the works of Hugo von Hoffmannsthal (*Andreas, oder die Vereinigten,* 1907-13) and Arthur Schnitzler (*Casanovas Heimfahrt*, 1918), Marcel Proust and Thomas Mann (*Der Tod in Venedig*, 1913), where the city is made to perform an uncanny, disquieting, and ultimately destructive function.

I have offered elsewhere a possible explanation of this prevailing attitude.[4] Islands are usually characterised by incrustation and stratification—the phenomenon whereby culture is incrusted on nature, and nature over culture, in an indissoluble way, or whereby cultural, historical, and artistic stratifications are ostensibly added onto geological stratifications. This condition, which is particularly present in Venice, favours or fosters a feeling of unease, dislocation, and unrest, in which premonitions or enactments of death find an easy way. In Venice there was for centuries an imposing series of historical, cultural and artistic incrustations and sedimentations over nature. The nature/culture oxymoron is predominantly and obsessively at work there: nature has been subjected to a drastic form of *acculturation*.

---

[4]   See my essay 'Literary Deaths in Venice', in *Venetian Views, Venetian Blinds,* eds Manfred Pfister and Barbara Schaff, Amsterdam, Rodopi, 1999, pp. 122-125. Maurice Barrès, in 'La mort de Venise' chapter of his *Amori et dolori sacrum,* Paris, Felix Juven, 1903, rpt. and ed. M.O. Germain, St. Cyr, 1990, sums up the *concetto* in the typically decadent phrase 'Désespoir d'une béauté qui s'en va vers la mort'; Venice appears as a Jezabel to him, and its places, especially its peripheral places, make it resemble Aigues-Mortes.

Her palaces appear as coral reefs, and such-like natural concretions. 'Reefs of palaces', Herman Melville called them in his poem 'Venice' (line 12); R. W. Emerson (who echoed Goethe)[5] in his *Journal* declared that he was ill at ease in a 'beavers' city'. In his turn, H. D. Thoreau in *The Maine Woods* (1858), proceeded half a mile up the Moosehorn, 'as through a narrow winding canal, where the tall dark spruce and firs and arbour-vitae, towered on both sides in the moonlight, forming a perpendicular forest edge of great height, like the spires of a Venice in the forest': the disquieting connection nature/culture goes on. Marcel Proust, too (echoing Ruskin), in *Du côté de chez Swann* (III, Noms de pays: le nom) wrote of Venetian palaces as 'those rocks of amethyst, like a reef in the Indian ocean', and in *Albertine disparue* they appeared as 'a chain of marble cliffs' ('une chaîne de falaises de marbre'). Throughout *The Cantos*, Ezra Pound played on the glimmering perception of palaces as forests of marble, or petrified forests.

Ruskin writes of Venice as of a *wilderness of brick* and a petrified sea, likens it to an opal and a coral reef, and specifies that the branches of forests had *physically* turned into marble. 'The whole architecture of Venice is architecture of incrustation', he had announced in a well-known passage;[6] both Proust and Pound would use the same word—incrustation—to define the inner nature of Venice.

---

[5]   Venice had been defined 'a republic of beavers' by Goethe in his *Tagesbuch der Italienischen Reise* (28 e 29 September 1786): 'under their feet the sand and the marshes became rock, their houses looking for air as closet-up trees' (IX, p. 64).

[6]   'The whole architecture of Venice is architecture of incrustation [...] the Venetian habitually incrusted his work with nacre: he built his houses, even the meanest, as if it had been a shell-fish,—roughly inside, mother-of-pearl on the surface: he was content, perforce, to gather the clay of the Brenta banks, and bake it into brick for his substance of wall; but he overlaid it with the wealth of the ocean, with the most precious of foreign marbles. You might fancy early Venice as one wilderness of brick, which a petrifying sea had beaten upon till it coated it with marble: at first a dark city—washed white by the sea foam.' (Ruskin, *Works,* IX, p. 323). On his vision of Venice in which the idea of death is inscribed, see *John Ruskin e Venezia. La bellezza in declino,* ed. Sergio Perosa, Firenze, Olschki, 2001. On the 'incrusted'

Conversely, in Venice nature has been subjected to a drastic form of *culturization*. It was built in the water; it is a water city—a contradiction in terms, rather than an oxymoron—on which a massive stratification of history, art and culture was piled. These stratifications of history and art were made *one* with the island; they make a splendid conglomerate and incrustation of it—as well as a *deadly oxymoron.*[7]

Given these views, and these premises, one can hardly think of a better place and a better cradle for death—indeed of a better place where literary deaths are bound to happen, haunting and hovering over writers and artists.

As for Henry James, we saw, Venice as the perfect seat for a deception and betrayal plot appears predominantly in *The Aspern Papers,* to some extent in 'The Pupil', and centrally in *The Wings of the Dove.* Kate and Densher's plot is hatched in London, but it is enacted in Venice, where Milly is in possession of the place, ensconced in her palace (II 132), but soon to be dethroned by cold-blooded schemes which are perfectly at home in the city.

That they are deception plots and schemes is made clear in several places: 'He [Densher] said to himself that he must make the best of everything: that was in his mind … It had done for the past, would it do for the present? … The necessity of making the best was the instinct …' (II 175).[8] Densher is placed, managed, 'manipulated' or perched by Kate

---

nature, even from a geological point of view, of Venice, see Adrian Stokes, *The Quattro Cento* [1932] and *Stones of Rimini* [1934]. University Park, The Pennsylvania State U. P., 2002.

[7]   'A stone fable', Rilke calls it, while Chateaubriand defines it an unnatural city, *une cité contre nature.* In the passage in which he equates the buildings of Venice to 'a chain of marble cliffs', Proust goes on to specify that they 'made one think of objects of nature, but of a nature which seemed to have created its works with a human imagination' (III, p. 644: 'une nature qui aurait créé ses oeuvres avec une imagination humaine'). In *Andreas, oder Die Vereinigten,* Hofmannsthal hints at an 'impossibility' of Venice, owing to her fusion of antique and oriental elements.

[8]   References in the text (volume and page number) are to *The Wings of the Dove. The Novels and Tales of Henry James,* New York, Scribner's, 1909, 2 vols.

('he was perpetually bent to her will', II 175-76) in such a position as to trap an unsuspecting victim: 'Since she's to die I'm to marry her?'— 'So that when her death has taken place I shall in the natural course have money?' (II 225). The answer is yes. The hypocritical scheme even provides for Milly to *offer* marriage, and for him not to make a move but simply to *accept* ('You think it then possible that she may *offer* marriage? ... It will be for me then to accept', II 230): hypocrisy and equivocation are in command. After Kate has come to his rooms, Densher is bound to a commitment whereby, in order to be faithful to her, he has to stay away from Kate and close to Milly: this is indeed a double or reversed form of deception, given that 'It was on the cards for him that he might kill her' (II 252), as will indeed be the case.

Later on, Densher himself openly declares that, while having a reason at Lancaster Gate, he has been 'up to something in Venice', to a 'game' or 'deviltry' (II 291-92). When his deception, 'deviltry' or plot is unmasked by Lord Mark, and Densher is denied access to Milly, he is significantly left with Pasquale and Eugenio—both insultingly characterised by James as unreliable and dubious characters of a slumberous and deceitful race (II 256).

To further my case about Venice as the privileged seat for treachery: Lord Mark, too, is presented as having been 'up to something' deceitful and dishonourable during *his* visit to Milly in Venice—marrying her for her money as she has just a few months to live ('having, for such a suit as his, not more perhaps than a few months to live', II 290). We are confronted with the display and deployment of a third element of duplicity. Even after his unmasking, Densher is asked to lie to Milly about 'everything', even about his engagement to Kate in order to save her life by a denial (II 322). The web of treachery is almost spiralling on itself.

So much for the plot-in-Venice motif—except to note that its peculiarity is that these plots, and especially the main one, are not conducted in a lurid, darksome or 'gothic' way, but in a purely rational way; they are conceived and controlled by the mind. They are *cold-blooded, cool* plots. This ties in with James's peculiar exhibition of the death-in-

Venice motif, in which, contrary to wide-spread patterns, the setting is characterised by wintry coldness and splashing rain.

James partook fully of the oxymoronic view of Venice as decaying in her glory and splendid in her decay, a city where beauty resides in decline, and decline is a form of beauty; a magnificent city with an in-built propensity to decay, brought under the shadow of death, imbued with, and immersed in, premonitions of death; indeed a most appropriate setting for death. In his 'Grand Canal' essay of 1892 he had written:

> Venetian life, in the old large sense, has long since come to an end, and the essential present character of the most melancholy of cities resides simply in its being the most beautiful of tombs. Nowhere has the past been laid to rest with such tenderness, such a sadness of resignation and remembrance. Nowhere else is the present so alien, so discontinuous, so like a crowd in a cemetery without garlands for the graves. (*Italian Hours*, ed. John Auchard, University Park, The Pennsylvania State U. P., 1991, p. 33: henceforth *IH*).

In keeping with the most deeply rooted archetype/stereotype about Venice, in that essay he also remarked on 'the general law that renders decadence and ruin in Venice more brilliant than any prosperity': 'Decay is in this extraordinary place golden in tint and misery *couleur de rose*.' (*IH* 47).

Elsewhere he mentioned the *locus classicus* of the gondola floating one to one's doom, and wrote perceptively of the 'poetry of misfortune'—the correlation between charm and decay, desolation and aesthetic beauty, which is such a prominent feature of the city, indeed 'the essence of her dignity':

> Is it the style [he asked himself] that has brought about the decrepitude, or the decrepitude that has, as it were, intensified and consecrated the style? Here is an ambiguity about it all that constantly haunts and beguiles. ... one clings, even in the face of the colder stare, to one's prized Venetian privi-

lege of making the sense of doom and decay a part of every impression. ('Two Old Houses', 1899, *IH* 61)

This was in line with accepted views of the ambivalent, amphibious, and therefore disturbing nature of the city. James added the specification that Venice might be better at night and in winter (p. 91)—and it is significant that in his better fiction he preferred to make use of Venice in its cold, wintry, rainy aspects.[9]

As we already saw (see above, ch. 4), in 'The Aspern Papers' (1888) James presented Venice as a city of darkness, mystery, and mystification—where the past of the Misses Bordereau is buried and the protagonist is lost in the maze of conscience. A mid-season Venice was the perfect setting for plots.

Three years later, in the short story 'The Pupil' (1891), Venice resurfaced as the topos for the young hero's crisis, and the city was cast in an almost sinister, autumnal light, cold, wind-swept, with the rain lashing the lagoon: 'One sad November day, while the wind roared round the old palace and the rain lashed the lagoon …The *scagliola* floor was cold, the high battered casements shook in the storm, and the stately decay of the place was unrelieved by a particle of furniture'. Though the death-in-Venice' conceit is barely present (the young pupil dies elsewhere), Venice significantly acquires a livid, lurid air: 'A blast of desolation, a prophesy of disaster and disgrace, seemed to draw through the comfortless hall'.[10]

This can already be taken as a pre-figuration of the meteorological and symbolic climate—wind and rain, deluge and high water—in which Milly's death in Venice is enacted in *The Wings of the Dove*.

---

[9] This, incidentally, was the Venice which was beautifully discovered and pictured in the same years by Whistler's *Nocturnes* and more specifically by Sargent's *Venice par temps gris* (a painting of 1880-81: today I would refer to Peter Milton's Drawings for *The Aspern Papers* done in the early 1990s).

[10] *The Complete Tales of Henry James*, ed. Leon Edel, Philadelphia, Lippincott, 1963, VII, p. 444.

Milly's premonition of her fate in Italy is Wagnerian ('It was the Wagner overture that practically prevailed up through Italy', I 114), yet her final tone is that of subdued surrender to silence and death. She is first 'successfully deceived' in England; Venice, as we know, only witnesses the final steps of her betrayal and of her extinction. But it is a crucial and influential setting.

The city is 'done' in the novel according to expectations and accepted 'rules' (the Rialto and the Bridge of Sighs, with a central role assigned to St. Mark's as 'a great social saloon, a smooth-floored, blue-roofed chamber of amenity', II 189). But when the crisis comes, a wintry coldness—as in the deception and betrayal plot—prevails:

> The weather, from early morning, had turned to storm, the first sea-storm of the autumn ...
> It was a Venice all of evil that had broken out for them alike ... a Venice of cold lashing rain from a low black sky, of wicked wind raging through the narrow passes, of general arrest and interruption, with the people engaged in all the water-life huddled, stranded and wageless ... out where the wind was higher, he fairly ... pulled his umbrella closer down. ...
> The wet and the cold were now to reckon with. (II 257, 259, 261)

'The great drawing room of Europe', 'greasy now with salt spray', is profaned by bad weather, and it is precisely in that emblematic climate that Milly hears of her betrayal from Lord Mark—so that it comes as no surprise that 'The vice in the air, otherwise, was too much like the breath of fate. The weather had changed, the rain was ugly, the wind wicked, the sea impossible, *because* of Lord Mark. It was because of him, *a fortiori,* that the place was closed' (II 263). I take it that this phrase is meant to emphasise the perfect coincidence of place and destiny, of locale and story.

The wind makes Milly face the wall (this image is used four times in the concluding sections of the novel), and when after three days, in an almost Shakespearean alternation of storm and calmness (or in Densher's hallucinatory oscillation between glitter and gloom, as all happenings are reviewed in his mind), 'The weather changed, the stubborn storm yielded, and the autumn sunshine ... came into his own again ... Venice glowed and plashed and called and chimed again' (II 294), the horrible feeling of an unprecedented, cold Venice in the rain is not totally dispelled. Its momentary sunshine, we are told, is a fool's paradise.

This death in Venice has then a cutting edge; it has nothing in common with the enervating, morbid, sirocco atmosphere prevailing in Thomas Mann and other great practitioners of the motif. It is a bang, not a whimper, in spite of James's confirmed reticence and his well-rehearsed 'conspiracies of silence'.

And let us recall that death also involves the love of the betrayers, of Kate and Merton (who wanders through desert *campi* and crumbling palaces, looking at their 'cold storeys'), because deterioration, doom and perdition set between them in an uncanny way: the city *is* for all of them a city of death,[11] as if an air of cold corruption and decline marked and enveloped people and places alike.

James even adds one of his twists, a hint of the *acqua alta* (high water) motif, and I am far from facetious in suggesting that it, too, contributes to qualify the overall, physical as well as symbolic, meaning of Milly's final surrender: it is almost a hint of a 'death by water' motif. If Milly is so profoundly connected and identified with the beautiful, rich but dying city—the death of one mirrors the decline of the other—it is also because of the 'sinking' fear which explicitly threatens both of them.

In 'The Grand Canal' essay James had remarked that the city 'contains most the bright oddity of its general Deluge air ... it has never got

---

[11] See Tanner, *Venice Desired*, p. 202: 'In *The Wings of the Dove* Venice is indeed a place of death—actual physical deterioration, pain, decay and collapse; and also more subtle forms of spiritual death and decline (Merton Densher also announces his own death while he is there)'—though Venice is also a place of love and carnality, where Merton and Kate enjoy physical love: the inescapable oxymoron obtains here, too.

over its resemblance to a flooded city … in which the houses look as if the waters had overtaken them' (*IH* 46). This is a commonplace (though at the same time, for Venetians, a daily preoccupation). Milly is fully protected in her palace, ready 'to sit there forever, through all her time, as in a fortress … remaining aloft in the divine, dustless air, where she would hear but the plash of the water against stone …' And yet, 'Ah, not to go down—never, never to go down!' she strangely sighed to her friend' [Lord Mark]' (II 147: the same invocation is repeated later).

Expressing the fear of 'sinking' in more dramatic, existential terms, James is careful in establishing the connection, making one threat or danger mirror the other. When the cold weather strikes the city, St. Mark's 'was more than ever like a great drawing-room, the drawing-room of Europe, *profaned and bewildered by some reverse of fortune*' (II 261; my italics)—almost on the verge of inundation or destruction.

As for Milly, we are warned by another striking image, just as revealing and unsettling as the previous one, that in her fortress of a palace 'She was *in* it, as in the ark of her deluge' (II 143). She is safe for the moment in an artificial way, but surrounded by a flood that threatens and may indeed engulf and bring her down, make her sink. Soon after, we are reminded that in 'the high-watermark of her security' was the sign of her 'reaching the view of the troubled sea' (II 143-44).

Milly has then to go down from the palace, to face the troubled sea of treachery and lost (or impossible) hope, to accept the high-water mark of her deception and dissolution. If I resist the temptation to interpret her death as a peculiarly feminine form of 'death by water',[12] it is because James has a further, final specification to make about her death; a specification which reinforces both the concept of the plot/conspiracy and that of the coldness of death, which are by archetype and stereotype enacted in Venice.

---

[12] This motif is more extensively dealt with in ch. 3, 'Death by Water', of Sergio Perosa, *From Islands to Portraits. Four Literary Variations,* Amsterdam, IOS Press, 2000.

In the very end we are told that Milly was separated from her dream of a future, 'not shrieking indeed, but grimly, awfully silent, as one might imagine some noble young victim of the scaffold, in the French Revolution' (II 370).[13] Heroic Milly's plight, in this case, may forcibly recall the conclusion of Poe's story 'The Pit and the Pendulum'. There, however, we have a last-minute escape, which is impossible for Milly. In James's novel, we are left to the very end with the prevailing sense of coldness and despairing death that runs through it, and that this final image evokes and reinforces—especially for those of us who visited that dismal, doomed, and haunting seat of revolutionary terror, the Conciergerie.

---

[13]   'She is like a creature dragged shrieking to the guillotine—to the shambles', James had written in a Notebook entry (*The Complete Notebooks of Henry James,* eds Leon Edel and Lyall H. Powers, New York, Oxford U. P., 1987, p. 103, 3 November 1894); he had used an image from the French Revolution for the plight of Mme de Vionnet in *The Ambassadors* as well.

7 *Henry James, Tolstoy and the Novel*

Two preliminary remarks are in order. The first concerns the title. The accent should be placed on the third part of it, that is 'the novel', as I will analyze the uneven relationship between James and Tolstoy above all in the light of a polemic and a debate on the mode, the form and the structure of the novel. The second precautionary remark is that James's opinions on Tolstoy are anything but flattering, and I want to make it clear that they are his and not mine, though I believe that there is no need to be frightened off when a great artist reacts negatively to a fellow artist: Tolstoy's own reaction to Shakespeare is another such example.

According to a newspaper account, Tolstoy was a great admirer of Henry James: but of Henry James *senior*, the father of the novelist, the Swedenborgian philosopher. As Edwin Markham reported in 1910,[1] a visitor in Tolstoy's house had been told that he considered Henry James senior the most suggestive writer ever produced by America.

Two of the three 'lettered' offspring of the philosopher enthusiastically reciprocated Tolstoy's admiration. At the beginning of her *Diary* (1886-87), Alice copied the description of Prince Andrei at Austerlitz

---

[1] Edwin Markham, 'Distinguished American Family', *Cosmopolitan*, 1 December 1910, p. 145, in F. H. Young, *The Philosophy of Henry James Sr.,* New York, Bookman Associates, 1951, pp. 1, 9.

from the French translation of *War and Peace*.[2] We also know that throughout his life the philosopher William James considered Tolstoy one of the world's greatest writers, to the point of identifying with his ideas and his vision of literature. Here is what William wrote in 1889 in an essay entitled 'What Makes A Life Significant':

> If any of you have been readers of Tolstoy, you will see that I passed into a vein of feeling similar to his, with its abhorrence of all that conventionally passes for distinguished, and its exclusive deification of the bravery, patience, kindliness, and dumbness of the unconscious natural man.

He then went on to ask himself:

> Where now is our Tolstoy, I said, to bring the truth of all this home to our American bosoms, fill us with a better insight, and wean us away from that spurious literary romanticism on which our wretched culture—as it calls itself—is fed? ... Must we wait for some one born and bred and living as a laborer himself, but who, by grace of Heaven, shall also find a literary voice?[3]

Tolstoy is seen as a religious prophet, as another Buddha or Christ or St. Francis or Rousseau, while *War and Peace* is considered 'assuredly the greatest of human novels' where 'the role of the spiritual hero is entrusted to a poor little soldier named Karataiev' whose sight, William James continues, notwithstanding his ignorance and dirtiness, 'opens the heavens, which have been closed, to the mind of the principal character'. What captured the interest of William James was Tolstoy's interest (expressed in chapter 10 of *My Confession*) in the humble, the peasants, the labouring folks who do not live by their intellect but accept the highs and lows of life with even-tempered and unshakable faith,

---

[2]   *The Diary of Alice James*, ed. Leon Edel, London, Hart-Davis, 1965, pp. 1-2.
[3]   William James, 'What Makes A Life Significant', from *Talks to Students on Some of Life's Ideals,* in *Writings, 1878-1899,* New York, The Library of America, 1992, p. 867.

who are filled, the philosopher wrote, with the fundamental virtue of humanity. One must add, though, that William James considered the philosophy of Tolstoy a 'false abstraction', savouring too much 'of that Oriental pessimism and nihilism of his'.[4]

One will have noticed that, in asking himself what American culture should do to create someone like Tolstoy, William James did not name his brother Henry, from whom he was separated by a cordial, but deep-rooted and absolute difference of opinion about almost all literary matters. Indeed, to come to the point, just as Henry James junior in his youth detested Whitman, so, throughout his mature years as a writer, he carried on a battle against the narrative model followed—and provided—by Tolstoy.

Why, then, dwell however briefly on a great writer's opposition to another, perhaps even greater writer? Not so much, one might say, to trace the history (in itself of limited interest) of this incomprehension, as to focus on the deep reasons of an antithesis which in the crucial years at the turn of the century figures as a radical divergence over the methods, aims and form of the novel. This divergence concerned the overall problem of 'how to write a novel', and it became crucial in the 19th century—almost a polarity of intentions and results.

In order to clear the field immediately of possible ambiguities, one should note that although his fiction was inspired by different themes, attitudes, and perhaps values from those of Tolstoy, Henry James never disparaged the latter's genius and greatness in his various statements. Rather, for reasons which will be clear shortly, he was opposed to the form and structure of the type of novel which Tolstoy proposed. Secondly, he denied that Tolstoy, in that historical moment, could provide a valid model for other novelists. Great in himself, Tolstoy, like Dostoevsky, was not useful as a 'subject of emulation'. His followers would be led down a blind alley. Balzac, as James noted in the very title of

---

4   *Ibid.*, pp. 868-70.

one of his essays, had a lesson to offer the novelist; but Dickens, Dostoevsky or Tolstoy did not.[5]

In the case in point, the opposite would occur: a 'school' of English novelists would recognize themselves (with some reservations) in
Tolstoy's model. In fact, at the beginning of the 20th century, James
opposed those novelists precisely because they were, in his opinion,
followers of the form of the novel which he identified as that of Tolstoy's. It is therefore not simply a question of investigating the obvious
differences of temperament and of artistic aims between the two, but of
discerning those aspects of this opposition that qualify and illustrate a
different stance toward 'doing' the novel.

Henry James had a preference for Turgenev, not only because they
both had similar temperaments and vaguely aristocratic sensibilities, but
also for three main reasons, perhaps not yet sufficiently clarified. James
recognized in Turgenev the same and, for him, crucial condition of the
expatriate writer. Secondly, according to a revealing statement that is often overlooked, James discerned an analogy between the type of the Russian character 'in formation' which Turgenev presented and the new type
of the American character, also in formation, by which he himself was
inspired. There is a very significant passage in which James writes that
'Mr. Turgenev gives us a peculiar sense of being out of harmony with his
native land—of his having what one may call a poet's quarrel with it'.[6]
If they had a novelist of such a large pattern, American readers would
probably have one like Turgenev; 'Russian society, like our own [that is
American society, James continued], is in process of formation; the Russian character is in solution, in a sea of change'. James, as an American
writer, felt naturally attracted by this type of character.

---

[5]   See Leon Edel, Introduction to Henry James, *The Future of the Novel,* New York,
        Vintage Books, 1956, pp. xiii-xiv; 'The Lesson of Balzac' (1905), rpt. *ibid.,* pp. 97-
        124, and in *Literary Criticism, European Writers and the Prefaces,* New York, The
        Library of America, 1984, pp. 115-39.
[6]   See his 1874 essay 'Ivan Turgenieff', in *Literary Criticism. European Writers*,
        pp. 969-99 (p. 975 for the quotation).

The third, and most important, factor is that James found in Turgenev the example of a novel built according to the principles of a strict coherence, harmony and structural finality in a period (the 1870s and 1880s) in which this artistic quality did not yet seem to him fully accepted or recognized in English circles. (Throughout his career, both theoretically and practically, James strove to endow the contemporary English novel with an artistic form). That is why James privileged Turgenev's model—not his value—and why, on the other hand, he shows his radical incomprehension of Tolstoy.

The first of his various statements—one might call them pronouncements—about Tolstoy, was in 1897: a rather late statement in an essay on Turgenev, in which Tolstoy was seen as his opposite. It would be too easy, James wrote, to say that Tolstoy was 'for home consumption' (obviously, in Russia) and Turgenev for foreign consumption. Rather, Turgenev was 'the novelist's novelist', while—here James' opposition stood out clearly—Tolstoy was 'a wonderful mass of life' totally devoid of method. The short passage is worth quoting in full because it already contains *in nuce* James's future strictures—including the ambivalences and hesitations revealed by his somewhat laborious metaphorical procedure:

> The perusal of Tolstoy—a wonderful mass of life—is an immense event, a kind of splendid accident, for each of us; his name represents nevertheless no such eternal spell of method, no such quiet irresistibility of presentation, as shines, close to us and lighting our possible steps, in that of his precursor. Tolstoy is a reflector as vast as a natural lake: a monster harnassed to his great subject—all human life!—as an elephant might be harnassed, for purposes of traction, not to a carriage, but to a coach-house. His own case is prodigious, but his example for others dire: disciples not elephantine he can only mislead and betray.[7]

---

[7]   Henry James, 'Ivan Turgenev' (an essay prepared for vol. XX of the *Library of the World's Best Literature*), in *Literary Criticism. European Writers*, pp. 1027-34 (pp. 1029-30 for the quotation). The oppositions in this passage are life/art; accident/

Less than two years later, in a letter dated 26 July 1899, in which James criticized the principle of 'going behind' or inside characters so as to analyze their psychological makeup, and in which he stated the need of a clear and unitary perspective in the elaboration of narrative material, Tolstoy was represented, this time along with Balzac, as an implicitly negative example in which 'promiscuous shiftings of standpoint and centre' occur. James traced these shiftings of viewpoint and center back to their being (Balzac and Tolstoy) 'not so much big dramatists as big *painters*', not so much 'theatrical' as 'pictorial', according to a deep-rooted distinction of his between the pictorial novel—which was illustrative, panoramic, documentary and processional—and the novel which was unified, instead, by the presence of a character involved in the action, from whose point of view it is presented.

Furthermore, he saw them (Balzac and Tolstoy) as 'the inevitable result of the *quantity of presenting* their genius launches them in. With the complexity they pile up they *can* get no clearness without trying again and again for new centres. And they don't *always* get it. However, I don't mean to say they don't get enough.'[8]

Here the two positions were further clarified. Tolstoy appeared as the opposite of the type of novel closely constructed around a center of consciousness and according to a single point of view, which at the turn of the century became James's major preoccupation and perhaps his major contribution to the 20th century novel. That is why, in his essay of 1903 on 'Emile Zola', when James placed Zola's *La Débâcle* alongside *War and Peace* as 'an incomparably human picture of war', he defined Tolstoy's work as a 'very much more universal but very much less composed and condensed epic'. This confirms what has just been said: James acknowledged that Tolstoy had a cosmic-historical

---

method; greatness of subject (all of human life)/the elephant that drags it; the immense event/the fatal event.

[8]   Henry James, *Letters,* ed. Leon Edel, Cambridge, The Belknap Press of Harvard U. P., 1984, IV , p. 112.

or epic-universal drive, but he insisted on what he considered a lack of composition and condensation around a single structural center.[9]

At the beginning of the 20th century, James's opposition became more marked. In his 1908 preface to *The Tragic Muse*, he made what is perhaps his best known or notorious statement, if read out of context. He was writing of one of his most pictorial, panoramic and processional novels, inspired by the representative amplitude of Tintoretto's 'Crucifixion' in Venice. Yet, he insisted on the fact that even this type of novel illustrating a social world must aspire to a compositional unity that can bridle, order and subdue the elusive wealth of life. For, according to James, without such compositional unity, only life remains; and if one has *only* life—James continued—as in Thackeray's *The Newcomes* or Dumas' *The Three Musketeers* or in *War and Peace*, what can it mean artistically? As he continued:

> what do such large loose baggy monsters, with their queer elements of the accidental and the arbitrary, artistically *mean?* We have heard it maintained, we well remember, that such things are 'superior to art'; but we understand least of all what *that* may mean, and we look in vain for the artist, the divine explanatory genius, who will come to our aid and tell us. There is life and life, and as waste is only life sacrificed and thereby prevented from 'counting', I delight in a deep-breathing economy and an organic form.[10]

Here James's opposition transcended mere personal idiosyncrasies. The 'complete pictorial fusion' to which he aspired in the Prefaces is an eco-

---

[9] 'Emile Zola' was included in *Notes on Novelists* (New York, Scribner, 1914), pp. 26-64; now in *Literary Criticism. European Writers*, pp. 871-99 (p. 898 for the quotation). Another passing reference to Tolstoy is in 'The Lesson of Balzac' (1905): if the lesson of Balzac is 'that there is no convincing art that is not ruinously expensive', in the light of Balzac's three major successors (George Eliot, Tolstoy and Zola), James is reluctant to see Balzac as 'the last of the novelists to do the thing handsomely; but I will say that we get the impression at least of his having had more to spend' (*ibidem*, p. 133).

[10] Henry James, *The Art of the Novel*, ed. R.P. Blackmur, New York, Scribner, 1934, p. 84 (*Literary Criticism. European Writers*, p. 1107-08).

nomic and organic form structured on the unitary principle of a center of interest and a limited point of view; on an absolutely unified perspective of presentation, on foreshortening, on the indirect method, and therefore on the representation of life as reflected in a consciousness rather than lived in action. It is pointless to pause here over the various aspects of the Jamesian theory of the novel.[11] Yet one point, perhaps, underlies his view of the novel that, at the turn of the century, was defined as 'artistic': the concept, already present in Flaubert and taken up by Joyce in *A Portrait of the Artist as a Young Man*, of a total and absolute artistic *illusion*, that creates its own self-sufficient and autonomous world. In that world, Flaubert said, the author is '*présent partout mais visible nulle part*'; Joyce said in almost the same words that there the author becomes 'invisible, refined out of existence, indifferent, paring his fingernails'.

Feeling that he himself represented a point of development or transition in the history of the novel precisely because of his insistence on the autonomy and objectivity of the fictional world projected by the novelist, James declared himself opposed to authorial intrusions and comments in the book, and to the idea that 'fiction' was make-believe (as for instance Trollope had maintained). And he was equally opposed to what he considered Tolstoy's fluidity or formlessness. If art is for him essentially form, construction, architecture, and composition, it aims at something other than the mimetic and, ultimately, at the non-representative. It does not reflect or represent life but transforms it, fixes it into something different. Art is coherence of parts, while life is fluidity. One fixes, the other flows. One captures and maintains the moment, the other overwhelms and carries on. James shared this position (and this inheritance) with Joseph Conrad and with the 'artistic' novelists of the turn of the century, notably (besides Conrad) Ford Madox Ford. It is

---

[11]   See, among others, my *Henry James and the Experimental Novel,* Charlottesville, Virginia U. P., 1978 and *American Theories of the Novel, 1703-1903*, New York, New York U. P., 1983.

an attitude that also reappeared in the first historical avant-garde—in Joyce, in Virginia Woolf or E. M. Forster.

Given this stand of James's, one can understand why the author of *Anna Karenina* and *War and Peace*, in spite of the vital and artistic turmoil that James recognized in him, appeared to him too fluid, too elusive. In a letter of 19 May 1912 he wrote:

> when you ask me if I don't feel Dostoevsky's 'mad jumble, that flings things down in a heap' nearer truth and beauty than the picking and composing that you instance in [R. L.] Stevenson, I reply with emphasis that I feel nothing of the sort, and that the older I grow and the more I *go* the more sacred to me do picking and composing become ... Don't let any one persuade you ... that strenuous selection and comparison are not the very essence of art, and that Form *is* [not] substance to that degree that there is absolutely no substance without it. Form only *takes*, and holds and preserves, substance—saves us from the welter of helpless verbiage that we swim in as in a sea of tasteless tepid pudding.[12]

And here James came out with his other notorious, chilling remark that 'Tolstoy and D[ostoevsky] are fluid puddings, though not tasteless'. As he reiterated in another letter of 21 August 1913, they seemed to him to waste the chance offered to the artist to 'close' his construction artistically:

> I have been reading over Tolstoy's interminable *Peace and War* [*sic*] and am struck with the fact that I now protest as much as I admire. He doesn't *do* to read over, and that exactly is the answer to those who idiotically proclaim the impunity of such formless shape, such flopping looseness and such a denial of composition, selection and style. He has a mighty fund of life, but the *waste*, and the ugliness and vice of waste, the vice of a not finer *doing*, are sickening. For me he makes 'composition' throne, by contrast, in effulgent lustre![13]

---

[12] See *Letters*, IV, pp. 618-19.

[13] *Ibidem*, IV, pp. 680-81.

Why such unprecedented harshness? The two letters were addressed to a still budding novelist, Hugh Walpole; and in those very years, immediately preceding World War I, James was actively involved in an intense debate, indeed a controversy, over the tendencies of the new English fiction. He was not at all pleased with what he saw around him. The very thing he had opposed all his life was taking root: the model of the new fiction writers had become none other than Tolstoy—with his wealth of life and affections, so directly reflected in his fiction, with that relative predominance of the author over the work, of personal intrusions over authorial distance, of the magmatic force of discourse over narrative composition, which James had fought against and feared.

His last attack against Tolstoy is most interesting precisely because James's opposition, which until then had remained personal and private, so to speak, had now become an *objective* opposition involving two different ways of writing a novel, almost a polarity that no longer concerned James or Tolstoy alone, but the contemporary tendencies of English fiction and the novel as a genre, as an artistic and communicative form.

In one of his articles entitled 'The New Novel' which appeared in the *Times Literary Supplement* in 1914 and which pertains to a much broader quarrel he carried on with H. G. Wells,[14] James recorded with very sensitive antennae the spreading in England of a type of novel saturated with the presence of the author, where interest in character dominated over the organization of plot, where social ideals were openly flaunted and where the magmatic force of life seemed to get the better of artistic attempts to order or compress. The 'new novelists' were H. G. Wells, Arnold Bennett, Hugh Walpole, Compton Mackenzie, and the then beginner D. H. Lawrence, all of whom shared what James called a 'value by saturation'. And if this new movement flourishing in Eng-

[14] See *Henry James & H. G. Wells. A Record of their Friendship, their Debate on the Art of Fiction and their Quarrel,* eds Leon Edel and G. N. Ray, London, Hart-Davis, 1958.

land was 'in favour of the "expression of life" in terms as loose as may pretend to an effect of expression at all', the inference to be drawn was this:

> We should have only to remount the current with a certain energy to come straight up against Tolstoy as the great illustrative master-hand on all this ground of the disconnection of method from matter ... of all great painters of the social picture it was given that epic genius most to serve admirably as a rash adventurer and a 'caution', and execrably, pestilentially, as a model ... All the proportions in him are so much the largest ... which fact need not disguise from us, none the less, that as Mr. H. G. Wells and Mr. Arnold Bennett ... derive, by multiplied if diluted transmissions, from the great Russian (from whose all but equal companion Turgenieff we recognise no derivatives at all), so, observing the distances, we may profitably detect an unexhausted influence in our minor, our still considerably less rounded vessels.[15]

Tolstoy was now placed above Turgenev: even for James he always remained the 'great Russian'. James recognized, however, that Tolstoy's lack of a compositional center was by that time accepted by the new English novelists, all intent on 'crowding the canvas'. And it was not so much an admission (to come to the end of this *excursus*) of personal defeat, as James's perceptive recognition of a contemporary historical tendency. In those critical years between the end of the 19th century and the beginning of the 20th, there were those who, like Conrad and Ford, continued along the road of the 'Jamesian' novel and those who, instead, followed Tolstoy—and rather closely at that.

In fact, as is evident from an essay of his on Gissing, which appeared in 1897, H. G. Wells was very well aware of Tolstoy's different 'structural conception'. This consisted, Wells wrote, in the grouping of

---

[15]   'The New Novel', in *Notes on Novelists,* pp. 328-29, and in *Literary Criticism. Essays, American Writers and English Writers,* New York, The Library of America, 1984, pp. 134-35.—A similar term, *leak,* was used for D'Annunzio (see chapter 8, below).

characters and incidents not about a misplaced will, a hidden murder or a lost child, but 'about some social influence or some far-reaching movement of humanity'.[16] For George Moore, Tolstoy gave the *true* life of his characters, i.e. their subconscious life. In a similar way Vernon Lee—a theorist who was writing at the turn of the century and was very often Jamesian in her outlook—recognized in Tolstoy's work not only wealth of characterization and the author's ability to *be* each of his characters, but also 'the force of accumulated action'.[17]

Studies on point of view and on the Jamesian novel at the turn of the 19th century have clarified—against the codifications of a Percy Lubbock or a Joseph Warren Beach—that *that* Jamesian form of the novel answered to specific expectations or even to the particular historical exigencies of the age and reflected a legitimate will to construct and affirm the artistic novel after the period of Victorian diffuseness.[18] A will or an exigency that found parallels in France, with Flaubert, as well as in other countries, and that undoubtedly led to great literary conquests a whole group of already mentioned twentieth-century writers.

But it was precisely a type or a kind, not an absolute form. In 20th-century England another great type or kind of novel coexisted alongside the 'artistic' novel. This type stressed a participating and even tumul-

---

[16] See Carlo Pagetti, *La nuova battaglia dei libri. Il dibattito sul romanzo in Inghilterra alla fine dell'Ottocento,* Bari, Adriatica, 1977, p. 297, and *G. Gissing & H. G. Wells. A Record of their Friendship and Correspondence,* ed. R. A. Gettman, London, Hart-Davis 1961, pp. 244-45.

[17] See Kenneth Graham, *English Cristicism of the Novel. 1865-1900,* Oxford, Clarendon Press, 1965, p. 41 (for G. Moore); and pp. 105-106, 136 and 138 (for Vernon Lee). For Hall Caine, Tolstoy represented, instead, romance *(ibid.,* pp. 68-69).

[18] See Walter Allen, 'Narrative, Distance, Tone and Character', and R. H. Fogle, 'Illusion, Point of View and Modern Criticism', both in *The Theory of the Novel. New Essays,* ed. John Halperin, New York, Oxford U. P., 1974, pp. 323-37, 338-52 and *passim*; Norman Friedman, 'Point of View in Fiction', in *The Theory of the Novel,* ed. P. H. Stevick, New York, Free Press, 1967, pp. 108-137; Dorothy Hale, *Social Formalism. The Novel in Theory from Henry James to the Present,* Stanford, Stanford U. P., 1998, chapter 1, among others. And see *Anna Karenina,* ed. George Gibian, New York, Norton, 1970, for an ample selection of essays.

tuous reflection of life in all its chaotic richness, an 'effusion of life' and the debate of ideas. It stressed an epic of the average man or a troubled mirror of the soul: to remain within the English context, one might include here even D. H. Lawrence (though his relations with Tolstoy were quite polemical, as essays by Raymond Williams and George Steiner bear out). In other words, Tolstoy, whom James thought had been thrown out the window (as a *model*, I must repeat, not as a *writer*), came back in through the main door. Ultimately, James's perception led him to foresee this development most clearly.

Besides, as the reader will have inferred, his 'opposition' was that which characterizes the artist rather than the critic. It was a difference of *poetics* more than of principles, a tactical or strategic difference, based on his aims as a novelist, not a denial or a repudiation of Tolstoy's greatness, which James, on the contrary, often underlined. The interesting thing is precisely the widening of the field of reflection and debate that such an opposition involved and permitted: the double perspective of the ways open to the novel that it favoured. Not only is there room for James and Tolstoy in the novel (God forbid!), but there is a need for both.

A NOTE ON JAMES'S LITERARY CRITICISM

In one of his occasional short essays, writing of periodical literature as 'a huge, open mouth which has to be fed', Henry James set the task for the ideal critic:

> To lend himself, to project himself and steep himself, to feel and feel till he understands, and to understand so well that he can say, to have perception at the pitch of passion and expression as embracing as the air, to be infinitely curious and incorrigibly patient, and yet plastic and inflammable and determinable, stooping to conquer and serving to direct—these are fine chances for an active mind... Just in proportion as he is sentient and rest-

less, just in proportion as he reacts and reciprocates and penetrates, is the critic a valuable instrument.[19]

Here, as elsewhere, he saw the task and the dignity of the critic as equal to those of the novelist: both led a kind of saturated, vicarious life, dealt with experience at first *and* at second hand, both must he supple and alert.

In a long life devoted almost exclusively to literature—as he wrote of Sainte-Beuve: 'he was literary in every pulsation of his being, and he expressed himself totally in his literary life ... he had no disturbing, perverting tastes; he suffered no retarding, embarrassing accidents ... he was not even married'—James wrote a vast amount of literary criticism, autobiographical and travel essays, art and drama reviews, on top of his rows of novels and stories and his stacks of letters. But it would be wrong to imagine him constantly at his desk or, in his later years, pacing about his room, dictating: we know of his many social engagements, of his moving restlessly between two continents, of his absorbing interest in human affairs and entanglements. There was no separation in him (as he projected it in his story 'The Private Life') between the man who creates in the dark intimacy of his room and the socialite who graces the ball or the parlour with his presence.

This wholeness added poignancy and range, I believe, to the more than three-hundred literary essays, prefaces and commentaries, which have been conveniently collected in two volumes of the Library of America in 1984. The range is impressive—from Epictetus to D'Annunzio, from Shakespeare to the question of women's massive contribution to nineteenth-century fiction, from theoretical definitions of novel-writing to discussions of the role of mass culture and mass production and of changing social conditions and manners. Practically all major novelists of James's time, European as well as American (with few exceptions),

---

[19]   'The Science of Criticism' (1891), in *Literary Criticism. Essays, American and English Writers*, p. 98.

are dealt with in his essays, which are marked by a personal accent and an easy-going, sometimes sharp or witty manner.

As he said, again, of Sainte-Beuve, James's 'very horror of dogmas, moulds, formulas' made him 'the least doctrinal of critics'. The tone of these essays is discursive and analytical, only slightly intellectual. In a period when biographical criticism seems on the increase, they ought to be required reading for the way in which they probe into the crucial relations between art and life, manners and motives, inspiration and execution; even for the economy and the astringency—yes, economy and astringency—with which James can sketch a writer's character, evoke a temperament, grapple with the works of a fellow author.

This is their first characteristic: James writes as a 'man of the trade' often in the habit, as he put it, 'of thinking of what, in the conditions, *he* would have done'. Secondly, in spite of his proverbial reticence and suppressions, James seems here fascinated with human and literary indiscretions. One episode may serve for all: George Sand's elopement to Venice with the young and unprotected Alfred de Musset, their quarrels and separation there in the midst of scandals, recriminations and open infidelities. James returns to this episode almost obsessively. Yet this reveals neither unsuspected pruriencies nor expected pruderies on his part: he is fascinated by the mysterious question of how the experience of life is transmuted into the substance of art, the turmoil of passion filtered by literature, the confusion of motives ordered by aesthetic perspective.

One of the most interesting lines of inquiry is James's life-long attempt at defining the role, aim, function and nature of fiction, both in essays dealing specifically with this topic and, by implication, in his studies of other writers. His views evolved in a notable way, but he always held the novel to be a 'capacious vessel', capable of taking in or accommodating almost anything, whose only danger was 'sailing too light'. It was to be allowed freedom of subject, form, expression and outlook, even in such taboo areas for the Victorian mind as sexual *mœurs* or the serious treatment of low life.

In his early phase James espoused the cause of literary realism to a degree perhaps unrealized so far. In his 1879 book on Nathaniel Hawthorne he rejected his great predecessor's 'want of reality' and 'abuse of the fanciful element', and saw his reliance on allegory and romance as a consequence of the lack in America of recognizable social signs and manners. After the Civil War, however, Americans had 'eaten of the tree of knowledge' and novelists had to face reality, to commit themselves to a representation of contemporary society, much in the way of their French predecessors and contemporaries: Balzac, with his 'grasp of actual facts', his 'complete social system', his 'overmastering sense of the present world'; Flaubert, with his impersonality and objectivity; even Zola, in spite of his 'monstrous uncleanliness' and sordidness of subjects, a master—as James was to maintain to the end of his life—of a 'totally *represented* world', at his best when promiscuous and collective.

James never doubted that 'art without life is a poor affair', that an 'air of reality (solidity of specification)' was essential to fiction. Realism, moreover, as the French showed, acknowledged and stressed the artistic nature of fiction—a far from undisputed notion at that time, as he noted in his crucial essay 'The Art of Fiction' (1884), where the claims of representative realism balance the claims of artistic expression.

It is true that James, equally thrilled and enthralled by George Eliot and her Anglo-Saxon *confrères* (he risked the witticism himself...), wanted to bring the question of morality, so neglected by the French, back into the picture. And it is also true that deep down he preferred the kind of 'delicate' realism that he found in Alphonse Daudet (who did see 'the connection between the feelings and external conditions') or, better still, in Turgenev—a kindred soul self-exiled from Russia just as James had expatriated himself from America (he preferred, however, to speak of dispatriation, rather than expatriation). This led him, even at an early stage, to stress the need for psychological analysis on the part of the novelist, a concern with consciousness, with 'that reflective part which governs conduct and produces character'. Besides being 'an object adorably pictorial', psychological analysis added perspective and completeness to realism; it allowed the novelist 'to survey the whole field'.

But it is only as he approached the 20th century that James considerably shifted his interest and emphasis from the object to the writer's vision, from represented to imagined reality, from the 'look of things' to searching analyses of motives; in short, from outer to inner reality. Fiction then became 'a personal, a direct impression of life' filtered by the writer's vision and often through a character's consciousness; facts were given or contemplated in the field 'rather of their second than their first exhibition'; they might even lose contours and consistency in the vagaries of consciousness and perception. And it is only then that James's so often exaggerated aestheticism (he was vociferous on at least two occasions against 'art for art') seemed to take the upper hand. The novel was then extolled not only as free and far-ranging in its representation of life, but as a form of 'rival creation'—giving us self-contained worlds of autonomous creation.

'Expression is creation ... it *makes* the reality', James wrote; it gives us 'another actual'. This was achieved through that unity of material and form, of style and idea, conception and language that he came to regard as of paramount importance now that the novel had become not only the genre of the age, but self-conscious in form, requiring structure and arrangements, composition and architecture—its 'costliest charm'. Relying on 'the mystic process of the crucible, the transformation of the material under aesthetic heat' was a way of stemming the vulgarization of mass culture: in any case, the subject must be fertilized by form. There is 'no complete creation without style any more than there is complete music without sound', James wrote a propos of D'Annunzio; even a 'slice of life' poses the question of where and how to cut it. If life is all saturation and confusion, he concluded, art is all discrimination and selection. But it is noteworthy that to the very end he tried consistently to balance their respective claims. Art, he wrote in one of the Prefaces to the New York Edition of his novels and tales, 'plucks its material ... in the garden of life—which material elsewhere grown is stale and uneatable. But it has no sooner done this than it has to take account of a process': the process, of course, of expression.

There is no doubt that the Prefaces are to be read as a plea for discrimination and conscious artistic application; charmingly personal and anecdotal as they are, they constitute an impassioned vindication of the creative value of fiction and a painstaking analysis of its ways and means, forms and techniques, aims and functions. They can be read as a manifesto of early modernism just as they prefigure crucial features and concerns of the latest narratology. Where else do we find so perceptively and abundantly discussed questions of point of view and foreshortening, of illustrative picture versus (or combined with) 'scenic form', of dialogue and time-passage, of the use of wonder and the appeal to consciousness, of mirrors of the subjects and so on and so forth? There is more of James in Genette than meets the eye.

Yet, one tends to overlook that the Prefaces end with a renewed acknowledgment of the 'lesson of Balzac', to whom is owed 'our richest and hugest inheritance in imaginative prose'. Just as, I think, we should read James's early criticisms of Hawthorne in the light of his appreciation of French realism, so should we read his Prefaces in connection with his later, comprehensive essays collected in 1914 in *Notes on Novelists*—re-visitations of Zola, Balzac, Flaubert, with their factual basis for fiction, saturation with life and awareness of social conditions. No wonder James saw the novel, at the end of his search, as elusive and ever-changing, constantly straining its mould, the 'most independent, most elastic, most prodigious of literary forms'.

A second perspective is given by the fact that James seems to be drawn to painstaking studies and eulogies of precisely those writers whom we tend somehow to consider outside the main concerns of his inspiration and who pursued different types of fiction. 'Compensation' may be at work here. Hawthorne is dealt with on repeated occasions as establishing a pattern to be superseded in modern times and in different social conditions. W. D. Howells is followed throughout his career as providing the example of the 'other' possibility—the writer who flourishes by staying at home, close to the sources of his native inspiration, 'heedless of foolish flurries from other quarters': exactly the opposite of James's international choice in life and fiction. (It is surprising, incidentally, in how many of these essays James faces the question of a national literature and a national consciousness, and his essays on American writers seem on the whole more deeply concerned and felt than the others).

British writers are appreciated either for their youthful promise (Kipling and Rupert Brooke) or for their imposing Victorian high seriousness (Matthew Arnold and George Eliot). R. L. Stevenson is cherished as the type of the sophisticated artist 'whose constant theme is the unsophisticated'. Walter Scott is praised as a born story-teller with no preoccupation with composition or form—just as George Sand is extolled as an *improvvisatrice* who writes as a nightingale sings, driven by passion and oblivious of checks. Among French writers, we noticed, James singled out the masters of 'scientific' realism or of local colour, like Pierre Loti (for one of whose volumes he wrote an introduction). And how shall we account for his belated interest in sensuous and unprincipled D'Annunzio, or indeed in the proto-feminist, the liberated and indiscreet Matilde Serao? Perhaps by the attraction of opposites, one may suggest (see chapter 9, below); or by James's delighted astonishment at the way in which these writers managed to combine vulgarity of subjects with literary skill, sordidness of situations with aesthetic (even aristocratic) pretensions.

He stayed, however, with his congenial models (with Alphonse Daudet, for instance, whom he also took the trouble to translate), and his most sincere and deeply felt tribute is perhaps to the genius of Turgenev—capable of 'watching the machinery of character', of combining moral meaning and form, at ease with the spectacle of life as well as with the life of conscience. James had his blind spots, too: Poe and Whitman, even Baudelaire, in his early stages, Tolstoy and Dostoevsky later on. But his criticism testifies to his catholicity and omnivorous taste. With an active mind, he explored the whole range, the mysterious sources and the inner workings of fiction.

8   *Henry James on D'Annunzio*

At the end of my previous essay I wondered how are we to account for James's belated interest D'Annunzio, or in the liberated and indiscreet Matilde Serao. Perhaps by the attraction of opposites, I proposed; more precisely, one might suggest, by James's delighted astonishment at the way in which these writers managed to combine vulgarity of subject with literary skill, sordidness of situations with aesthetic (even aristo-cratic) pretensions. Throughout his life James felt that respectability could be a blight on literature, and wrote against the Anglo-Saxon 'con-spiracy of silence' in sexual matters—a conspiracy of silence which D'Annunzio had triumphantly overcome.

The picture is naturally much more complex when we examine at close range James's long essay on D'Annunzio, completed in 1903 (in spite of the date he put at the head of the essay), published the follow-ing year in the *Quarterly Review* and reprinted in his *Notes on Novelists* of 1912. As often in such encounters between gifted writers, the essay throws as much light on James and his view of the novel as it does on D'Annunzio and his fictional achievement. James's essay dealt with five of D'Annunzio's better known novels to date (*Il piacere, L'innocente, Il trionfo della morte, Le vergini delle rocce, Il fuoco*), with only pass-ing references to two of his plays (*La Gioconda, Francesca da Rimini*) and to the total exclusion of his poetry. Although the caption listed their English (and one French) translations, Leon Edel notes that James had read the novels 'in the original (they remained in his library heavily marked)', and in his essay he preferred to use the Italian titles.[1]

Quite perceptively, James presented D'Annunzio as a 'case', the best case of the aesthetic writer (or, if you will, of the fin-de-siècle decadent) in his purest form. At home, James was confronted with a similar case—that of Oscar Wilde—but we can surmise that he chose not to deal with him for several reasons: first, Wilde's notoriety was socially and morally too much for him; second, Wilde did not appear to be a fully-developed or flourishing *novelist* (but, rather, a dramatist). Moreover, the writer seeking 'beauty at any price, beauty appealing alike to the senses and to the mind', throwing 'a straighter and more inevitable light on the aesthetic consciousness' could be studied better on the Continent (in such countries as France or Italy) than in England. Indeed, in the fullness of his devotion to aestheticism and the life of the senses D'Annunzio provided a kind of example and even an anti-dote for British fictional restraint and deprivation: he was 'as a literary figure, the highest expression of the reality that our conditions were to fail of making possible', 'the measure of our shortcomings in the same direction' (p. 909).

D'Annunzio showed 'an artistic intelligence of extraordinary range and fineness concentrated almost wholly on the life of the senses'. 'The only ideas he urges upon us are the erotic and the plastic [James went

---

[1]   Now in *Literary Criticism. European Writers and The Prefaces,* New York, The Library of America, 1984, p. 907-43 (hereafter page references in the text); see also P. Meixner, 'James on D'Annunzio—"A High Example of Exclusive Estheti-cism"', *Criticism,* 13 (1971), pp. 291-311.—Previous articles on D'Annunzio had appeared in *The Yellow Book* (October 1886), pp. 284-99, on his poetry, and in *The Quarterly Review* (July 1900), pp. 107-28; Ouida [Marie Louise de la Ramé], in 'The Genius of D'Annunzio', *Fortnightly Review* (March 1897), pp. 349-73, related him to French and Russian writers, and anticipated James in noting the 'bad smell' he shared with Zola; H. D. Sedgwick, in 'D'Annunzio the Novelist', *Atlantic Monthly* (October 1897), pp. 508-22, insisted on his new style and compared him with James: both lived in a hot-house atmosphere of excessive refinement where only special creatures could live (p. 513).

on: I take 'plastic' to indicate his pictorial quality], which have for him about an equal intensity, or of which it would be doubtless more correct to say that he makes them interchangeable faces of the same figure'. From the beginning, however, James sees the tragic potential of such a concentration on the life of the senses, the suffering, rather than the enjoyment, inherent in this choice. He stresses 'the manner in which the play of the aesthetic principle in him takes on, for positive extravagance and as a last refinement of freedom, the crown of solicitude and anxiety' (pp. 909-10).

In *Il piacere*—an early novel which is 'a sort of prophetic summary of his elements. All that is done in the later things is more or less done here'—Andrea Sperelli 'pays, pays heavily ... for an unbridled surrender to the life of the senses" (p. 913). In *L'innocente*, the characters are seen as victims of their own sensibility, exasperated, erotic, hysterical, cut off from any personal source of life that does not poison them (p. 919). The same would be true of *Il trionfo della morte* and *Il fuoco*, although in a more complex and mature way. We can spot here more than a touch of James's concern with the moral, as well as aesthetic, life of the mind, with both intellectual and sensual awareness, and with the full, rather than limited, range of experience. As this was the main point developed in the final part of his essay, I mention it here only in passing, and will take it up later on.

At the outset, James reaffirms his lifelong conviction that a novelist—any novelist—must be granted his *donnée,* his postulates, his subject, and must be judged by his treatment of them: 'his treatment of it [the subject] ... is what he actually gives; and it is with what he gives that we are critically concerned' (p. 918). In this sense, D'Annunzio's postulates, *données,* and subjects—in particular, his obsession with sexual passion—are seen and accepted with relief, almost with expectation and satisfaction, by an elderly James who, at the beginning of the new century, was all in favor of a greater range and freedom for the novel, including those areas so far excluded by British and American respectability. These were the years in which James was pleading that the novel

embrace the fullness of life, and D'Annunzio was a case not to be overlooked in this regard.

More specifically, now, D'Annunzio was admired by James for three
aspects of his 'case'. In *Il piacere*

> The author's three sharpest signs are already unmistakable: first his rare
> notation of states of excited sensibility; second his splendid visual sense,
> the quick generosity of his response to the message, as we nowadays say, of
> aspects and appearances, to the beauty of places and things; third his ample
> and exquisite style, his curious, various, inquisitive, always active employ-
> ment of language as a means of communication and representation. So
> close is the marriage between his power of 'rendering', in the light of the
> imagination, and whatever he sees and feels, that we should much mislead
> in speaking of his manner as a thing distinct from the matter submitted to it.
> The fusion is complete and admirable, so that, though his work is nothing if
> not 'literary', we see at no point of it where literature or where life begins
> or ends… It is brought home to us afresh that there is no complete creation
> without style any more than there is complete music without sound; also
> that when language becomes as closely applied and impressed a thing as
> for the most part in the volumes before us the fact of artistic creation is
> registered at a stroke (p. 914).

For those familiar with James's critical views, the third point is the
clearest mark of artistic greatness. It is the mark of Shakespeare (James
repeated much the same thing in his essay on *The Tempest*, as we shall
see in the next chapter) and of the best novelists. The task of 'rendering' imaginatively what one sees and feels was the novelist's greatest
challenge (as expressed for instance in Conrad's influential Preface to
The Nigger of the 'Narcissus', 1897); the fusion of life and literature,
of matter and manner, was James's own ideal since he began theoriz-
ing on the novel. Art without life is a poor affair, he had written in an
early dialogue on George Eliot's *Daniel Deronda,* and in other essays
collected in *Notes on Novelists* he was to repeat and enlarge on the need
of a full apprehension of life for all aesthetic purposes. One lengthy

quotation that James offers from *Il piacere*—Sperelli leaving the Roman palace after the initiation vouchsafed to him—is a clear example of what James considered good fictional *showing* rather than *telling* (pp. 916-17).

In D'Annunzio one has then creation *with* style, language as a triumph of expression. The first two points in my long quotation, however, allow for particular specifications and gradual qualifications.

D'Annunzio's plastic, pictorial, and visual sense is for James—that inveterate lover of Italy and Italian landscapes—a triumph of rendering. There is a feeling of ecstatic recognition in the way in which James revels in the golden presence of Rome in *Il piacere* or the gloomy presence of Venice in *Il fuoco*. The writer of *Italian Hours*, the novelist who had used Rome and Venice as well as many other Italian backgrounds in his novels, finds in D'Annunzio a kindred spirit and perhaps even a superior master. Above all, however, James values in D'Annunzio the way in which his local landscapes and atmospheres, triumphantly rendered in visual terms, influence and impinge on the secluded, closeted lives of his characters, and on their mental dispositions. The whole category of the phenomena of 'passion'—so prevailing in D'Annunzio, as it was in Matilde Serao (p. 915), to whom James also devoted an essay—is seen as both connected to, and tragically secluded from, the beauty of its physical surroundings.

James is very good in pointing out that the states of feeling, ecstasy, and suffering of D'Annunzio's characters take place in a sphere of exasperated, claustrophobic sensibility, which becomes their prison and their doom, as well as their mark. The prevailing relation between his men and women is not only sexual; it is the relation of the erotically exasperated *with* the erotically exasperated: a vicious circle in all senses (p. 918). D'Annunzio's characters, in these five novels, are 'deprived of any enlarging or saving personal relation, that is of any beneficent reciprocity'. That is why they are often reduced to homicidal madness (pp. 918-19).

Their obsession with the world of the senses—of all the senses—'yields them such a crop of impressions' that they can live and vibrate and react by themselves. (This is for James a sign of novelty, a marked difference from the novels being written in Britain and America, where he found a predominant habit of dealing with man dramatically in his social or gregarious dimensions, in action, and mixing with his kind [p. 921]). But theirs then becomes a closed and haunted world, a world of gloom and exasperation, of dark and secluded rooms, *un'atmosfera di serra* (*serra* is a better word for my purposes than *hothouse*). Even the outer beauty of Italy becomes for them an 'enclosing cage of golden wire', emphasizing their prison of bitterness and woe:

> The innumerable different ways in which his concentrated couples are able to feel about each other and about their enclosing cage of golden wire, the nature and the art of Italy—these things crowd into their picture and pervade it, lighting it scarcely less, strange to say, because they are things of bitterness and woe. (p. 920)

The element of suffering breaks through again here; indeed, it breaks through beauty and passion.

A fourth point, however, is forcibly made by James in this context, where he speaks in his own voice and through his personal predilection for the reflected, rather than the immediate, side of life. I mean his predilection for facts given or contemplated (as he put it in his Prefaces) in the field 'rather of their second than their first exhibition'. If in *The Triumph of Death, The Flame of Life*, and *L'innocente* 'the temporarily united pair devour each other, tear and rend each other, wear each other out through a series of erotic convulsions and nervous reactions', these 'are made interesting … almost exclusively *by the special wealth of their consciousness*' (p. 920, my italics).

Among the five novels, James singles out for special recognition and praise those two in which a central awareness and the play of consciousness are present: *L'innocente* and *Le vergini delle rocce. Il trionfo della morte* and *Il fuoco* appear as the amplest and richest, for their mixture of every element of personal charm with the local influence, for the inexhaustible magic of Italy they evoke, for their style (pp. 924-26). The first presents the only exhibition of human relation other than acutely sexual, a magnificent visual strength, and it is pervaded by what we would now call an overwhelming death wish (p. 927). The second shows the lesson that love is a source of suffering, not of enjoyment, but it is marked by 'no moral sense proportionate to the truth', and by too raw a sense of life. This is something which James had disclaimed throughout his life: 'We get the impression of a direct transfer, a "lift", bodily, of something seen and known, something not really produced by the chemical process of art, the crucible or retort from which things emerge for a new function' (p. 930). In both these novels there are almost Zolaesque elements.

In *The Virgins of the Rocks,* instead, and partially in *L'innocente,* the hero is a central consciousness—for James, the saving grace and the modern touch for the novel. 'It is all a mere affair of the rich impression, the complexity of images projected upon the quintessential spirit of the hero, whose own report we have—an affair of the quality of observation, sentiment and eloquence brought to bear', James writes (pp. 932-33). Thus,

> The book is a singularly rich exhibition of an inward state, the state of private poetic intercourse with things … It represents the aesthetic consciousness, proud of its conquests and discoveries, and yet trying, after all, as with the vexed sense of a want, to look through other windows and eyes. (p. 934).

Here D'Annunzio surpasses himself and overcomes his limitations: he becomes as much as possible Henry James.

James can, however, go deeper than this form of personally biased recognition and near identification. This is only one side of the 'case'. The deeper aspect of D'Annunzio's 'case' lies in the intriguing and

surprising fact—to which James devoted the final, and most interesting part of his essay—that the highest claims for aesthetic beauty and
refinement coexist, or are intermingled with, a strong element of ugliness and vulgarity. James's exquisite critical expertise is excited by this
'anomaly', by the realization of the coexistence of opposites, the discovery of the worm in the bud that eats or endangers the effect of beauty. He had already found Zolaesque effects in *The Triumph of Death,*
in the description of the 'local Lourdes' in the Abruzzi (p. 929). In all
D'Annunzio's novels, however, James now finds 'a singular incessant
leak in the effect of distinction so artfully and copiously produced'—
indeed, a 'bad smell' that must be accounted for:

> There is no mistaking it; the leak of distinction is produced by a posi-
> tive element of the vulgar; and that the vulgar should flourish in an air so
> charged, intellectually speaking, with the 'aristocratic' element, becomes
> for us straightway the greatest of oddities and at the same time, critically
> speaking, one of the most interesting things conceivable. (pp. 935-6)

This anomaly, or this dualism, is due less to D'Annunzio's insistence
on the sexual relation, to 'the space he allots to love-affairs' (p. 936),
than to 'the weakness of his sense of 'values' in depicting them' (p.
937). This weakness, however, stems from that insistence, in the sense
that D'Annunzio's heroes and heroines are engrossed in the sexual
relation to the exclusion of all other relations. James sees them as
deprived of any 'general history', they are only products or victims
of their senses; whereas for him 'relations stop nowhere', in fiction
as well as in life, and the task of a novelist is to depict the web and
complexity of those relations—not a single overpowering thread. It is
not only that James sees in D'Annunzio an inadequacy or a failure to
deal with the deep and moral side of man (and woman), a confirma-
tion of the truth he had expounded at the end of his essay 'The Art
of Fiction', that 'No good novel will ever proceed from a superficial
mind'. The isolation of D'Annunzio's characters and plots within the
stifling compass of a single passion results in a failure of 'rendering'

and of 'showing', in a failure of *artistic* as well as *moral* poignancy and complexity.

Andrea Sperelli and Donna Maria are not really *done,* in *Il piacere.* We are only *told* about their natures, there is no march, no drama, no real development for either of them (pp. 937-38). No 'provision has been made in it for some adequate inwardness', James noted (p. 940). In *Il fuoco*, 'The pang of pity, the pang of pity that springs from a conceivable community of doom, is … altogether wanting' ('He takes for treatment a situation that is substantially none' [pp. 939-40]). Even in *L'innocente,* which 'of the group, comes nearest to justifying its idea', the 'connections are poor with the higher dramatic, the higher poetic, complexity of things'. D'Annunzio 'treats 'love' as a matter not to be mixed with life', whereas, for James, the effect of comedy or tragedy is 'determined by the interference of some element that starts a complication or precipitates an action' (pp. 940-1). Nothing of the kind seems to happen in *Il fuoco* or, for that matter, in the other novels.

Here lies the gist of James's criticism of D'Annunzio, of the anomaly he finds in him. An obsession with the love relation and sexual passion as *such* limits D'Annunzio's range and complexity, endangers his distinction and his aesthetic control, opens the door to vulgarity. A love 'relation' unrelated to anything in heaven or on earth undermines the charm of the achievement, we read at the conclusion of James's essay, where, as is usual with him, he insists on what *he* would have done, as a novelist, with the other's premises and *données.* In D'Annunzio, 'That sexual passion from which he extracts such admirable detached pictures insists on remaining for him *only* the act of a moment, beginning and ending in itself and disowning any representative character'; whereas, in James's well-known dictum,

> it finds its extension and consummation only in the rest of life. Shut out from the rest of life, shut out from all fruition and assimilation, it has no more dignity than—to use a homely image— the boots and shoes that we see, in the corridors of promiscuous hotels, standing, often in double pairs, at the doors of rooms. (p. 942)

The stuff of poetry is not in 'detached and unassociated' views of what goes on inside those rooms, it is in what 'the participants do with their agitation',[2] and this, in turn, 'is never really interesting save when something finely contributive in themselves makes it so'. This 'absence of anything finely contributive in themselves ... is the open door to the trivial' (p. 943).

James thus moved from an initial recognition of D'Annunzio's high aestheticism and artistic distinction to a charge (almost) of triviality. This seems to me typical of James's attitude to aestheticism: a profound appreciation of its potentialities for visual, plastic, sensuous, artistic renderings, and a deep-seated distrust of (or at least uneasiness about) its capacity to apprehend the fullness of life, reality in all its aspects— psychological as well as aesthetic, intellectual as well as physical, moral as well as sentimental. Much as James was attracted by aestheticism— and his essay on D'Annunzio is a fine proof of it—he was always concerned with its limitations, always in favour of a fuller view of human life, of a deeper engagement with both inner and outer reality.

The irony of all this lies in the fact that another well-known aesthete, Max Beerbohm, was to immortalize James precisely in the posture he had attributed to D'Annunzio, kneeling massively in front of a hotel room with a double pair of boots and shoes in front of it, peeping through the keyhole.[3] Did Beerbohm perhaps see in James the same limitations James had found in D'Annunzio—which would only prove

---

[2]   On *indirectness*, see *Literary Criticism. European Writers*, p. 1149 and *passim*; the principle is related to that of the limited point of view and the center of consciousness. Two letters to Mrs. Humphrey Ward of July 1899 emphasize its necessity (*The Letters of Henry James*, ed. Percy Lubbock, New York, Scribner's, 1920, II, p. 322; *The Letters*, ed. Leon Edel, Cambridge, The Belknap Press of Harvard U. P., 1984, IV 109-12); in the second letter, while criticizing one of her novels, James admits that in such cases he always takes the stand of how he himself would have 'done' it—which is partially what he does with D'Annunzio.

[3]   The drawing is in *Beerbohm's Literary Caricatures*, ed. J. G. Riewald, London, Allen Lane, 1997, p. 225, Table 80. Beerbohm had sketched D'Annunzio in 1904 (*ibidem*).

that critical strictures often reflect personal fears as well as personal biases—or did he detect a closer similarity between the two?

This is a matter worthy of further speculation, for comparatists. I have chosen to deal, rather, with James's beautiful essay on D'Annunzio for what it tells us about James *as well as* D'Annunzio, their times and their cultural milieu. I have preferred this to pursuing possible links and analogies between the two writers. One could have dealt with some analogies existing between James's *The Tragic Muse* (1890), with its powerful presentation on the histrionic and the artistic temperaments, and *Il fuoco* (1900); or one could have dwelt on the strange similarities that can be detected in the endings of James's *The Other House* (1896) and *L'innocente* (1892), in both of which a young innocent is murdered and sacrificed by interested or guilt-ridden grown-ups who are made to pay for their crimes only morally and psychologically. One could have treated as well the likely influence of *Il fuoco* on James's final masterpiece, *The Golden Bowl* (1904): not so much on account of the obvious question of the central symbols of the *calice di Murano* and the bowl, which are broken in the course of both novels (on which Giorgio Melchiori has written perceptively),[4] as for the 'drama of silence', the closed-in atmosphere, the struggle of exasperated souls that characterizes James's novel in a fairly clear D'Annunzio fashion.

I preferred to concentrate instead on the play of minds and sensibilities, of converging views and diverging tastes, of adhesion and repulsion, that is enacted in James's important essay on D'Annunzio, because here, as in James's other essays on Balzac and Maupassant, Flaubert and Zola, George Eliot and Hawthorne, and so many others,

---

[4] Giorgio Melchiori, 'James, Joyce e D'Annunzio', in *D'Annunzio e il simbolismo europeo*, Milano, Il Saggiatore, 1976: Joyce would have considered *Il fuoco* as a step forward after Flaubert in the art of the novel; Barbara and Giorgio Melchiori, *Il gusto di Henry James*, Torino, Einaudi, 1974, pp. 233-36. Adeline Tintner, in 'Henry James, *The Story in It* and Gabriele D'Annunzio', *Modern Fiction Studies*, 28-2, (1982), pp. 201-14, analyzes James's 1902 short story in order to show the totally different methods of the two writers.

we find one of those encounters of lively minds, or even one of those fine consorts of voices, on which the life of literature and of criticism still thrives.[5]

---

[5] Important studies of the relation are Mario Praz, *Gabriele D'Annunzio e la letteratura anglosassone* (1963), in *Il patto col serpente,* Milano, Mondadori, 1972, pp. 399-421, and in *Gabriele D'Annunzio e la cultura inglese e americana*, ed. Patrizia Nerozzi Bellman, Chieti, Solfanelli, 1990, for D'Annunzio's possible influence on George Moore, Frederick Rolfe, Ronald Firbank, Joyce, Ford Madox Ford, D. H. Lawrence, for Pound's and Hemingway's interest in him, for possible links of *Il piacere* with Wilde's *The Picture of Dorian Gray*, some similarities with contemporary British visual culture, as well as for D'Annunzio's interest in Whitman, Browning, Swinburne, Romaine Brooks and her 'Amazons', and others.

9 Henry James and Shakespeare

1

In his story 'The Birthplace' (1903) Henry James dramatizes the plight of the guardian of the house of the Bard—never mentioned, though recognizably Shakespeare: 'the early home of the supreme poet, the Mecca of the English-speaking race' (*CT* XI 405).[1]

The protagonist, Morris Gedge, is infatuated with him, possessed by him, feeling that the Bard is everywhere and haunts the house. But then

---

[1] Abbreviations are as follows: *CT* = *The Complete Tales of Henry James*, ed. Leon Edel, London, Hart-Davies, 1962-64, 12 vols.; *LC1* = *Literary Criticism. Essays on Literature, American and English Writers*, *LC2* = *Literary Criticism. French Writers, Other European Writers, The Prefaces*, both New York, The Library of America, 1984; *L* = *Letters*, ed. Leon Edel, Cambridge, The Belknap Press of Harvard U. P., 1974-84, 4 vols; *A* =*Autobiography*, ed. F. W. Dupee, New York, Criterion Books, 1956; *SA* = *The Scenic Art. Notes on Acting & the Drama: 1872-1901*, ed. Allan Wade, New Brunswick, Rutgers U. P., 1948; *TW* =*Collected Travel Writings. The Continent*, New York, The Library of America, 1993; *WJ&HJ* = *The Correspondence of William James and HJ*, Charlottesville, Virginia U. P., 1992-94, 3 vols.; *Edel* = Leon Edel, *Henry James. A Biography*, Philadelphia, Lippincott, 1953-72, 5 vols.—On Henry James's views of Shakespeare, William T. Stafford, 'James Examines Shakespeare', PMLA 73 (1958), pp. 123-28, and three essays in *The Henry James Review*: by Larent Cowdery, 3 (1982), pp. 145-53; by Nim Schwartz, XII (1991), pp. 69-83; by Neil Chilton, XXVI (2005), pp. 218-28.

he gradually realizes that the Bard is not there at all, that the Chamber of Birth is empty, that there is 'nothing' there—there are only the immortal people *in* the work, but nobody else. So Morris becomes 'the disaffected guardian of an overgrown legend' (as James put it in a later Preface, *LC2* p. 1096) and gives up the Show (The Biggest on Earth)— only to be compelled by practical and family reasons to resume it. But then he does it on the grand scale, turning into the greatest inventor of magnified fibs and made-up, fanciful stories. Thus he becomes famous, in England and across the Atlantic, like a TV anchorman of today, thriving on virtual reality. His salary is doubled.

The fable has a double edge: it has to do with James's life-long opposition to the biographical exploitation of authors, but also, uncannily, with what we may call the Bard's contagion: he transmits to votaries the taste for invention. He transforms adepts and admirers into creators in their own right.

James may be taken as a case in point, doubling with Shakespeare, as it were, throughout his life—interpreting and envisioning him as a 19th-century novelist, fascinated and dismayed by the discrepancy between Shakespeare's overwhelming artistic power and his disarming scantiness as a man. We find Shakespeare in his life as a theatre-goer, in his readings, letters, memoirs, travel essays, and in his fiction. James seems to pursue the image, the phantom, the ghost of that queer monster, the artist, 'the master and magician of a thousand masks', which he would pull from his face—a fellow-writer and a *confrère*, gradually becoming a double, an alter ego, a *Doppelgänger*, an ante litteram apotheosis of the *romancier artiste*.

'I walked arm-in-arm with Shakespeare', he boasted from Newport when he was twenty (*L* I 49). In his 1905 essay 'The Lesson of Balzac', he would call him the 'great story-teller, great dramatist and painter, great lover, in short, of the image of life' (*LC2* p. 122: please note the terms), who was already exploring 'prodigious consciousness', characters that attain a keen and painful awareness of themselves. Finally, Shakespeare was extolled as 'the supreme master of expression', described and analysed in terms closely reflecting the novelist's own tenets and practices.

2

The 'prime initiation' was the 'scarce tolerable', 'sacred thrill of the green curtain' rising on *The Comedy of Errors*, when he was eight, as revealed in the first volume of his unfinished autobiography, *A Small Boy and Others*. James was probably telescoping even earlier theatrical experiences in small community halls, Assembly Rooms, Lecture Rooms, Academies of Music, Museums, Lyceums, that in those years served for 'legitimate' theatres.

There he saw and admired *Much Ado About Nothing* and *Midsummer Night's Dream* ('the illusion was that of a multitude and a pageant', *LC1* p. 1082), where the visual impact predominated on the dramatic effect, as in the 'prodigious' *Henry VIII*, seen in London, 'doubtless at its time the last word of costly scenic science': 'we did nothing for weeks afterwards but try to reproduce in water colours queen Katherine's dream-vision of the beckoning, consoling angels, a radiant group let down from the skies by machinery then thought marvellous' (*A* pp. 179-80).

The children had been equally fascinated by a 'steel-plated' volume of Shakespeare, whose 'plates were so artfully coloured and varnished', that it was 'a shock at the theatre not to see just those bright images ... come on' (*A* p. 56; 'I cherished the scene ... while I panted towards the canvas on which I should fling my figures', James specified; 'The picture, the representative design, directly and strongly appealed to me, and was to appeal all my days'; 'the picture was still after all in essence one's aim', *A* pp. 149-50). He was always attracted by the great Victorian canvasses on Shakespearean themes. 'I could never have enough of Maclise's Play-scene in Hamlet', he confessed (*A* p. 178); in 1900 he found Edwin Austin Abbey's Shakespearean paintings 'diabolically clever and effective ... I came away ... with the sense of how it's not the age of my dim trade' (Edel V 35).

His theatre chronicles (for *The Nation, The Atlantic Monthly, The Galaxy*, etc., posthumously collected in *The Scenic Art*) also emphasize the visual and picturesque impact, but its excesses caused dire results. These productions appeared as 'the last word of picture making on the stage', as 'a series of exquisite pictorial compositions'; moreover, they were interspersed with entr'actes, preludes, interludes, interpolations, embellishments and embroideries of all sorts, ballets, dances. Hence a marked discrepancy between what attracted the audience and Shakespeare's poetic excellence: 'the poor great poet has strange bedfellows' (*SA* pp. 168-69, 147).

'The intensity of our period is that of the "producer's" and machinist's', James wrote (*A* p. 204); modern acting was bombastic and high-flown. The 'picturesque actor' depended 'for his effect upon the art with which he presents a certain figure to the eye, rather than upon the manner in which he speaks his part'. Great actors of the time like Ernesto Rossi and Tommaso Salvini, for instance, would perform their roles in Italian to enthusiastic and totally uncomprehending audiences, while the other actors answered them in English, or rather 'in a language that sometimes failed to be English' (*SA* p. 169).

These *mises en scène* offered 'as little as possible the mirror up to nature'. Plays were converted into gorgeous and over-weighted spectacles; they were 'the last word of stage-carpentering, and full of beautiful effects of colour and costume', not acted, but 'costumed'; 'Scenery and decorations' prevailed over 'elocution and acting, the interpretation of meanings, the representation of human feelings' (*SA* pp. 163-65). The productions were triumphs of theatricalism and overacting. As James puts it: 'Realism is a very good thing, but it is like baking a pudding in a porcelain dish: the pudding may be excellent, but your dish gets cracked.' (*SA* p. 34). He is then led to conclude that the distortions of the contemporary stage are inimical to Shakespeare's elevated poetry and divine elocution, while his supreme qualities would in any case be antithetic to staging, joining a long list of 19th-century writers, from Coleridge and Lamb downward, who considered Shakespeare as intrinsically unsuited for the stage. '*King Lear* is not a play to be acted … *Lear* is a great and terrible poem—the most sublime, possibly, of all dramatic poems'; 'it is, in my opinion, impossible to imagine a drama that accommodates less to the stage' (*SA* pp. 178-79, 190).

Statements to this effect thickened with time: 'the represented Shakespeare is no longer to be borne ... there is absolutely no representing him'. 'I like Shakespeare better—let me hurry to declare—"for reading"' (*SA* pp. 287-88). Or: 'To be played at all, he must be played ... superficially'. This sounds like heresy to us, who consider Shakespeare a man of the theatre, deeply involved in the demanding, sordid and exhausting business of staging plays, but James never relented in this rather romantic (and rather aristocratic) view.[2]

The impossibility of representing Shakespeare on account of its sublime poetry and the sorry state of the British and American theatre was also reinforced in his essays 'After the Play' (1889) and 'The Blight of the Drama' (1897). All in all, the Comédie Française fared better, and should have been imitated in England and the US; even a 'French' actor (Charles Fechter, in 1877) as Hamlet was 'less foreign and more comprehensible' in his speech than what floated in the thankless medium of English actors (*SA* pp. 105).

3

When young James wrote that 'Shakespeare's word carries weight; he speaks with authority' (*LC1* p. 1276), he was expressing the aim of any writer. 'Authority' comes from 'author', and in an author it is not only legitimate, but especially recommendable. When insisting in 1902 that

---

[2] In a 1913 letter he wrote that the Drama was distinguished from the Theatre: his own plays 'were inevitably the Theatre-stuff ... but they are now, enjoying complete immunity from performance as they do, Drama-stuff' (quoted in Henry James, *The Complete Plays*, ed. Leon Edel, Philadelphia, Lippincott, 1949, p. 10), and next year he reiterated: 'I am not sure that beyond a certain point scenic refinement and development are not really inimical to its—the Drama's—intrinsic life' (*L*, IV, p. 709).

'the plays and the sonnets were never written but by a *Personal Poet*, a Poet and Nothing Else',[3] however, he was disingenuous. This Poet was made to serve in many other capacities—painter, storyteller, psychologist, divine musician (seldom playwright).

In his critical statements, too, James emphasized his visual and pictorial, rather than dramatic, side. Shakespeare's equivalent was Tintoretto, he found, with his immense pictures and canvasses swarming with figures: 'if Shakespeare is the greatest of poets Tintoretto is assuredly the greatest of painters. He belongs to the same family and produces very much the same effect' (*L* I 138). This is in a youthful letter. In a travel essay of 1872: 'You get from Tintoretto's work the impression that he *felt,* pictorially, the great, beautiful, terrible spectacle of human life very much as Shakespeare felt it poetically' (*TW* p. 343). 'You seem not only to look *at* his pictures, but *into* them' (*LC1* p. 140), he would add.

Both playwright and painter had a three-dimensional view and anticipated what would become the greatest value for James: an insight into the inner life of their characters (*L* I 140). He paired himself off with the two of them: 'I'd give a great deal to be able to fling down a dozen of his pictures into a prose of corresponding force and colour' (*L* I 139-40).

Another equivalent for Shakespeare was Balzac, who shared with him an 'art of complete representation'. In the Preface to *The Princess Casamassima* James puts Shakespeare at the head of a list of novelists: 'as most of the fine painters of life, Shakespeare, Cervantes and Balzac, Fielding, Scott, Thackeray, Dickens, George Meredith, George Eliot, Jane Austen, have abundantly felt' (*LC2* p. 1092). James was implicitly at the end of the line. Dickens and Balzac have no rivals but themselves and Shakespeare, James writes at one point, and he presents them as his true followers and heirs, or kindred spirits. 'Balzac, in the maturity of his vision, took in more of human life than any one, since Shakespeare,

---

[3]   Henry James, *Selected Letters*, ed. Leon Edel, Cambridge, The Belknap Press of Harvard U. P., 1987, p. 343.

who has attempted to tell us stories about it' (*TW* p. 24).[4] His 1905 essay seems almost extravagant in its finding in Balzac a depth of psychological insights in line with Shakespeare's.

In this idea of a 'charged consciousness', in the inner thrust and third dimension of his characters, James constantly doubles with the Bard. As early as 1864 he had defined the psychological novelist as one who exercised 'scrutiny, in fiction, of *motive* generally': the action had to rest, 'not only exclusively, but what is more to the point, avowedly, upon the temperament, nature, constitution, instincts' of one's characters (*LC1* p. 591). In 'The Art of Fiction' (1884) he insisted that 'A psychological reason is, to my imagination, an object adorably pictorial ... The moral consciousness of a child is as much part of life as the islands of the Spanish Main' (*LC1* pp. 61-62).

The interesting point is that when in the Prefaces James expands on the theory and practice of the 'psychological' novel, he finds his precedent, a double or a *Doppelgänger*, in none other than Shakespeare. There are two conclusive references. One in the Preface to *The Princess Casamassima*: 'the figures in any picture, the agents in any drama, are interesting only in proportion as they feel their respective situations ... Their being finely aware—as Hamlet and Lear, say, are finely aware— *makes* absolutely the intensity of their adventure, gives the maximum of sense to what befalls them' (*LC2* p. 1088). The other in the Preface to *The Tragic Muse*, where James dwells on 'the prodigious consciousness of Hamlet, the most capacious and the most crowded, the moral presence the most asserted' (*LC2* pp. 1112-13).

James's final view is that of Shakespeare as the abstract Master of Expression. His 'special introduction' to *The Tempest* for Sir Sidney

---

4   In a 1875 essay, taking his cue from Hippolyte Taine, James noted that 'after Shakespeare, he [Balzac] is our great magazine of documents on human nature', adding, on his part, that 'Shakespeare's characters stand out in the open air of the universe, while Balzac's are enclosed in a peculiar *artificial* atmosphere ... But it is very true that Balzac may, like Shakespeare, be treated as a final authority upon human nature' (*LC2* pp. 67-68).

Lee's edition (1907), admittedly, wanted to pull down the thousand masks of the master and magician: in doing so, James repeatedly finds his own. Throughout the essay, he seems to be speaking of himself, using for Shakespeare the very terms and tenets that he applied to his own fictional ideals. On the one hand, he is obsessed by Shakespeare's having inexplicably shut himself off at the peak of his achievement, by his 'abrupt and complete cessation' (*LC1* pp. 1207), the 'impenetrability of silence in which Shakespeare's latest years enfold him' (p. 1026). '*How* did the faculty so radiant there contrive, in such perfection, the arrest of his divine flight?' What became of the checked torrent? In an afterlife, what other mills did it set turning? (pp. 1119-20). On the other hand, *The Tempest*—'one of the supreme works of literature', 'the finest flower of his experience'—appears as the culmination of an almost abstract art, and as the prototype of James's own *roman artiste* (artistic novel): the play and the subject itself are seen at the beginning as 'intact and unconscious, seating as unwinking and inscrutable as a divinity in a temple ... The divinity never relents—never, like the image of life in The Winter's Tale, steps down from its pedestal' (p. 1206).

As for the author, 'so steeped in the abysmal objectivity of his characters and situations', he is a diver: we witness 'a series of incalculable plunges' of the man into the artist and of the artist into his innumerable creatures—Romeo and Juliet, Shylock, Hamlet, Macbeth, Cleopatra, Antony, Lear, Othello, Falstaff, Hotspur: 'but what he sinks into, beyond all else, is the lucid stillness of his style' (p. 1209). Hence *The Tempest* is a triumph of self-satisfaction: in spite of its being concocted on demand for a Court occasion it became 'a charming opportunity to taste above all for *himself*, for himself above all ... of the quality of his mind and the virtue of his skill ...Innumerable one may always suppose those delicate debates and intimate understandings of the artist with himself'.

Shakespeare is thus exposed as 'a divine musician, who, alone in his room, preludes or improvises at close of day. He sits at the harpsichord, by the open window, in the summer dusk; his hands wander over the keys'; when he finds and holds his motive, 'then he lets himself go, embroidering and refining' (p. 1210). It is 'a private occasion, a concert for one, both performer and auditor, who plays for his own ear, his own hand, his own innermost sense, and for the bliss and capacity of his instrument' (p. 1211).

This seems to us verging on nonsense, considering how deeply and even 'sordidly' involved Shakespeare was in the reality and the compromises of the Elizabethan theatre, as an actor, a shareholder, a playwright working often (as in this case) on commission and to please patrons and protectors, in a political and social situation fraught with the highest risks and complexities.

Still, James sees Shakespeare speaking superlatively 'of that endowment for Expression, expression as a primary force', as from another planet, 'working predominantly in the terms of expression, *all* in the terms of the artist's specific vision and genius' (p. 1211). 'He points to us as no one else the relation of style to meaning and of manner to motive'; 'these two things, on either side, are inseparable', they are compressed as body and soul, so that a consideration of them as distinct would be a gross stupidity (p. 1212), James continues, 'doubling' what he had all his life insisted upon or claimed for the artist, the novelist, himself: the joy of the absolute value of Style, the ideal of an abstract and purely formal artist, surrendering to the highest sincerity of virtuosity, the perfect coincidence of manner with motive, of subject with form. In 'The Art of Fiction' he had warned that 'The story and the novel, the idea and the form, are the needle and the thread'. In his 1902 essay on Flaubert he had written that 'expression is creation, it *makes* the reality'; we know 'nothing except by style' (*LC2* pp. 340), and in the same year, on D'Annunzio: 'we should much mislead in speaking of his manner as a thing distinct from the matter ...there is no complete creation without style any more than there is complete music without sound ... the fusion is complete and admirable' (*LC2* pp. 914). Or, in the Preface to *The Awkward Age*: 'it helps us ever so happily to see the grave distinction between substance and form in a really wrought work of art signally break down' (*LC2* pp. 1135).

James created or recreated Shakespeare *in his own image*, a replica
of *himself*. His view of him as a purely 'musical' artist, in the manner
envisaged by Walter Pater (*'All art constantly aspires towards the condition of music'*),[5] is reinforced by his totally ignoring what happens in
the play—James never actually tells us what it is about—and by a similar disregard for the very matter of Shakespeare's plays: 'The subjects
of the Comedies are, without exception, old wives' tales'; 'The subjects
of the Histories are no subjects at all; each is but a row of pegs for the
cloth of gold that is to muffle them' (Style, I presume); *The Merchant of
Venice* is much more than its 'witless "story"', the two parts of *Henry
IV* are 'a straight convenient channel for the procession of evoked images'; *The Tempest* itself is 'a thing of naught' (*LC1* pp. 1213). What
saves them is the personal tone, the brooding expression; again, Style.
Virtuosity and independence of style is what James finds and extols in
Shakespeare, 'a vaulting spirit', invisible to us like Ariel—a brother,
a twin, a double in the realm of expression. His successes might even
have ravaged him as a man: James wonders what might have been the
'effect on him of being able to write Lear and Othello' (pp. 1218).

Though he would finally envisage Shakespeare as leaving the window of his secluded room, joining and being lost in the crowd in the
street, James gives a view of him as the practitioner of a non-referential,
absolute and supreme art, much in keeping with *fin-de-siècle* aestheticism and pure poetry, totally de-contextualized, and I would even say,
de-textualized.[6] And he was so obsessed with Shakespeare's total disap-
pearance as a man in his plays, that he was briefly tempted by what he

---

[5]   Walter Pater, *The Renaissance*, Oxford, Oxford U. P., 1986, pp. 85-88.

[6]   The extent of this de-contextualization is signalled by the fact that Sidney Lee himself was one of those who, in those years, emphasized the 'American' sources or
roots of the play (the Bermuda pamphlets, particularly that of William Strachey):
Kipling, so much admired by James, had devoted a letter to the *Spectator* (1898,
and later a Poem, 'The Coiner') to this fact. The first to suggest it had been another
American writer, Washington Irving, in two essays of the 1840s. See *The Tempest*,
eds Virginia Mason Vaughan and Alden T. Vaughan, The Arden Shakespeare 3rd
Series, 1990, pp. 99-101; Hobson Woodward, *A Brave Vessel*, New York, Viking,

himself called the *Bêtise*, the Baconian theory, the idea that the plays and the sonnets were written by Sir Francis Bacon, which was widely held in America in those years. He possibly felt that Shakespeare, with his lack of schooling and a limited access to knowledge, could not have written such sublime plays and poems. Where could he have found such wealth of dramatic knowledge and poetic range? Yet, if the 'lout from Stratford', as James once called him, 'the transmuted young rustic', working 'under sordidly professional stress', could not have written those plays and sonnets, neither could have the 'the ever so much *too* learned Francis'; 'I find it *almost* as impossible to conceive that Bacon wrote the plays as to conceive that the man from Stratford, as we know the man from Stratford, did'.[7]

The mystery remained, and thickened.

4

James was equally close to Shakespeare in his fiction, which shows contacts and affinities with him. About a contested Raphael Madonna he joked that it was 'no more Raphael than *Daisy Miller* is Shakespeare' (Edel III 211); a disclaimer, but the connection was made, especially as the story was conceived as an *étude* in the French manner, with few incidents, essentially a history of 'moral intercourse' (*LC1* p. 604). In various cases, he seems to have been 'instigated' by Shakespeare.

2009; *'The Tempest' and its Travels*, eds Peter Hulme and William H. Sherman, Philadelphia, Pennsylvania U. P., 2000

[7] See Henry James, *Letters*, ed. Percy Lubbock, New York: Scribner's, 1920, 2 vols., I p. 424 (1903), and: 'the plays and the sonnets were never written but by a *Personal Poet*, a Poet and Nothing Else, a Poet, who, being Nothing Else, could never be a Bacon ... The difficulty with the divine William is that *he* isn't, wasn't, the Personal Poet of the calibre and the condition, any more than the learned, the ever so much *too* learned, Francis', *Selected Letters*, p. 343 (1902).

Shakespearean echoes and allusions, overt or buried, are frequent in his novels and tales. They have been noted and charted, and listing them is not in order here.[8] But I will recall that his 'Master Eustace' (1871) is 'like Hamlet—I do not approve of mothers consoling themselves'; that in *The Portrait of a Lady* Henrietta Stackpole cries out 'You were Prospero enough to make her [Isabel] what she has become', to Ralph, who defines himself as 'Caliban to her Ariel'; that the 'publishing scoundrel' in *The Aspern Papers* is twice related to Romeo in the garden; that in *The Ambassadors* Mme de Vionnet, suggests to Strether 'the reflexion that the *femme du monde* ... was, like Cleopatra in the play, indeed various and multiform', and it would have been an impoverishment not to have known her (Book VI, iii: this seems to me to betray a rather bookish idea of the *femme fatale*). As for *The Tragic Muse*, the novel in which the relation with the Bard is 'thematized', in her attempt to become a Shakespearean actress (more in the way of the Comédie Française than of the British theatre), Miriam Rooth is coached in Rome by a 'famous Signor Ruggieri', who is very reminiscent of Ernesto Rossi—all pantomime and no elocution, as we have seen— and before triumphing as Juliet, her first role is that of Constance in *King John*.

Structurally, there was no lesson James learned from Shakespeare's plays: his 'scenic method', developed in the 1890s, was derived from the well-made plays of Scribe and Sardou; Shakespeare inspired him, rather, for the 'illustrative method' and pictorial mode of his early and central novels, while the two methods, by his own admission in the Prefaces, were combined in the novels of his major phase. Shakespeare presented him, instead, with 'an immense gallery of portraits' (*LC1* p. 1202)—'characters born of the *overflow* of observation' (in 'Daniel Deronda: A Conversation', 1873, *LC1* p. 991). I prefer to concentrate therefore on the mediated way in which James seems to have drawn inspiration from Shakespeare for two central and crucial types of char-

---

[8]   See Sergio Perosa, *Henry James e Shakespeare,* Roma, Bulzoni, 2011.

acters: 'frail vessels' and 'superfluous men'. Both can be traced back to
him, through the mediation of contemporary novelists.

The first definition is George Eliot's: 'In these frail vessels is borne
onward through the ages the treasure of human affection' (*LC2* p. 1077,
Preface to *The Portrait of a Lady*). They are young, sensitive, intelligent—sometimes presumptuous—young women, who find it nobler in
the mind to suffer the slings and arrows of outrageous fortune, than to
take arms against a sea of troubles, and by opposing, end them. They
suffer as much as they shine; they are heroines of renunciation, but of
value. James offers an almost endless row of them, from Mme de Cintré and Catherine Sloper to Daisy Miller, Isabel Archer, Fleda Vetch,
Mme de Vionnet and Milly Theale, to some extent, possibly even Maggie Verver. But their antecedents, prototypes, or kindred spirits are to
be found in Shakespeare: Ophelia, Desdemona and Imogen (whose
'fragrance' he had noted early, *LC1* p. 1351), Portia. In the readings of
Fanny Kemble—the only tolerable Shakespearean 'shows' for him—
James had cherished 'the Juliets, the Beatrices, the Rosalinds, whom
she could still made vivid without accessories except the surrounding
London uproar'. They are characters who, like 'the Isabel Archers, and
even much smaller female fry, insist on mattering' to themselves and
others, he specified (*LC2* p. 1077).[9]

They are centrifugal as well as centripetal. Centrifugal, in that they
are surrounded by 'a hundred other persons, made of much stouter stuff,
and each involved moreover in a hundred relations which matter to *them*
concomitantly with that one, 'Cleopatra matters,—James continued—
beyond bounds, to Antony, but his colleagues, his antagonists, the state
of Rome and the impending battle also prodigiously matter'; in *The*

---

[9] 'It may be answered, meanwhile, in regard to Shakespeare's and to George Eliot's
testimony, that their concession to the "importance" of their Juliets and Cleopatras
and Portias (even with Portia as the very type and model of the young person intelligent and presumptuous) and to that of their Hettys and Maggies and Rosamonds
and Gwendolens, suffers the abatement that these slimnesses are ... never suffered
to be sole ministers of its appeal' (*LC2* p. 1078).

Merchant of Venice Portia matters to Antonio, Shylock, and the Prince of Morocco, but for these there are other concerns as well: 'for Antonio, notably, there are Shylock and Bassanio and his lost ventures and the extremity of his predicament', which, 'by the same token, matters to Portia—though its doing so becomes of interest all by the fact that Portia matters to *us*' (p. 1078).

Centripetal, in that they must be made not only the centre of all relations, but centres of interest and centres of consciousness. This was a difficult task—never attempted by Scott, Dickens or Stevenson, James noted—but if the difficulty is braved, as Shakespeare *and he* had done, the 'frail vessel' becomes precisely 'of importance to itself'. 'Place the centre of the subject in the young woman's [Isabel] own consciousness,' he had told himself, 'and you get as interesting and as beautiful a difficulty as you could wish. Stick to *that*—for the centre; put the heaviest weight on that scale, which will be so largely the scale of her relation to herself' (p. 1079). Their inner life *is* the story, it absorbs and sucks in, as it were, all other incidents (as in Isabel's meditative vigil in chapter 42, her imagination being positively 'the deepest depth of the *imbroglio*); their *seeing* is more important than their doing. And when James specifies that 'The novel is of its very nature an "ado", an ado about something …Therefore, consciously, that was what one was in for—for positively organizing an ado about Isabel Archer' (p. 1077), that 'ado', which is not 'about nothing', sends you back compulsively to Shakespeare.

'Superfluous men' (*lišnij čelovek*) first appeared in Turgenev (who in 1851 had published a novella called 'Diary of a Superfluous Man'), and became a throng in mid-19th-century Russia.[10] They are characters marginalized by choice, poor health, mostly by historical circumstanc-

---

[10]   Typical 'superfluous men' are Rudin, in Turgenev's novel of that name, and many others of his characters, Besuchov in Tolstoy's *War and Peace*, Levin in *Anna Karenina,* most of the Karamazovs, the student in Chekhov's *The Cherry Orchard* and Colonel Veršinin in *Three Sisters*, Gonciarov's Oblomov, etc. Forerunners were in Puškin's *Eugene Onegin* (Lenskij), in Lermontov's *A Hero of Our Time,* perhaps

es, isolated and made useless (*hommes inutiles*, as George Sand called them) by the lack of social, political, and working roles; unquiet and tormented characters, wandering in the distress of the mind rather than active in the turmoil of existence, floating in emotional void with no real purpose in life. Here I touch more on similarities than differences. In Russia they are usually nobles, motivated—indeed, un-motivated— mainly by political conditions and absolute rule. In James they are idlers, aesthetes, and wealthy *flâneurs*, tycoons who went through the fierce competition of business, but still relegated to, or choosing to rest in, the margins of life; some are simply forlorn souls. Though he never used the term itself, he was well aware of these malcontents and disaffected heroes.

Writing about Turgenev, he identified them as morbid characters, 'fatally complex natures strong in impulse, in talk, in responsive emotion, but weak in will, in action, in the power to feel and do singly' (*LC2* p. 977). Their primary prototype, however—as Turgenev had made clear in his short story 'A Russian Hamlet' and in his 1860 lecture on 'Hamlet and Don Quixote',[11] where characters of the first type are those who think, are aware, see everything, but are impotent and condemned to inactivity, indolence, and immobility, watching themselves all the time—was none other than Hamlet, a discontented hero, barred from a role in Court, unable to act, thrown back on himself, brooding and reflexive, a paragon of *intériorité* and a prototype of inwardness (p. 1095). He was their prototype in psychology—'devoured by reflection', morose, crafty and cruel—as well as in pathology: 'A core of negativity is lodged in him', Turgenev noted; the head, rather than the heart, predominates; self-analysis becomes crippling.

---

in George Sand's '*hommes inutiles*'.—James found them present in George Eliot's *male* characters.

[11] 'Hamlet and Don Quixote', in *The Essential Turgenev*, Evanston (IL), Northwestern U. P., 1994, pp. 547-64. 'A Russian Hamlet' was later collected in *A Sportsman's Sketches*, 1852.

Hamlet is many other things—shrewd, cunning ('I have that within that passeth show', I, ii, 85), cruel, sarcastic, ruthless, violent ('Yet have I in me something dangerous', V, ii, 1-37), even savage ('Now could I drink hot blood', III, ii, 379-90). He is a scholar, courtier, soldier, even a boaster; in spite of his hesitations, he is active throughout the play and finally, in his way, successful. But he *is* a self-proclaimed melancholy, marginalised, and dispossessed Prince ('Sir, I lack advancement', III, ii, 331; Claudius 'popp'd between th'election and my hopes', V, ii, 65), characterised at the outset by his 'nighted colour', 'vailed lids', 'a heart unfortified, a mind impatient' (I, i, 68, 70, 96). Fortune to him is a strumpet (II, ii, 235), Denmark, a prison, where he feels 'most dreadfully attended' (*ib*, 269). In his soliloquies he proves a malcontent: 'How weary, stale, flat, and unprofitable / Seem to me all the uses of this world' (I, ii, 128 ff.); 'I have of late … lost all my mirth … and indeed it goes so heavily with my disposition that this goodly frame the earth seems to me a sterile promontory, this most excellent canopy … but a foul and pestilent congregation of vapours', where man, 'this quintessence of dust', 'delights not me' (II, ii, 295-310). He sets himself a task as a restorer of right against 'the drossy age' (V, ii, 186): famously, 'The time is out of joint. O cursed spite, / That ever I was born to set it right' (I, v, 196-97). This, and his being eminently self-searching, immersed in his consciousness, ill at ease among the evils of the age, give him a strong title to being father to 'superfluous men'.

Consciousness, 'in the sense of a reflecting and colouring medium', again defines the value and the humanity of these characters: 'their adventures and their history', James felt, was 'determined by their feelings and the nature of their minds' (p. 1095). They are interesting, he insisted, 'only in proportion as they feel their respective situations', reaching 'the power to be finely aware and richly responsible'—which connects them, explicitly, with Hamlet (p. 1088). You recall, in his Preface to *The Princess Casamassima*: 'Their being finely aware—as Hamlet and Lear, say are finely aware—*makes* absolutely the intensity of their adventure, gives the maximum of sense to what befalls them'

(p. 1088). In that to *The Tragic Muse* he extolled 'the prodigious consciousness of Hamlet, the most capacious and most crowded, the moral presence the most asserted in the whole range of fiction'.

Their closest heir is 'little' Hyacinth Robinson in *The Princess Casamassima*, a discontented, tormented young man of illegitimate birth, left wondering, questioning, doubting, feeling, rather than doing, who in the end, disaffected with his revolutionary task, does commit suicide. Just like the 'frail vessels', such 'superfluous men' live not in the immediate, but in 'the reflected field of life, the realm not of application, but of *appreciation*'(p. 1091), and are put in a web of relations with others (including fools). There is an array of such characters, in James's fiction, and in this Preface he acknowledged some fifty of them.

In an enormous variety of types, and in different degrees, you have, among others, Rowland Mallet and Lambert Strether, Winterbourne and Ralph Touchett, possibly Prince Amerigo himself (led to inaction and a life of dissipation by the lack of a role commensurate to his title), or Stransom in 'The Alter of the Dead' and John Marcher in 'The Beast in the Jungle'—the man to whom nothing was to happen (pp. 1095-96). They are all very different in their roles, but belong to the type—while the closest remains Hyacinth Robinson. We should of course make nice distinctions among them, especially when 'centres of consciousness' turn from dull to 'intelligent observers', or from marginal spectators to central concerns (as was the case of their prototype Hamlet). But both are saved—or damned—precisely by the degree, range, and depth of their consciousness.

As for deeper structures, James often echoed the Shakespearean theme of duplicity, swindle, deceit and deception, cheating and plotting (in the double sense of conspiring and putting on the scene). Advisedly, I believe, James uses the Italian term *imbroglio* for Isabel. Dubious and duplicitous characters act as agents of devastating dramas for friends and relatives.

Iago is in these cases often the prototype. *The American*, for instance, has a recognizable Shakespearean subtext harking back to *Othello*, that has been often stressed and analyzed: Newman is 'insidiously beguiled and betrayed ... cruelly wronged' by persons close to him (p. 1054), as indeed had been the case with the Moor (though Mme de Cintré is more, though not totally, in the line of Ophelia, rather than Desdemona, and is literally sent to a nunnery). *The Portrait of a Lady* is an existential as well as psychological drama, in which Isabel is in every sense the innocent and sacrificial victim of vicious and duplicitous dealings. In both cases, Iago is an evoked or implied master of villainy: collectively, as it were, in the Bellegardes, openly and particularly in Gilbert Osmond, doing evil for the taste and the sake of it.

This, I realize, is very slippery ground, and I won't venture too far on it. But let me quote one of James's earliest critics, R. P. Blackmur, certainly not a friend of Maggie's, who noted that 'In Shakespeare good and evil make an endless jar; in James, and especially in *The Wings of the Dove* and *The Golden Bowl*, they make an almost purulent infection in each other which somehow seems a single disease. Yet the infection drawn from the good is worse than the that drawn from the evil'.[12] This may sound excessive, but it suggests a further, deeper, and closer link with Shakespeare.

5

I have three final notes for my conclusion.

The two writers share the taste for experimentation: for each, 'Every attempt is a wholly new start' (to apply to them T. S. Eliot's dictum). As soon as success is achieved in one genre, subgenre, structure,

---

[12]   R. P. Blackmur, *Studies in Henry James*, New York, New Directions, 1983; Maggie, he continues, 'destroys all the values between the two pairs ... all that would make life tolerable and desirable between her husband and herself. There is no beauty in her daily life; so, like, Iago, she removes it from possibility—so far as they believe her—from the lives of her father, from Charlotte, and from her husband' (p. 227).—James had noted 'the Medusa face of life' in her eyes.

type of drama or, respectively, novel, new forms and ways of expression must be pursued and found. Each writer is driven to a variety of genres and modes: Shakespeare by the needs of the Elizabethan theatre (though this applies to anyone writing for the stage): the list of his types of plays is as long as that recited by Polonius in *Hamlet*. James tried all sorts of 19th-century novels—romantic, realistic, 'analytical', *dialogué*, illustrative, scenic, even *noir*, the ghost story and the anti-novel: it was for him the most comprehensive and elastic of literary forms. 'The novel is of all pictures the most comprehensive and the most elastic. It will stretch anywhere—it will take in absolutely anything. All he needs is a subject and a painter. But for its subject, magnificently, it has the whole human consciousness' ('The Future of Novel', 1899, in *LC1* p. 102).

Both aimed at 'the art of complete representation' and revised endlessly, either by choice or on demand (Shakespeare, of course, on account of his 'sordid profession'). Just as we have three *Hamlets* and two *King Lears*—that we can read, especially now with computers, as parallel texts—so, with James, we are allowed to choose among, to revel in or to suffer through, the serialized version, the first book version, the revised, the New York Edition. Both stretched the possibilities of language to the utmost limit and to breaking point. In late Shakespeare, it has been said, we have too much thought for his expression; in later James, we might venture to submit, too much expression for his thought. What T. S. Eliot wrote of 'the other task of the poet' in Shakespeare's last plays, from *Cymbeline* to *The Tempest*: 'that of experimenting to see how elaborate, how complicated, the music could be made without losing touch with colloquial speech altogether', seems applicable to later James. Peter Rawlings has written that James seems to 'recruit Shakespeare in the proximity of the unutterable'. Both writers, however, with an awareness, I believe—as James put it in a fragment of a 1911 letter—that 'expression is, at the most insurmountably, a compromise.' 'Poetry strains expression to the cracking point', he continued: 'with Dante [the first time he mentions him!] and Shakespeare it cracks and splits perpetually, and yet we like it so tortured and suffering.'[13]

Finally, an imaginative parallel, indeed an uncanny doubling, is drawn by Virginia Woolf. In a letter of 25 August 1907 she recounts how she went to tea with James at the Rye Golf Club, and how the Master, before starting off in one of his winding, endless, hesitating and exasperating sentences, which she duly mimics, *'fixed me with his staring blank eye—it is like a childs* [sic] *marble'*. At the outset of her 'androgynous' novel *Orlando* (1928), she shows Shakespeare in the retinue of Queen Elizabeth, at the servants' table at Knole Manor: 'he held a pen in his hand, but he was not writing: He seemed to be rolling some thought up and down ... *His eyes, globed and clouded like some green stone of curious texture, were fixed.'*

Woolf links them in a flash through their eyes.[14]

---

[13] See T. S. Eliot, 'The Music of Poetry', in *On Poetry and Poets*, New York, Farrar Straus and Cudahy, 1957, p. 29; Peter Rawlings, *Henry James and the Abuses of the Past,* New York, Palgrave Macmillan, 2005, pp. 80-98; Henry James, *Life in Letters*, ed. Philip Horne, London, Penguin, 1999, pp. 502-03.

[14] Virginia, Woolf, *The Flight of the Mind. Letters 1888-1912*, ed. Nigel Nicolson, London, The Hogarth Press, 1975, p. 306; *Orlando*, Harmondsworth, Penguin, 1942, pp. 13-14.—In a different way, but on three occasions, Ezra Pound, too, focuses on James's eyes: at the outset of his pioneering 1918 essay 'Henry James', where he refers to his long-winded conversation, massive head and *gli occhi onesti e tardi* (from Dante's *Purgatory*, VI 63, 'honest and grave eyes'); in section 7, *I Vecchii*, of his poem *Mœurs contemporaines* ('Blagueur! "Con gli occhi onesti e tardi"'); and in Canto VII ('And the great domed head, *con gli occhi onesti e tardi'*).—The first dozen pages of Gertrude Stein's 'Henry James' (written 1932-33, published in *Four in America*, 1947) are ostensibly devoted to Shakespeare: it seems the embryo of a 'Duet', but this and what follows is conducted in Stein's peculiar and idiosyncratic manner, with has no or little relevance to what I tried to describe in this essay.

PART THREE

10   *Henry James and Unholy Art Acquisitions*

1

In 'The Curse of Minerva' (1811), Byron inveighed against Lord Elgin's acquisition of the Greek marbles for the British Museum in no uncertain terms: it was sacrilegious lust, blacker than Eratostratus, worse than both Turk and Goth; they were 'pilfer'd prey'. This was rather unusual for the times: no one had taken exception, for instance, to the British Consul Joseph Smith's 'depredations' of Venetian art in the 18th century, mostly for the royal collections. Public and private collecting went unchallenged in the 19th century.

Henry James originally had few doubts, qualms or indignation about it. Indeed, in a well-known episode in his *A Small Boy and Others*, the Galérie d'Apollon at the Louvre strikes him as offering a happy bridge to Style and 'a general sense of *glory*', 'what I can only term a splendid scene of things'. Here he reports the 'most appalling yet most admirable nightmare' of his life, a 'dream adventure' founded in an act of life-saving energy in which he routs and defeats a frightful apparition 'that retreated in terror before my rush and dash'. The significance of the Louvre, of its 'great insolence' and 'imposed applause, not to say worship', was reasserted in *Notes of a Son and Brother*.

In letters, art and travel essays, autobiographical writings, and in his fiction, James enthused over European galleries and museums—the

British Museum and the National Gallery, the Pitti Palace, the Uffizi, and so forth. He was rather sceptical or non-committal about *American* museums, on the other hand, at least in his early statements. In the notorious list of items of high civilisation that were missing in America published in his *Hawthorne* book (1879, quoted in chapter 2), he specifically added two items that were not in his original Notebook entry: 'no museums, no pictures'.

As for art collections, James expressed no qualms in his early articles on 'The Metropolitan Museum's "1871 Purchase"' of 175 pictures, mostly of the Dutch and Flemish school (while the museum was still a 'charming little academy in Fifth Avenue'), or on 'The Wallace Collection' (1873) and 'The Old Masters at Burlington House' (1877): this exhibition of privately owned 'art-wealth' showed how 'In England it has not been the sovereigns who have purchased, or the generals who have "lifted" ... the English gentlemen have bought—with English bank notes—profusely, unremittingly, splendidly'. His other articles, on showings at the Boston Atheneum of French and Italian paintings owned by Mr. Quincy Shaw, or on the acquisition for a sizable sum of Meissonier's *Friedland* by a Mr A.T. Stewart of New York, were equally unconcerned.[1]

---

[1]   These articles are collected in Henry James, *The Painter's Eye. Notes and Essays on the Pictorial Arts*, ed. John L. Sweeney, London, Hart-Davis, 1956.—Quotations are so thick and interwoven in this essay, that no single bibliographical references are given. However, I give here the main sources: *Autobiography*, ed. F. W. Dupee, New York, Criterion Books, 1956; *Hawthorne*, in *Literary Crticism. Essays, American and English Writers,* New York, The Library of America, 1894; *Letters*, ed. Leon Edel, Cambridge, Massachussets, The Belknap Press of Harvard U. P., 1974-84, 4 vols; *Italian Hours*, ed. John Auchard, University Park, The Pennsylvania State U. P., 1991; *The Complete Notebooks*, eds Leon Edel and Lyall H. Powers, New York, Oxford U. P., 1987; *The American Scene,* in *Collected Travel Writings. Great Britain and America,* New York, The Library of America, 1993; *Novels*, New York, The Library of America, 1983-2010, 6 vols.; *Complete Stories 1998-1910,* New York, The Library of America, 1996-1999, 5 vols.—Letters are identified by date and recipient.

In this case, indeed, 'the spell of our disjunction from Europe in the enjoyment of collections has been broken', he wrote; 'one takes ... an acute satisfaction in seeing America stretch out her long arm and rake in, across the green cloth of the wide Atlantic, the highest prizes of the game of civilisation'. He was dimly aware that in the Grosvenor Gallery love of pictures might be indistinguishable from love of money and commercial speculation: if its origin was 'rather in the love of pictures than in the love of money', 'In so far as [its] beautiful rooms in Bond Street are a commercial speculation, this side of their character has been gilded over.' This was reinforced by the awareness that there was crudity and levity, a show of low civilisation, in the English Art world (as witnessed by the Whistler vs. Ruskin trial in 1878: the whole affair was 'decidedly painful, and few things ... have lately done more to vulgarise the public sense of the character of artistic production'), and that it was difficult to draw the line between fair and fictitious value—though a unique thing would deserve a unique price, he admitted, even if sometimes an elevated one.

The note of an inborn and growing American propensity for appropriation, cultural and otherwise, had already been touched upon in a well-known letter of 20 September 1867 to Thomas Sargeant Perry: 'to be an American is an excellent preparation for culture. We have exquisite qualities as a race, and ... we can deal freely with forms of civilisation not our own, can pick and choose and assimilate and in short (aesthetically etc.) claim our property wherever we find it' (for American writers, the condition of achievement would be 'a vast intellectual fusion and synthesis of the various National tendencies of the world').

This was echoed in his 1873 essay 'The Autumn in Florence', later collected in *Italian Hours*, about the art-wealth of Florence that *could* be taken to New York without noticing:

> here and there, one comes upon lurking values and hidden gems that it quite seems one might as a good New Yorker quietly "bag" for the so aspiring [Metropolitan] Museum of that city without their being missed. ... what

dishonour, could the transfer be artfully accomplished, a strong American light and a brave frame would, comparatively speaking, do it. There and then it would shine with the intense authority that we claim for the fairest things.

Years later, in another essay of that book, 'Two Old Houses' (1899), however, the pitiless way in which Venice treasures had been 're-moved' was evoked as a painful and irreparable experience: one of the sisters he is writing about was perhaps old enough to have seen the work of an early Venetian master 'taken down from the room in which we sat and—on terms far too easy—carried away for ever; and not too young, at all events, to have been present, now and then, when her candid elders, enlightened too late as to what their sacrifice might really have done for them, looked at each other with the pale hush of the irreparable'.

Just as this 1899 passage contrasts markedly with the 1873 essay, a letter of 26 December 1898 to Charles Eliot Norton expatiates on the danger of too much and too ready acquisitiveness:

> It's strange the consciousness to an American today, of being in a country in which the drift of desire … is that we *shall* swell and swell, and acquire and *re*quire, to the top of our opportunity. My own feeling, roughly stated, is that we have been not good enough for our opportunity—vulgar, in a manner, as that was and is; but that it may be the real message of the whole business to make us as much better as the great grabbed-up British Empire had, unmistakeably, made the English.

He may have had in mind here the 1898 Spanish American war, but the feeling of unease about American appropriations is generalised. This turn from the early enthusiastic and acritical view of art-wealth and collecting to a later sceptical, embarrassed, and dismayed awareness of the problems involved, seems to reflect both a historic and a personal experience.

The historic change was the appearance in force in the later part of the 19th century, of the American 'robber barons' turned into art collectors, bent on an unprecedented acquisition of art treasures of all kinds, mostly from Europe and the Orient. It has been estimated that the fifty museums existing in America at mid-century had risen to six-hundred in 1910 and would rise to 2500 in 1914; this in turn reflected a shift from privately owned collections to public, endowed, art institutions. In either case, the process implied, among other things, the issue to which we have become so sensitive today: snatching art-works away from their real home, and the related question of an insatiable, greedy 'bagging', 'banking', 'hoarding', as James variously termed the phenomenon. America was its spearhead, while in Europe—notably in Italy and in England—the new art of connoisseurship would help in an unprecedented and correlated way. The two aspects mingled and coalesced across the Atlantic: witness Giovanni Morelli (aka Lermonliev) in Italy, and his 'pupil' Bernard Berenson, on either side of the ocean.

It seems that James was brought to face the question historically and privately in his dealings with an eager and inspired art collector with whom he consorted and flirted, at least by letter, from 1879: the celebrated 'Mrs. Jack', Isabel Stewart Gardner, 'Cleopatra of the Charles River' (as Mary Berenson called her), whom to all appearances he loved and appreciated as a hostess, but whom at the same time he tended to be wary of, fearing her as a first-hand example of a potentially 'destructive' collector: destructive, that is, in terms of European spoilations and American acquisitions.

There is an entry of 15 July 1895 in his *Notebooks* that, however guardedly and at second remove, but with a sense of oppressive concern, well-nigh equates her with the new 'barbarians' looting the world from, and for, the shores of America: 'the deluge of people, the insane movement for movement, the ruin of thought, of life, the negation of work, the "where are you going?", the age of Mrs. Jack, the figure of Mrs. Jack, the American, the nightmare—the individual consciousness—the mad, ghastly climax of denouement. ... The Americans looming up—

dim, vast, portentous—in their millions—like gathering waves—the barbarians of the Roman Empire'.

James was, in a way, confronting the shift from an established Art world to a fast-growing Art Market (strictly connected as it was here with an unprecedented expansion of of private collections and public museums), for which he was probably unprepared. This growing awareness may account also for his notable change in his view of art museums and collecting, at least across the Atlantic, and in his way of dramatising it in his later fiction.

His startling, though perhaps perceptive and prophetic, 'treatment', in *The American Scene* (1904), of the Metropolitan Museum, which had been expanded and moved uptown from its original location on West 14th Street, is a case in point and an example of a change in attitude as to the national ways and potentialities of cultural acquisition, which would be reflected in his novels. In contrast to the British Museum, say, or the National Gallery of London, or the Uffizi, the 'new' Metropolitan posed to James the question of 'historic waste' and of the 'sacrifice to pecuniary profit', the drama of an expense that does not educate, or of an education without regard to cost. It loomed for him on Fifth Avenue and the edge of Central Park as an example of purchase and acquisition, rather than collecting; it figured almost as 'making up' for past neglect of art.

The relevant passages leave not much for doubt or nice distinctions, and have been duly noted and discussed by critics:

> It spoke with a hundred voices of that huge process of historic waste that the place in general keeps putting before you; but showing it in a light that drew out the harshness or the sadness, the pang, whatever it had seemed elsewhere, of the reiterated sacrifice to pecuniary profit. For the question here was to be of the advantage to the spirit, not to the pocket; to be of the esthetic advantage involved in the wonderful clearance to come … One never winces after the first little shock, when Education is expensive—one winces only at the expense which, like so much of the expense of New York, doesn't educate; and Education, clearly, was going to seat herself in these marble halls … and issue her instruction without regard to cost.

It strikes James not only that 'almost no past acceptance of gifts and bequests "in kind" has been without weakness', but, more forcefully, 'that Acquisition—acquisition if need be on the highest terms—may, during the years to come, bask here as in a climate it has never before enjoyed. There was money in the air, ever so much money—that was, grossly expressed, the sense of the whole intimation.' And the money, James continues, almost in a crescendo of misgivings and premonition, 'was to be all for the most exquisite things—for *all* the most exquisite except creation, which was to be off the scene altogether'; so that, even if 'Education was to be exclusively that of the sense of beauty', he is left wondering a little about the 'contradiction involved in one's not thinking of some of its prospective passages as harsh'. The 'trade-value' is that of 'pure superfluity and excess'—'acres of canvas and tons of marble to be turned out into the cold world as the penalty of old error and the warrant for a clean slate'. Sacrifices 'dwindled to nothing', he concludes—'though resembling those of the funeral-pile of Sardanapalus'.

Here, too, as usual in *The American Scene,* James is harping on the contrast between the old world and the new, between old homeliness and spreading, 'imperial' drives. But he is also facing the possible embodiment of market and exhibition values over aesthetic concerns, the rampant new mode of excess, and acquisition substituting for artistic creation.

It may be a reflection of old-age grumpiness (in a similar way, and in the same years, according to Lady Ottoline Morrell, he found Waddesdon Manor, the country estate that Baron Ferdinand de Rothschild had turned into a 'private museum', then owned by Alice de Rothschild, lifeless and stale, observing that 'Murder and rapine would be preferable to this'). It may also be a compound of his life-long quarrel with and growing distrust of his native land, with accumulating fears about the power and treacheries of art-collecting, and with doubts about proclaimed values of authenticity and connoisseurship. If so, the compound is socially and, for James, literally explosive—except when mitigated, controlled and assuaged through the moderating process he could exercise in his fiction. Because the connoisseur mingles with the dubious aesthete and may verge on the market agent, the collector, whether real or metaphoric, may be selfish in his choices and vicious in his dealings; art does tragically impinge on life, and in all cases cherished 'values' can be jeopardised, compromised, or doomed.

2

These aspects are taken up, explored, and dramatised in various ways in his fiction. The most salient examples will suffice, with the customary warning that James tackles the topic both 'realistically' and metaphorically, and that his tortuous ambivalence at any given moment lurks in the path. Reassurance is restored by the fact that his fictional path follows closely the 'critical' one.

Early American collectors are acceptable. In *Roderick Hudson* (1876), Rowland Mallet, a collector in a relatively modest way, 'had an uncomfortably sensitive conscience', possibly an excessive one; he has 'a turn for doing nice things'. Being fond of the arts and with a passionate enjoyment of pictures, he feels 'that it would be the work of a good citizen to go abroad and with all expedition and secrecy purchase certain valuable specimens of the Dutch and Italian schools ... and then present his treasures out of hand to an American city' (not yet the 'American City' of *The Golden Bowl*) for an art-museum. He prefigures future James collectors, in intention if not in performance. His generosity will go to provide a promising American painter with the money to realise himself in Europe: as in the case of Ralph's generosity toward Isabel in *The Portrait of a Lady* (1881), the 'fortune' given proves the cause of destruction.

Europeanised Americans are a different matter. Gilbert Osmond is an amateur and a connoisseur, but turns a villain wanting to 'collect' fine people, notably Isabel (who is significantly termed an 'original') as he collects fine objects: 'he perceived a new attraction in the idea of taking to himself a young lady who had qualified herself to figure in his collection of choice objects by rejecting … a British aristocrat'. The sly collector, however, so 'rare' as to be a 'specimen apart', is also the object of Isabel's wish to 'collect' him, and I find Jonathan Freedman's summary of the situation particularly apt: 'Seeking to collect a collector, she finds herself collected'.

Apart from Osmond's cruelty and malice, the whole situation of the novel refers to questions of art: Ralph is correct in telling himself that 'A character like that [Isabel] is … finer than a work of art', while Osmond may well insist with her that 'one ought to make one's life a work of art'—with all the negative connotations of such an assumption. And it should not surprise us, in this context, that in her early crisis Isabel finds peace and a lyric space for herself in the Capitoline Museum, where she can listen to the 'eternal silence' of Greek sculptures.

Other characters, in James's novels, are even more openly caught in the complexities of art-wealth and art treasures, realistically as well as metaphorically. I cannot refrain from mentioning Hyacinth Robinson's dramatic exposure in *The Princess Casamassima* (1886) to the accumulated treasures of Venice—an art-museum if ever there was one—which are perceived as based on social and economic exploitation, on ruthless acquisition: 'What an enchanted city … what a revelation of the exquisite!', he writes in his 'Letter from Venice', noting 'the splendid accumulations of the happier few, to which, doubtless, the miserable many have also in their degree contributed'.

'They seem to me inestimably precious and beautiful', he avers, 'and—shall I tell you *le fond de ma pensée* …?—I feel myself capable of fighting for them'. His fellow revolutionaries seem to hold them too cheap, but he renounces his revolutionary pledge when confronting 'The monuments and treasures of art, the great palaces and properties, the conquests of learning and taste, the general fabric of civilisation as we know it, based, if you will, upon all the despotisms, the cruelties, the exclusions, the monopolies and the rapacities of the past, but thanks to which, all the same, the world is less impracticable and life more tolerable.' Unholy acquisitions they may well be—but their value is irresistible, and one should rest at comparable peace with their acceptance.

A fuller fictional engagement with art-collecting and acquisition is to be found, ten years later, in *The Spoils of Poynton* (1897)—'a story of cabinets and chairs ands tables', James wrote in the later Preface, where he also noted that art 'hoards and "banks"', and engenders a 'sordid situation'. Here we have collecting in a minor key, mostly in interior decoration, the valuable furniture and art-works of a fine old house (even if as a 'source' for Mrs. Gereth's 'record of a life' at Poynton James may have had in mind the Wallace Collection, of which he had written with admiration). Yet the drama hinges squarely and destructively on a fight for the possessions of those 'old things' and 'household goods'. James's Preface stresses 'the sharp light it [the situation] might project on that most modern of our passions, the fierce appetite for the upholsterer's and joiner's and brazier's work, the chairs and tables, the cabinet and presses, the material odds and ends. A lively mark of our manners indeed the diffusion of this curiosity and this avidity'. The short novel has basically to do with that question, and with the ravages of the art-passion and art-collecting.

James emphasises the value of the house that Mrs. Gereth is in danger of losing—'there was nothing really in England to compare with Poynton. There were places much grander and richer, but there was no such complete work of art'—as well as 'her personal gift, the genius, the passion, the patience of the collector … that had enabled her to do it all with a limited command of money'. Yet her passion turns into an obsession, a way of discriminating those who do not share it: 'Here are things in the house that we almost starved for. They were our religion, they were our life, they were *us*!', she cries out. She identifies herself with the collection, and trouble is to be expected. Her insistence on keeping the collection firmly in the hands of those who appreciate it, ends in the wreck of lives, love, and finally of the precious things themselves, which are destroyed by fire (ironically, after they have been removed from and finally restored to the rightful house).

The next example reflects James's later view of American art-collecting, when it becomes so much involved with acquisition per se and the art-market, when the shift is from private to 'public' collecting. (Walter Benjamin had noted in *Paris. Capital of the Nineteenth Century*, that museums reflect the bourgeois obsession with accumulating and exhibiting commodities, and that in them art treasures are freed from their original function and forced into a new, constrictive order, while the collector 'merely confers connoisseur value on them, instead of intrinsic value'.) As settings or pursued avocation, museums and collections often acquire a sinister light and dubious connotations, in keeping with the negative connotations James expressed in the *American Scene*.

It has been noted by Adeleine Tintner and Tamara Follini, respectively, that, in 'Julia Bride' (1908), the Metropolitan Museum becomes the proper setting for petty lying and moral thievery, the scene where 'money values ruthlessly enclose' the two characters, who act as 'two traders in the great market-place of the museum'. While, in *The Ambassadors* (1903), Strether wishes to be 'under the charm of a museum', in *The Wings of the Dove* (1902) Densher feels ill at ease and trapped as in a museum by the power of financial and artistic wealth in Palazzo Leporelli.

The theme is directly confronted in *The Golden Bowl* (1904) and *The Outcry*. In the former, one of the four main characters is a recognisable, late 19th-century American collector on the grand scale—a far cry from Rowland Mallett—who 'has an easy way with his millions' and can command art treasures and people alike. Adam Verver wishes to endow his native city (not now Roland's unspecified 'American city' but 'American City') with 'the collection, the Museum ... of which he thinks more ... than of anything in the world ... the work of his life and the motive of everything he does', and has things 'stored in masses' all over Europe. 'We're like a pair of pirates—positively stage pirates', his

daughter Maggie tells him—pirates who rejoice when they find the buried treasure (similar hints are scattered in the novel). He also 'collects'
Prince Amerigo for her (as Isabel had wanted to 'collect' Osmond, and
he Isabel): 'You're at any rate a part of his collection ... one of the
things that can only be got over here', the Prince is told: 'You are a
rarity, an object of beauty, an object of price ... You're what they call
a *morceau de musée*'. 'The instinct, the particularly sharpened appetite
of the collector, had fairly served as a basis for [Verver's] acceptance of
the Prince's suit.'

Verver's marriage to Charlotte, poor as she is, and hater of America
as she declares herself, is also a gross acquisition. He *holds* all of them;
Charlotte, in particular, will end up being held by 'a long silken halter
looped round her beautiful neck', kept 'virtually at bay', totally possessed and finally 'removed, transported, doomed' to American City,
in charge of the Museum (references to her 'doom' are also frequent
in the novel). He is the fictional rendering of a Carnegie, a Morgan,
a Rockefeller, and is identified with Homer, Keats and Cortez at one
shot: 'To rifle the Golden Isles had, on the spot, become the business
of his life'. In Portland Place, he 'had pitched a tent suggesting that of
Alexander furnished with the spoils of Darius'. (Fawns, too, the country seat, probably based on Weddesdon Manor, becomes a place for the
art of dissimulation, where in Part II Maggie and Amerigo enact 'their
forfeiture, in so dire a degree, of any reality of frankness'.)

Verver combines greatness and self-absorption, romantic vision and
self-interest, the consummate collector and the connoisseur: 'he had
in him the spirit of the connoisseur', we are told, and—keeping up the
comparison with Alexander—perceives 'with the mute inward gasp
akin to the low moan of apprehensive passion, that a world was left for
him to conquer'. He looks down on the kingdoms of the earth as from
a platform: 'he was equal, somehow, with the great seers, the invokers
and encouragers of beauty—and he didn't after all perhaps dangle so far
below the great producers and creators' (sellers go to him, and not he to
them, being 'approached privately and from afar').

The reader is encouraged to read a rich meaning into the character of the Patron of the Arts: his plan 'was positively civilisation condensed', 'a sort of religion he wished to propagate'. However—and here shines James's great art of ambivalent characterisation—he is 'a taster of life economically constructed'; he applies 'the same measure of value to such different pieces of property as old Persian carpets, say, and new human acquisitions', which become 'the pride of his catalogue' and which he reviews with the collector's and the possessor's gaze. His passion 'had constituted the kind of acquisitive power engendered and applied', and he is described as 'caring for precious vases not less than for precious daughters'.

Maggie, too, incidentally, is given an 'impunity of appropriation': in her re-capture of the Prince she shows 'the note of possession and control'; she, too, leads poor Charlotte 'by the neck': 'I lead her to her doom', she muses. In the final scene, she views them both 'as high expressions of the kind of human furniture required', harmoniously fused 'with the decorative elements'—though to 'a view more penetrating ... they also might have figured as concrete attestations of a rare power of purchase'. The sentence, so conclusive for my purpose, is in every sense chilling: '*Le compte y est.* You've got some good things', Verver comments. Indeed, Charlotte and the Prince look like 'a pair of effigies of the contemporary great on one of the platforms of Madame Tussaud': the sign and the chill of a lifeless museum is on them.

Art collecting has turned considerably to a question of acquisition and possession, involving human lives as well as art treasures, whose value has become more and more financial and social: that is why in all cases—with the Prince, Charlotte, the bowl, the art-works—the issue of 'authenticity' constantly arises.

3

In *The Outcry* (1911) James faced the real, not the metaphorical, issue of unholy acquisitions: it proved less powerful and less 'realised'. This is a topical novel on the art-drain; the 'leak there appears no means of stopping' swept art treasures from Europe to America and fostered a new manifestation of James's cherished 'international theme'.

The ravages of the 'robber barons' turned collectors had become conspicuous: by 1912, 52 Rembrandts, 21 Rubens, 11 Holbeins, 3 Velasquez, 7 Vermeers, among others, had found their way to the U. S.— duly purchased, and sometimes saved from neglect, loss or destruction. Bernard Berenson, whom James may have had at least partially in mind, and who had been quite active as an expert connoisseur in such 'removals', had justified them in a 1905 article in *The Sun*, 'Italian Art and Milanese Collections', precisely on the ground that those paintings were not properly cared for in their original countries and would be thus saved from abandonment, neglect or gross restorations; that their owners were eager to sell them as they were unwilling to spend money for their safekeeping, relying for that on their governments, rather than on private enterprise, as the Anglo-Saxons did.

Yet such 'removals' would acquire a sinister hue as 'raids', 'depredations' and 'spoils', particularly in Great Britain. Even if by then James had realised that European art-wealth, too, was often based on plundering ('We largely took it from somewhere, didn't we?', Lady Grace acknowledges in *The Outcry*), the aggressiveness of American collectors seemed to spur him, though in his story there is no clash between good and evil doers, but rather an amused and amusing dramatisation of the issue.

In 1907 an outcry had been raised in London about the Duke of Norfolk's intention to sell for a sizable sum of foreign money a painting by Hans Holbein, loaned till then to the National Gallery: an anonymous purchase for the nation kept it eventually in England. James wrote first a three-act play for the Duke of York Theatre, which failed to reach the stage owing to the death of Edward VII in 1910, and then re-wrote it as a novel the year after, keeping the long dialogues, simply inserting descriptions of characters and 'such a running comment as merely represents decent interpretation & expression', as he put it in a letter to Edith Wharton of 25 October 1911.

He set it in England, writing on 21 March 1914 to Harley Granville-Barker that 'It's essentially of this, our own, air and these conditions—an Anglo-American *opportune* comedy or *pièce d'occasion*', whose subject and interest and irony 'relate but to England and her art-wealth and the U. S. and their art-grab and their grab-resources'. On the dust jacket, taken apparently from his prospectus for the book, the English theme is asserted over the international one: it deals with the question 'of the degree in which the fortunate owners of precious and hitherto transmitted works of art hold them in trust, as it were, for the nation, and may themselves, as lax guardians, be held to account by public opinion'; the drama would be a 'study of the larger morality of the matter ... almost a national as well as a personal crisis'. And he relied heavily on a modern setting—the London of cars and the Tube, of telegrams and newspapers, galleries, exhibitions and advertising.

Two interesting topics emerge: the contrast between Old World traditions, including the 'transmitted' possession of art works, and an American *nouveau riche* art-collector eager to 'grab' them for enormous sums of money; and the modern connection of collecting with the new expertise of connoisseurs on the way to become art-experts, who may tilt the contrast for one or the other of the contenders (a melodramatic family contrast mingles with both aspects: a daughter is to be 'sacrificed' for her sister in a loveless marriage, and her dowry is to be provided by the sale of a valuable picture; she loves, instead, a young connoisseur, who dabbles in attributions, and contributes directly to plot complications).

The issue of the art drain is thus spectacularly dramatised: yet, contrary to some recent readings of the novel (among others, Toby Litt's and Jean Strouse's respective introductions to the Penguin and the New

York Review of Books editions of the novel), the drama tends to balance one position against the other. *The Outcry* is no *roman à thèse*.

Lord Theign, the custodian of tradition who feels he is the quintessence of the nation, is quite willing to sell a precious painting in order to cancel his daughter Kitty's debts. With all his grand manner, he is autocratic and supercilious, wishing to impose his standards, driven by a 'perversity of pride', ironically ready to sell at his own undisputed will, but at his own, limited, 'conservative' price—not at the price the American collector wants to offer. Theign insists upon flying in the face of Opinion, and acts out of defiance, ignoring the pressure from the public outcry; when finally he donates the contested painting to the nation, it is for the 'glory of the greatest gift'.

As for his counterpart, the American Breckenridge Bender, the collector, he is paired off with him at the end: 'our awful American—!', Lady Grace exclaims; 'Not to speak of our awful Briton!', is the retort. Bender is variously described as a 'bloated alien', one of the despoilers and the 'conquering horde', 'a corrupter of our morals and a promoter of our decay'. But he is presented as genial, quaint, with a rough-edged distinctness, substantial, powerful, easy, with no physiognomy, perhaps, but with a 'voracious integrity'. His distinguishing trait—which works both positively and negatively—is that he is interested in buying only at preposterous prices, with enormous checks: he has 'no use for a ten thousand picture', 'he wants to give millions', 'He wants, you see … an *ideally* expensive thing'. He is the biggest buyer; he is after 'the grand publicity of the Figure'. The more he pays for a painting, the more it acquires value in his eyes (and in the eyes of art lovers).

Therefore he is pleased with adversity, glad to kick up a row; he *revels* in publicity and the public outcry, the noise of the press, the clamour of gossip, indiscretion; notoriety is for him added value, a measure of success. He is definitely a new type—despised as much as prophetic. The happy ending is implicit in these premises, and in the fact that the novel originated as a stage comedy; even if Bender is thwarted and defeated in the end, it would be myopic to see him as the villain of the story. The starting point and the underlying assumption about such art-acquisitions is that they are unholy; but the accidentals of the story present a much more shaded and less negative picture. Moreover, Bender's willingness to pay only preposterous prices for his 'spoils' poses and exemplifies a new issue, which James as usual was able to sense and prefigure ahead of his times.

Lord John, a European, cries out at one point 'What values are *not* pecuniary?' If it was thought that monetary values would compromise artistic value, Bender is there to enact—as will be more and more the case—the reverse: the cost of acquisition *gives* value to the painting, a large sum of money paid for it makes the painting valuable, and not vice versa. Art appreciation begins to diverge markedly from its financial value, in the sense that the latter more and more determines the former.

This is where the second, related topic of the 'beautiful and wonderful new science of connoisseurship' merges decisively with the question of art collecting. Hugh Crimble, the moneyless lover of art (who will marry Lord Theign's daughter), the 'new man' who rides a bicycle with pins on his trousers, is the new type of connoisseur (Rosier in *The Portrait of a Lady*, a minor collector with an 'instinct for authenticity' [added in the New York edition], is a pre-figuration of him), whose expertise will be directed to the question of right attribution and authentication. For the Italian expert whom Crimble will consult, James probably had Giovanni Morelli in mind.

By establishing the attribution and authenticity of the painting, such a connoisseur establishes simultaneously the artistic and *financial* value of the painting: willingly or unwillingly (as Alide Cagidemetrio has noted) he becomes a market agent for the collector; he participates in 'the new, modern market activity'. This is fully faced in the novel, and Bender makes no bones about it: 'you *have* got an eye for the rise in values', he tells Hugh, and is willing to grant him 'unearned increment'. Things are then becoming more and more complex: in James's easy 'comedy of manners', connoisseurs—in spite of their good intentions, and Hugh has plenty of them—end up by being unwillingly complicit in the bigger question of unholy acquisitions, the art drain, and the substitution of money value for artistic value.

James comes close to suggesting that it was doomed to become an unholy alliance—though stopping short, because of the happy ending, of the problem. Yet all the potential of the new historic and social drift is there (the borderline between authenticity and counterfeiting, forgery and the fake, is a thin one, and one must be always ready to face the oxymoron of an 'authentic fraud'). We are accustomed to James's narrative—as well as moral—twists. When we would expect him to be at his severest, he is at his most lenient, almost non-committal. A streak of mild irony, humour, and even sarcasm, runs through the novel, which exploits sensational features: an unsigned, forgotten check, the Prince appearing at the end to appease all fears, final marriages for almost all the characters.

A perfect balance, however, is kept on the central issue. Dedborough Place is a suggestive name, the British order does express pride, the Britons, who hold art treasures 'in trust' in their family collections, may eventually give them to the nation, but after much debating, and for dubious reasons: they are far from 'pure' themselves. As for Bender, the acquisitive American, he believes he is not after all producing more evil than they do or did in terms of unholy art acquisitions: 'If you drag their value to the light why shouldn't we want to grab them and carry them off—the same as all of *you* originally did?', he claims—with some degree, it seems to me, of authenticity as well as brazenness.

11   *Manners and Morals in James and Others*

My title may recall Lionel Trilling's "Manners, Morals, and the Novel" (1947, republished in *The Liberal Imagination*, 1950), but it has little to do with it: it was invented on the spur of the moment over the telephone when I was invited to contribute to a symposium. Its final part nods to James's own title, *A Small Boy and Others*, in which the Others may prove more important than himself.

Manners, as indicated in the epigraph, are meant in their simple meaning of acceptable ways of outward behaviour; morals, in that of ethical or responsible behaviour: it would be of little use (at least for my purposes) to try to define them more strictly. Originally, 'manners' almost coincided with 'morals', possibly owing to their identification with *mores, mœurs* (*OED*: 3.†a. A person's habitual behaviour or conduct; moral character, morals –1794. †b. Conduct in its moral aspect … –1776. d. Good customs or ways of living 1579). Then their meanings diverged, almost in an oppositional way: this will be the basis for my exposition, with an obvious warning—needless to say, I am dealing with representational practices or fictional representations: in one word, with literary texts.

1

We are all too familiar with the standard or stereotypical love scene in the movies or TV series: soft (but not too soft) music, intense stares in the luminous eyes, a rug on the floor, in front of a mildly roaring fireplace; two figures in some degree of nudity, with glowing skins. Bright, watery eyes and glowing skins are *de rigueur*. When we see this, we know what's going on: the two people involved are or are in the process of becoming lovers.

It was much simpler—or more complicated, and much more difficult for us—in the 19th century:

> Just beyond the threshold of the drawing-room she stopped short, the reason for her doing so being that she had received an impression. The impression had, in strictness, nothing unprecedented: but she felt it as something new, and the soundlessness of her step gave her time to take in the scene before she interpreted it.
>
> …
>
> Madame Merle was standing on the rug, a little way from the fire, Osmond was in a deep chair, leaning back and looking at her. Her head was erect, as usual, but her eyes were bent on his. What struck Isabel first was that he was sitting while Madame Merle stood; there was an anomaly in this that arrested her.
>
> …
>
> the thing made an image, lasting only a moment, like a sudden flicker of light. Their relative position, their absorbed mutual gaze, struck her as something detected. But it was all over by the time she had fairly seen it. Madame Merle had seen her and had welcomed her without moving; her husband, on the other hand, had instantly jumped up.
>
> …
>
> "I came to see you, thinking you would have come in; and as you hadn't I waited for you," Madame Merle said.
> "Didn't he ask you to sit down?" Isabel asked with a smile.(*N*, II 611-12)[1]

---

[1]   Volume and/or page references in the text are to Jane Austen, *Emma,* London, Col-

This is chapter XL of Henry James's *The Portrait of a Lady* (1881). We have the fire, the rug, the absorbed mutual gaze (his looking up, her eyes bent on his)... But Isabel, and the readers, suspect and learn what's going on, or what went on, by witnessing a breach in manners, good breeding, accepted rules of civility: a *standing* woman and a man leaning back in an easy chair could only mean or suggest a degree of intimacy or familiarity between the two far greater than acceptable. That was the 19th century equivalent of seeing, in today's movies or soap operas, a naked couple in bed or on a rug.

A breach in manners, in *galateo*[2]—that is—was a sure sign of a breach in morals, the manifestation, the epiphany of something going wrong in ethical behaviour. When violated, an accepted standard of civility between the sexes, whereby the man would stand if the woman is standing, becomes a sure indication of morality defied, compromised, denied. In other words, manners and morals were ostensibly linked as in a double cross: one was the outer sign of the other.

This connection—whereby manners (civility) are revealing signs of morals, usually on the negative side: the breach, the rupture of either— was typical of late 19th-century fiction and of James.

---

lins, 1953; John Cleland, *Memoirs of a Woman of Pleasure*, with an Introduction by Peter Quennell, New York, Putnam, 1963; Henry James, *The Complete Notebooks*, eds Leon Edel and Lyall H. Powers, New York, Oxford U. P., 1987 (= *CN*); Henry James, *Complete Stories,* New York, The Library of America, 1996-1999, 5 vols; (= *CS*);. Henry James, *Novels*, New York, The Library of America, 1983-2010, 6 vols (= *N*); F. S. Fitzgerald, *The Last Tycoon and The Great Gatsby*, New York, Scribner's, 1951; Philip Dormer Stanhope, Earl of Chesterfield, *Letters to his Son*, ed. Oliver Herbrand Gordon Leigh, New York, Tudor Publishing, 1901.

[2] There is no etymological connection to be established between *galateo* (Giovanni della Casa's *Galateo* was so called because written at the suggestion of Galeazzo [*latine* Galateo] Florimonte, bishop of Sessa) and *galante* (from old French *galer*, to amuse oneself)—though of course the connection is made in the popular mind and works subliminally in conversations and literary texts: *proposte galanti* followed for quite a while the strict rules of *galateo*, and *galateo* had always an implication of *galanteria*.

Earlier, the parallel was there, but the connection was far from negative:

> After tea, and taking a turn in the garden, my particular, who was the master of the house, and had in no sense schem'd this party of pleasure for a dry one, propos'd to us, with that frankness which his familiarity at Mrs. Cole's entitled him to, as the weather was excessively hot, to bathe together, under a commodious shelter that he had prepared expressly for that purpose, in a creek of the river, with which a side-door of the pavilion immediately communicated.
>
> …
>
> it reached sufficiently into the water, yet contain'd convenient benches round it, on the dry ground, either to keep our clothes, or …, in short, for more uses than resting upon. There was a side-table too, loaded with sweetmeats, jellies and other eatables, and bottles of wine and cordials, by way of occasional relief from any rawness, or chill of the water, or from any faintness from whatever cause; and in fact my gallant, who understood *chère entiére* perfectly, … had left no requisite towards convenience or luxury unprovided.
>
> As soon as he had look'd round this inviting spot, and every preliminary of privacy was duly settled, strip was the word. (pp. 267-68)

This is from the best text of 18th-century porno fiction, John Cleland's *Memoirs of a Woman of Pleasure* (1748-49: the years of Henry Fielding's *Tom Jones*), where all rioting of the flesh and the most advanced sexual exploits and transports are carried out, in spite of the heat they generate, coolly and with the utmost civility, the best breeding, perfect manners. *Galateo* goes hand in hand here with physical enjoyments of the most daring type, and it does almost point to a kind of pacified 'morality'.

Courtesy of gestures and of moods is in full sway, neatness and cleanliness are the rule, in the girls' bonnets as well as their shifts, in the very premises, in the ornate gardens, gazebos and private pools. The girls are expected and required to take up well-modelled attitudes, answer with elegant and polite turns of phrases (and bodies), control their spotless appearance in the mirrors, undress and put on their clothes with grace, and they do it to perfection. After their transports of joy, their first urge is to compose themselves, smile, smooth their hair, sip a cordial. As the author himself wrote:

> for it is to be noted, that though all the modesty and reserve were banished from the transactions of these pleasures, good manners and politeness were inviolably observed; here was no gross ribaldry, no offensive or rude behaviour, or ungenerous reproaches to the girls for their compliance. (p. 201)

One must indeed succeed in reconciling the gratification of sensuality—we further read—with the delicacy and the refinement of taste. (I mention *Fanny Hill* not only for the pleasure of it, but because, as we learn from Peter Quennell's "A Note on the American History of *Memoirs of a Woman of Pleasure*", it had a remarkable diffusion and exercised an influence in the American colonies and in 19th-century America: Cleland, p. 22). Not only is vice not punished in this novel, and we have the most romantic of happy endings, but, for our purposes, we have an example in which the most binding 18th-century *convenances* and *bienséances,* as well as *savoir faire,* are applied to what can be considered a reverse or perverse morality.

Contrary to what would happen in the twentieth century, when vulgarity and a dismissal of civility are felt to be the mark of and the gateway to sexual liberation (H. D. Lawrence's *Lady's Chatterley's Lover* and Joyce's *Ulysses* are cases in point), and contrary to 19th-century fiction, in which, as we saw, poor manners are a sign of a lapse in ethics and morality, in the 18th century manners, on their way to becoming the ruling guidelines of behaviour and proper conduct, may go and indeed go hand in hand with freedom from moral ties. Perfect manners are paired with horrible morals, which they conceal or disguise: civility has nothing to do with morality.

Impeccable manners obtain among the rogues, highwaymen and hussies of John Gay's *The Beggar's Opera* (1728), even when Macheath's two women quarrel fiercely for him. The separation of civility from morality is posited and exemplified by Lord Chesterfield's *Letters to his Son* (1732-68), while the equation or the coincidence between good manners and loose morals is at work in such novels as *Les liaisons dangereuses* (1782). Chesterfield—who in Samuel Johnson's dictum taught "the morals of a whore, and the manners of a dancing master"—wrote (as we heard already) that "A man of the world must, like the chameleon [*sic*] be able to take every different hue; which is by no means a criminal or abject, but a necessary complaisance: for it relates only to manners, and not to morals" (Stanhope, p. 128). Laclos's masterpiece is a hymn to good manners used and wisely exploited in the pursuit of profligate morals: these are ruined, while the others shine to perfection.

As we reach the 19th century, however, good manners and forms of civility are instead seen in close dialectical relationship with questions of morality. They are sides of the same coin: an 'impropriety' belongs to both realms. For the origin of this equation—whereby a breach in one is a breach in the other—here is Jane Austen, who may be said to have erected a monument to their interdependence: the well-known episode in chapter 43 of *Emma* (1816)—Knightley's so strongly-felt remonstrance to Emma about her 'indiscretion' with Miss Bates:

> "Emma, I must once more speak to you as I have been used to; a privilege rather endured than allowed, but I must still use it. I cannot see you acting wrong, without a remonstrance. How could you be so insolent in your wit to a woman of her character, age, and situation? Emma, I had not thought it possible."
>
> ...
>
> "Oh!" cried Emma, " I know there is not a better creature in the world; but you must allow, that what is good and what is ridiculous are most unfortunately blended in her."

"They are blended," said he, "I acknowledge; and, were she prosperous, I could allow much for the occasional prevalence of the ridiculous over the good. Were she a woman of fortune, I would leave every harmless absurdity to take its chance; I would not quarrel with you for any liberties of manner. Were she your equal in situation—but, Emma, consider how far this is from being the case. She is poor; she has sunk from the comforts she was born to; and if she live to old age must probably sink more. Her situation should secure your compassion. It was badly done, indeed!"

...

She was forcibly struck. The truth of his representation there was no denying. She felt it at her heart. How could she have been so brutal, so cruel to Miss Bates! How could she have exposed herself to such ill opinion in any one she valued! And how suffer him to leave her without saying one word of gratitude, of concurrence, of common kindness! (pp. 295-96)

From this point onward, manners—whether good or bad manners, civility or lack of civility—become pointers, signs, signifiers of moral stances. They *tell* (as James would have said), they direct meaning and generate response, clarify or obscure. Manners, when rigidly codified and observed as they were in the 19th century, and not before—in the eighteenth century, as we know, noblemen could defecate in public on their stools, while graciously conversing, and do what they do in *Fanny Hill* with a smile—create systems of meaning: in literary texts they reflect questions (and questionings) of morality or lack of morality, in good or even in bad ways (*Daisy Miller* may be a case in point here: see below).

For all this to happen, however, the so-called 'society' novel or the novel 'of manners' had to be firmly established. This happened around mid-century in England and in the second half of the nineteenth century, after the Civil War, in America, as James extensively argued in his 1979 *Hawthorne* book. In full-fledged society novels or novels of manners (which, incidentally, are set in urban milieus rather than in the country), manners, good breeding and polite behaviour became pointers—rather than bad travesties—of moral issues.

James—to come now to my main example—made the most of it throughout his fiction. There is a *macro-text* in which the connection is used to explore, set in motion, and dramatize the crucial (for him as well as for us) relation between America and Europe. We can visualize a scissors-like movement between manners and morals, whereby the axis of Europe moves high in manners but low in morals, while the axis of America goes up in morals but low in manners:

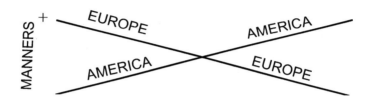

The key-texts are *Roderick Hudson, The American, Daisy Miller, The Portrait of a Lady*, in his first phase, *The Ambassadors* and especially *The Golden Bowl* in his 'major' phase, in which the moral issues are reversed (though the contrast had always a problematic character). The important point to bear in mind is that characters involved in breaches of morals—which are betrayed, revealed, made manifest by breaches in manners—are often Europeanized Americans, who have absorbed, as it were, the worst possible qualities of the two diverging traditions.

2

For our purposes, I will touch briefly on some aspects of the connection I have described in some novels and novellas, mostly on the 'international theme'.[3]

---

[3]   The manners/morals relation I am trying to describe obtains specifically in James's 'society novels'; it does not apply in his many works dealing with artists (there

In *The American* (1877) morals are high, even too high, in Christopher Newman—but his obtuseness in manners, his wilful blindness in questions of etiquette and *savoir faire* prove disastrous. The old-generation Bellegardes are plainly wicked, perhaps even murderous, and they hide and defend their poor morality with an *excess* of manners: their *grand manners* are an overbearing travesty even of elegance—and yet they work successfully against Newman's social naiveté, his lack or dismissal of sophistication. There was too much of romance, as James maintained, in his delineation of Newman and of the plot. Yet even in its crudeness, Christopher's revulsion at stooping down to the Bellegardes's moral level, his refusal to breach high standards of ethical conduct, does not redeem his hopeless lack of social graces.

To celebrate his engagement he is willing to give a "festival", hiring "all the great singers from the opera, and all the first people from the Théâtre Français", to which he will invite "all my friends, without exception: Miss Kitty Upjohn, Miss Dora Finch, General Packard, C. P. Hatch, and all the rest" (*N*, I: 700): the list of names prefigures the ludicrous list of people "going", rather than being invited, to Gatsby's parties, and thereby making them socially outrageous (Fitzgerald, 211-13: see below, note 7). And at the formal party the Bellegardes give instead, Newman behaves in such a way to almost force them to break the engagement;[4] in turn, his disgust at their low morals, when he dis-

the relation is mostly between life and art, aestheticism and morality: Roderick Hudson, for instance, has admittedly a "sacred fire" and "no manners"), and in his many works dealing with the supernatural or the uncanny (in which the relation is between this and the other world, or between conscience and hallucination: see *The Turn of the Screw*), where questions of manners would be misapplied.

[4] For a list of Newman's social blunders and "ignorance of polite manners": "He at first mistakes Urbain for the butler; he is on terms of easy familiarity with cicerones, guides, couriers, and the coquette Noémie Nioche. He telegraphs his engagement to America before it is formally announced and then brandishes the congratulatory replies in the face of Mme de Bellegarde. He threatens to stage an engagement party at his hotel, unaware that the 'everlasting proprieties' require that Mme de Bellegarde give it. He parades the old marquise around the room on the evening of the

covers the nest of vipers in their family, is sufficient to make him forgo the advantage he has on them and any wish for revenge or 'restitution' (chapters XXIV-XXV).

Similar situations and issues are dramatized in two early *novellas*. In *Madame de Mauves* (1874), the protagonist's refusal to accept or to adopt European manners, with their accompanying concessions to loose morals, brings her unfaithful husband to suicide. Moral rigour and domestic silence are used, perceived and presented as a kind of straitjacket, in a way that prefigures, in part, Maggie's adoption of the rule of silence to restrain the Prince in *The Golden Bowl. An International Episode* (1879) pits two bourgeois American ladies against the ways of British aristocracy, whose 'high manners' are felt and perceived as a possible threat to social intercourse and well-being: " 'They meant to overawe us by their fine manners and their grandeur, and to make us *lâcher prise* ... they meant to snub us.' 'I saw no attempt to "overawe" us,' said the young girl. 'Their manners were not fine.' 'They were not even good!' Mrs. Westgate declared" (*CS*, II 398). In the end, the young girl, Bessie Alden, behaves as Newman had done, with a 'noble' rejection of aristocratic 'grandeur' (and possible marriage) which stresses her superiority in morals as well as civility: she too withdraws from the social fray and goes back to America in disdain, rather than accede to a travesty of gentility, though no real *moral* issues are at stake for her here.

Daisy Miller (1878) dramatizes the manners/morals quandary in an exemplary way: here judgments of morality are tragically misled by a biased misreading of socially awkward, naïve, or defiant behaviour. Daisy is declared and shown to be very common and rather vulgar (chapter 1), and her 'innocence' of manners is said to betray a notable degree of wilful 'ignorance' (chapter 2). It is true that she is 'condemned' by the strictures of Europeanized Americans (including Winterbourne, the

party, mortally embarrassing her in the presence of her guests" (James W. Tuttleton, *The Novel of Manners in America*, Chapel Hill, North Carolina U. P., 1972, p. 67).

detached and wavering narrator) who mistake her social defiance for moral depravity. But her predicament is clearly indicative of a situation in which breaches of manners are construed as breaches of morality— much in the way of what we saw in the episode of *The Portrait of a Lady* quoted at the outset. Here morals are on Daisy's side, and depravity (or a misconception) of manners on the side of her critics: still, the outcome is tragic, because the social force and the constriction of manners, no matter how falsely applied, carry an overwhelming victory.

Even in a purely American novel like *Washington Square* (1880) the lack of style and social accomplishments of Catherine Sloper is pitted against her father's formidable shrewd eye and overbearing manners. He is right in surmising or detecting the 'mercenary' motives of her suitor, Morris Townsend, that he is 'not a gentleman', that he is vulgar and too familiar, that his 'naturalness' is a disguise for questionable aims. Yet in the end Doctor Sloper's moral stance betrays a great deal of social awkwardness (he is certainly "not polite" to his daughter and her suitor, chapter 12), while Catherine's surrender to high standards of conduct in refusing Morris, is construed by him as a breach of manners: "'She doesn't care a button for me—with her confounded little dry manner'" (*N*, I 189), again positing a possible coincidence of manners and morals.[5]

In the long story *The Point of View* (1882), on the contrary, American 'open' and natural manners are eulogized. With all their liberty and simplicity of behaviour, American girls are protected instead of being trapped by the gentle, humane, bourgeois manners of the place (*CS*, II 537-38), which are nearer to reality, whereas "an aristocracy is bad manners organized": aristocrats "may be polite to themselves, but they are rude to every one else" (*CS*, II 561)—a clear breach of social as well as ethical consistency.

---

[5]   In *The Europeans* (1878), which stages an 'international' comedy in New England on the Bohème *vs.* Puritans theme, Puritan morality goes hand in hand with stiff manners; the Baroness Eugenia is suspected of an 'impropriety', but the only danger to proper manners is that of an "abuse of hospitality".

American girls, however, are still trapped in or by manners. In *Daisy Miller* the signs were read falsely, and questions of manners impinged on moral judgment. In *The Portrait of a Lady* scene I quoted they were read properly, but throughout that novel social graces, *bon ton* and *aplomb* are a deception, a means of betrayal for the 'villains', Osmond and Madame Merle. They use "the achieved manners of an old civilization" much in the way of the older Bellegardes, to cover devious behaviour and treacherous aims. Beautiful manners are a perfect accomplishment for, say, the Touchetts (in the Gardencourt opening scene and elsewhere), in spite of their being an estranged couple, and are deployed and displayed with insouciance by Lord Warburton. Numberless analyses of the novel expatiate on these aspects.

But please note: Isabel's much-debated decision in the end to remain with her deceitful and oppressive husband, to continue being a 'lady' (as the over-determined title implies or requires), is motivated as much by points of civility and good-breeding as by an adherence to moral values:

> When a woman had made such a mistake, there was only one way to repair it—just immensely (oh, with the highest grandeur!) to accept it. One folly was enough, especially when it was to last for ever; a second one would not much set it off. (*N*, II 609; "just immensely (oh, with the highest grandeur!)" was added in the revised New York Edition).

Previously, she had assured Ralph: "I shall never complain of my trouble to you!" (*N*, II 550), and she would later reinforce this point: "She didn't wish him to have the pain of knowing she was unhappy; that was the great thing" (*N*, II 639). In other words: the moral problem of which future life she is going to embrace is solved on grounds that partake as much of elegant behaviour and style, of civility and social manners (or *mœurs*), as of ethics. It is as if Isabel had absorbed those aesthetic values of conduct that had so much attracted her in Osmond and Merle, and were to use them in the end to guide her life: manners are just as important in her final decision as morals.

As I already suggested, this is because in James—and in the *fin de siècle*—there is a strong tendency to equate, if only for fictional purposes, perfection of manners with perfection of morals. Oscar Wilde may have gone back to the 18th-century view that perfect manners could be a cover and a disguise, or indeed a varnish, for outrageous morality—but he was more prone to *substituting,* in fact, civility and high breeding for morals. With James, questions of good manners are superimposed on moot points of morality.

This is borne out by texts of his 'middle period'. In *The Aspern Papers* (1888), for instance, the protagonist deserves the charge of being a "publishing scoundrel", only if he resorts to the means of the detective and the 'peephole'—i.e., if he behaves with a disregard for taste and refined manners. If he were to behave impeccably from a *social* point of view, he could get away with securing the papers and the other treasures of the American poet he is after. (This same principle, incidentally, applies to the pursuit of the Narrator in James's later novel *The Sacred Fount*, 1901: the *style* redeems any possible indiscretion of his quest.)

'Respectability'—i.e. refined manners used to conceal and disguise her indiscretions—had been pursued by the protagonist of *The Siege of London* (1883), an American woman who wanted to be socially reinstated in Europe. In an opposite way, the young American heroine of *A London Life* (1889), Laura Wings, seems to misread signs and manners all around her, as if horrors were lurking behind them, and is so obsessed by fears of an overriding corruption, that while her 'corrupt' sister Selina peacefully thrives in society with her supposedly wicked behaviour, Laura has to escape back to America in shame and disarray. Here, too, questions of manners and morality seem to overlap, to the point that their separation is blurred: "She had often been struck with it before—with that perfection of machinery which can still at certain times make English life go on of itself with a stately rhythm long after there is corruption within it" (*CS,* III 450).

Again, the "sinking of manners" in *The Reverberator* (1888), is due to the growing invasion of publicity and the newspapers.[6] Yet here the young American woman who is guilty of a journalistic indiscretion—an unforgivable breach in manners if ever there was one, that would have condemned her to social ostracism and worse, as in *Daisy Miller*—is accepted in the end by the scion of a French noble family, in total reversal, for instance, of what had happened in *The American*.

In other important and crucial texts of the middle period, shades of ethical judgment are still conveyed by means of insisted social awkwardness and *gaucherie*. In *The Bostonians* (1886) Verena and the Tarrants are tainted by poor manners on account of their social insecurity and marginality, of their consorting with 'objectionable' people and endeavours—the underworld of mesmerism and 'public performances' (this also applies to some extent to the 'feminists', who are presented as gauche and socially deficient). There, rather than in their ethical or political views, seems to lie for James their condemnation. But where we do find good, indeed impeccable, manners—in Basil Ransom the Southerner, in Olive Chancellor the New England intellectual—they appear more *de façade* than of substance, and are used by these two characters, openly or covertly, as overpowering means of possession and possessiveness, of subjugation and constriction: a development to which James gives full swing in later novels.

He begins openly, that is, "to strip the façade of manners", as Balzac had done.[7] In *The Spoils of Poynton* (1897), to give another example, Mrs Gereth objects violently to Mona—who is to inherit her treasures

---

6   "One sketches one's age but imperfectly if one doesn't touch on that particular matter: the invasion, the impudence and shamelessness, of the newspaper and the interviewer, the devouring *publicity* of life, the extinction of all sense between public and private. It is the highest expression of the note of 'familiarity', the sinking of *manners,* in so many ways, which the democratisation of the world brings with it." (*CN*, p. 40).—Given the complexity, narrative and otherwise, of James's later novels, in my further exposition I can proceed only by drastic simplifications, and must forgo quotations.

7   See Peter Brooks, *The Melodramatic Imagination. Balzac, Henry James, Melodrama and the Mode of Excess*, New Haven, Yale University Press, 1976.

and 'beautiful things' without appreciating them—precisely because Mona is not up to her aesthetic as well as social pretension, and not on other grounds. Questions of 'taste' and 'style' are expected or supposed to carry it over law and ethical customs. As with Olive Chancellor, Mrs Gereth's 'taste' verges on or becomes a kind of arrogance, her 'style', a form of possession, in the full sense of the word: legal and moral obligations are sacrificed or suppressed in the name of 'higher manners' which become more and more dubious and constrictive.

To close with the three novels of the major phase: questions of intermingled manners and morals become central in new ways. In *The Ambassadors* (1903) the education of Chad Newsome in Paris, at the expense of poor and sacrificed Mme de Vionnet, is purely on the level of social refinement, the appreciation and adoption of good manners, the acquisition of *savoir faire,* the ways of the world, personal elegance and *allure*—and an undisguised dose of selfishness –, while the woman and the city can only *give,* minister and contribute to his social advancement and well-being. From this point of view, Mme Merle's and Osmond's situation in *The Portrait of a Lady* is confirmed: social graces, *galateo,* manners, reinforce an attitude to the world which can do without or diminish moral awareness and concern, but the application is reversed: Chad, the American, is here in the acquisitive and predatory position, while Mme de Vionnet, the European, is the victim or the giver.

A subtle game of manners as well as of morals is enacted in *The Wings of the Dove* (1902). Kate Croy and Merton Densher are clearly defined as not up socially, trapped in a kind of cheap respectability, possibly even low in morality; but it is clear that their constrained manners and later moral deceptions are due to their lack of means and social possibilities, while Milly Theale's graces, social possession, and perfect manners, in every sense of the word, including her generosity to her betrayers, for good or worse prove destructive of the deceivers' future prospects and happiness. Kate and Merton are finally carried away and destroyed by the sway of manners and morals higher than those they can possibly envisage or sustain.

Finally, in *The Golden Bowl* (1904), the lack of social *expertise*—not of social graces—in Maggie Verver may bring her to let her husband, the Prince, consort too much and too freely with Charlotte Stant. But when she realizes—much in the way of Isabel Archer—what has been happening in her marriage, it is precisely by resorting to an iron-willed exercise of social graces and binding good manners, by having recourse not so much to a 'conspiracy of silence', as to a masterly use and adoption of silence and the *non detto* as a means of conviction and coercion, that Maggie can triumph over her marital difficulties and accomplish the recapture and the retention of her husband.

My words are used advisedly. Hyper-civility and good manners exercise here a powerful force in the direction of moral stability and domestic enforcement; manners were never before so forcefully, so effectively, and so equivocally, allied to moral and ethical aims. But they become and are used as a cage and ultimately a prison, as a superior form of restraint and constriction ('restraint' carries Shakespearean echoes and implications, sexual, social, and legal, from *Measure for Measure*). Nancy Bentley has written of "the well-mannered violence" and "the discipline of manners" in this novel: the word 'discipline', too, is appropriate and self-explaining, much in the same vein.[8]

---

8   Nancy Bentley, *The Ethnography of Manners. Hawthorne, James, Wharton*, Cambridge, Cambridge U. P., 1995: "What allows Maggie to triumph over Charlotte is … her position in the network of social forms, the 'silver tissue of decorum' that works to repress acknowledgment of the sexual betrayal. Manners are thus the very medium in which the novel's characters try to exert force on one another. One sign of the rise of Maggie's 'feverish success', for instance, is the enhanced sensitivity with which Charlotte begins to ritually observe the grades of disparity between their respective social positions" (pp. 92-93, where she also quotes Mark Seltzer: in James's novel, power is 'finally indistinguishable from manners'). Bentley expatiates on this in chapters 2 and 3, where Edith Wharton's novels are also examined: here, more than elsewhere, manners prove a restraining power and a moral constriction.

3

By way of a coda, rather than a conclusion: the idea that good manners should coincide with good morals, but in doing so they end by imposing vicious and dramatic restrictions, by exercising unbearable violence and restraint, is brought to completion, indeed to its farthest extreme, by Ford Madox Ford, James's admirer and disciple. In his masterpiece, *The Good Soldier* (1915), an absolute respect for manners exercises a total repression of spirit and passion in the protagonist, in ways that are comparable with *The Golden Bowl*. But here the outcome is openly tragic: the minuet of manners to which the various characters subject themselves, willingly or unwillingly, proves a constraining prison, a ferocious drama of coercion and repression. The excess of social delicacy and scruples wrecks the lives of almost everybody concerned in the plot, and on the very verge of the outbreak of World War I seems already to pose the question: what is civilization worth?

This is reinforced in Ford's subsequent tetralogy of novels, *Parade's End* (1924-28), where the perfect manners and stylish, even too scrupulous behaviour of Tietjens—a relic of 19th-century values and beliefs if ever there was one—are literally and tragically trounced and destroyed by the rampant immorality of his wife, her coterie, and his opponents, who also act under the disguise of similarly impeccable manners, but viciously flout morals, decency and decorum in their totally irresponsible behaviour. *Some do not...* is the title of the first volume: some, and Tietjens in particular, will not yield to the overwhelming corruption in manners and morals brought about by the new times and the war; a series of refusals of moral inconsistency under the shield of still perfect manners will mark his social descent and the ruin of his life. By renouncing all, however, his final defeat turns into a kind of moral, if not social, victory, though the price to be paid is enormous; if gentility is defended and maintained, the loss of life and love is overwhelming.

Finally, in the masterpiece of another, later and indirect follower of James, in F. S. Fitzgerald's *The Great Gatsby* (1925), the game of manners and morals is played to its tragic outcome, and in an almost exemplary way for his times. Their interplay is absolute, and the whole gamut of possibilities is dramatized.

Gatsby's fake manners are a travesty and a disguise of his poor morality—in spite of his steadfast dedication to a single dream. His fantastic mansion is "a factual imitation of some Hôtel de Ville in Normandy" (p. 170), his speech is affected and often ludicrous in its social pretension (the 'old sport' form of address, etc.), the showy clothes he wears and the colour of his shirts are preposterous; his guests conduct themselves at his parties "according to the rules of behaviour associated with an amusement park" (p. 196), and their very names in the list that Fitzgerald draws is sufficient to qualify Gatsby's total 'innocence' of manners and social graces, in a way that seems a big step forward on Christopher Newman's naiveté.[9] He is so low in manners and morals, that in his defeat he is at least partially saved by his romantic dedication to Daisy.

High-class, snobbish and supercilious manners characterize the Buchanans: Daisy is elegant, airy, as sweet as honey, and yet basically careless and irresponsible; Tom is hard, cruel, and racist in attitude and behaviour, and can be as vulgar and violent with his mistress as any low-bred rogue (witness his connection with his mistress, her husband and her friends). In spite of high-flown pretensions to gentility, they form a kind of 'secret society': she is offended by Gatsby's caravanserai of a mansion and his style of life, and makes him dismiss both during the brief resumption of their affair; Tom's 'hard malice' smashes eas-

---

[9]   "From East Egg, then, came the Chester Beckers and the Leeches, and a man named Bunsen, whom I knew at Yale, and Doctor Webster Civet, who was drowned last summer up in Maine. And the Hornbeams and the Willie Voltaires, and a whole clan named Blackbuck ... Clarence Endive was from East Egg ... the Cheadles and the O. R. P. Schraeders, and the Stonewall Jackson Abrams of Georgia, and the Fishguards and the Ripley Snells ... From West Egg came the Poles and the Mulreadys and Cecil Roebuck and Cecil Schoen and Gulick the State senator and Newton Orchid, who controlled Films Par Excellence, and Eckhaust and Clyde Cohen and Don S. Schwartze (the son)", and so on, in an almost two-page-long piece of bravura (pp. 211-13).

ily through Gatsby's weak and romantic defences—so that he is finally left "watching over nothing" (p. 275) and murdered with the Buchanans' connivance, to say the least: "They were careless people, Tom and Daisy—they smashed up things and creatures and then retreated back into their money or their vast carelessness" (p. 300).

Their friend Jordan Baker, such a lovely golfer, with all her charm, is also "incurably dishonest" (p. 209) and irresponsible. The only character in whom decent manners and decency of conduct coexist is the narrator, Nick Carraway, who feels 'uncivilized' in front of the Buchanans, would instinctively call for the police, but can suspend judgment; who has a tentative affair with Jordan, but leaves her after the tragedy has happened, and can divide his allegiance equally in the end: "You're worth the whole damn bunch put together", he can tell Gatsby (p. 281), but can also shake hands with Tom, "rid of [his] provincial squeamishness forever" (p. 300). In Nick, civility of manners and moral awareness coincide—except that he is, if not a loser, an outsider in the struggle of life, and goes back alone and partially defeated to the country, where games of manners and of morals are much less likely to engage our imagination.

12 *Discontinuous Autobiographies: James and Others*

1

> My first memories are fragmentary and isolated and contemporaneous, as
> though one remembered some first moments of the Seven Days. It seems
> as if time had not yet been created, for all thoughts connected with emotion
> and place are without sequence.

This is the opening sentence of W. B. Yeats's *Reveries over Childhood
and Youth*, and my discontinuous autobiographies are meant in this
sense: fragmentary, blending past and present, without sequence.

I will concentrate on cases which deal primarily with the education
of a youthful genius, with the rise and emergence of a writer—self-
portraits of the writer as a young man—, and which are concerned with
evocations of memory, the wooing, luring and enticing of recollections,
rather than their possession (see note 1, below). These autobiographies
are written less from a position of authority and achievement than from
a standpoint of insecurity, uncertainty, unstableness—psychological or
otherwise—, as a troubled interrogation of the past, rather than a re-
appropriation of it.

They are found primarily at the end of the nineteenth century and
the beginning of the twentieth—precisely when ideas of duration and/
or stream of consciousness began to obtain, and would soon be guid-

ing principles for writers. This is a surprising and interesting aspect. Tension arises from the clash of the continuity and amalgamation which subsumes the flow of recollections, once it is started, and the stops, gaps, jumps, fits and starts implied in unprompted memory; of Bergsonian *durée* and what Proust called *intermittences du cœur*; of solid chunks of recollected past and the vagaries of casual memory, the disconnected narration of its findings.

Romantic and Victorian autobiographies are generally written by artists in a position of pre-eminence and control, reviewing the past from achieved and recognized success: Goethe (*Dichtung und Wahrheit*, 1811-32), Wordsworth (*The Prelude*, 1799-1850, notably in verse), Chateaubriand. As a quick example I take his *Mémoires d'outre-tombe* (1848-50), Book I, Les années de jeunesse, 1768-91, on two accounts.

First: autobiographies are by definition and necessity unfinished. The final and crowning event—the protagonist's death—cannot be reached, let alone narrated, unless one were to resort to some kind of 'mesmeric revelation' à la Edgar Allan Poe. At most, one can write 'Testamentary Acts', as Michael Millgate has called them.[1] Chateaubriand writes *de l'outre-tombe,* from 'beyond death, alone in front of eternity', erecting a funereal monument to his grandeur and drawing a document of epoch-making events, displaying his material with assurance, always with the big historical figures he had dealings with in attendance, moving in war and peace in four continents, relating himself to classical and medieval writers: 'Ces *Mémoires* seront un temple de ma mort élevé à la clarté de mes souvenirs' (chapter 1). Frightening: and 'clarity' is not exactly what we find in them.

Second: he organizes the flow of memories in an 'unité indéfinissable' according to a telescoping system: 'ma jeunesse pénétrant dans ma vieillesse', prosperity—he continues—into misery, tribulation into happiness, and vice versa: 'mon berceau a de ma tombe, ma tombe

---

[1]   Michael Millgate, *Testamentary Acts. Browning, Tennyson, James, Hardy*, Oxford, Clarendon Press, 1992.

a de mon berceau' (Préface testamentaire, 1833; Avant-Propos, 1846). Each of his chapters begins from where and when he is writing—a present of elevated activities and places of eminence: embassies, imperial courts, capitals—moving back to the crucial events of his youth, and from there opening giddy vistas on far distant, historical times: family genealogies reaching back to the Middle Ages, the feudal past, the age of discoveries, the kings of France, etc.

There are moments of unprompted (involuntary? unintended? see note 2, below) memory à la Proust (the chirping of a thrush making the past re-emerge, ch. 3), but this telescoping of events—present, personal past, historical perspectives reaching far back in time—gives the narration a controlled drive and a sense of finality: his memoirs are the lower part of an hourglass (he states in ch. 5), but he will not turn it back when all the sand has trickled through. The adolescent moves between Britanny and Paris, is exiled by the Revolution, becomes an emigrant in America, where he is charmed by the wilderness and the Founding Fathers; yet in spite of all drawbacks and disillusionments encountered there, on his return to France in January 1792 he emerges primarily as writer: 'J'amenais avec moi ... deux sauvages d'une espèce inconnue: Chactas et Atala'—the characters of his first novels, *Atala* (1801) and *René* (1805)[2]—, so that the first circle of greatness is completed.

This will be the ending of quite a few autobiographies of the young genius; but it is given here almost as a matter of course, a rightful achievement, not as an agonized conquest.

There are special cases, however, of discontinuous autobiographies. One is S. T. Coleridge's *Biographia literaria* (1817), more *literaria* than biography, a series of critical and philosophical dissertations rather than an autobiographical record. While exploring the genesis of the intellectual world of the artist, he makes his metaphysical work into an

---

[2]   These 'années de jeunesse' were published separately (Paris, Hachette, n. d.). In the Pléiade edition, Paris, 1966, they comprise Tome I, livres 1-8, p. 283 for the final quotation.

expression of his life: the search is for *ego cogitans*. The narrative line thus moves disconnectedly from chapter to chapter, ending with the inclusion of youthful letters (Satyrane's Letters), so as to 'present myself to the Reader as I was in the first dawn of my literary life', and with the insertion of unconnected material.

Another is De Quincey's *Confessions of an English Opium-Eater* (1822, originally a series of articles), where discontinuity is inherent in the upsurge and superimposition of memories and sensations which are due not so much to literary, psychological or existential motivations, as to the *derèglement* of the senses and the mind induced by laudanum. The distinction is of great importance, although Georges Poulet (in *Mesure de l'instant*), remarks that it was De Quincey's romantic sensibility that fostered new concepts of a time totality in simultaneous experience of past memories and present perceptions.

De Quincey adopts principles of expansion and distortion, a 'spiralling mode' which I have visualized elsewhere ('turning and turning in the widening gyre', as Yeats would say).[3] He writes as if he were 'thinking aloud', without worrying about who may follow him: dreams and visions allow for the contemplation of one's whole life, past and present, they merge and coalesce in moments of revelation. Yet his 'Preliminary Confessions' ('Introductory Narration' in the 1856 edition), which even in the short 1822 text extend for some 200 pages, register typical passages of the youthful education of a writer. According to Spengemann's *Forms of Autobiography* (1980), they can be said to move from historical recollection to philosophical self-exploration and to poetic self-expression, especially in the desultory, though beautiful, final additions in the much enlarged text of 1856.

These two cases, however, are admittedly over-determined: by Coleridge's incurable vagaries of the enquiring mind, in one, by De

---

[3]   See Sergio Perosa, 'Deformazioni in De Quincey', in *Gli universi del fantastico*, eds Vittore Branca and Carlo Ossola, Firenze, Vallecchi, 1988, pp. 323-37.—I am not concerned with his *Autobiographical Sketches*, which are by definition discontinuous.

Quincey's dependence on opium, in the other. (Incidentally: ever since Northrop Frye's *Anatomy of Criticism* struck us in 1957 in graduate school, I have been fully aware of the rightful distinctions to be drawn between autobiography, memoir, confession, and adhered to them in previous essays. If I disregard them now, it is because in literary matters categorizing is as good in the observance as in the breaking.)

2

Discontinuous autobiographies of the youthful genius emerge with late Victorian and early twentieth-century writers. I'll consider three exemplary cases: John Ruskin's *Praeterita* (1885-89), Henry James's *A Small Boy and Others* (1913), W. B. Yeats's *Reveries over Childhood and Youth* (completed in 1914), in which discontinuity has different motivations.

Ruskin's *Praeterita*, too, was written under the stress of a partially deranged mind (which increases abnormally the disparity between his present reconstruction and what happened in the past), and was originally published in instalments. It follows no chronological order and is 'selective' in what it tells us of his development: a high level of distortion is to be reckoned with.

Besides being selective and idiosyncratic, it is also heterogeneous, according to the accepted modes of its times, because it freely includes letters or passages of letters, past diary entries, often in contrast with present, 'reformed' views, digressions and intellectual discussions, jumps in time and subject, merging and dislocations, especially towards the end. It almost breaks down in the proposed Appendix, *Dilecta*.

It is above all discontinuous by personal, avowed choice, and by the workings of deep-seated repressions and removals. 'I think my history will, in the end, be completest if I write as its connected subjects occur to me, and not with formal chronology of plan', he declared.[4] (The subtitle reads 'Outlines of / *Scenes and Thoughts* / Perhaps / Worthy of Memory / In my Past Life'.) At the outset he avers that he will write as he pleases of 'what it gives me joy to remember', 'passing in total silence things which I have no pleasure in reviewing'. The tone is flippant, but repressions and removals of this kind, given their obvious psychological and psychoanalytical motivations and implications, delete crucial aspects of his life, so that the story line is desultory and disconnected—indeed disfigured—in more than one way.

Two, as we know, are his fundamental omissions: that of his disastrous, non-consummated marriage to Effie (and ensuing scandal), where silence might have been standard procedure for Victorian times; and that of Venice itself, the starting point and the main ground of his achievement as a writer. 'At the very end', as Tony Tanner remarked, 'he effectively bracketed the whole [Venice] affair out of his life'.[5] The absence of Venice is ominous and even more conspicuous than that of Effie, not only for its distorting effect on Ruskin's narrative, but because it highlights a further point of interest in my discussion: it shows, and is the outcome of, the position of insecurity and dissatisfaction from which the autobiography is written.

The endearing early memories of childhood and youth, and of the education of the budding scholar, in spite of all his difficulties and shortcomings, vouch for the undoubted acquisition of intellectual eminence. Yet the standpoint of this autobiography is of doubt, promises betrayed, inconclusive achievement.

At one crucial moment Ruskin writes of 'three centres of my life's thought: Rouen, Geneva and Pisa'. They 'have been tutoresses of all I

---

[4] *The Complete Works of John Ruskin*, ed. E. T. Cook and Alexander Wedderburn, Oxford, George Allen, 1903-12, vol. XXXV, p. 128, I, vii, §148 (hereafter *CW*, with references in the text).—For a fuller treatment of what follows, see my 'La grande assente: Venezia e *Praeterita*', in *Ruskin e Venezia. La bellezza in declino*, ed. Sergio Perosa, Firenze, Olschki, 2001, pp. 147-64.

[5] *Venice Desired,* Oxford, Blackwell, 1992, p. 69.

know, and were mistresses of all I did, from the first moment I entered their gates' (p. 156, I, ix, §180)—not Venice: 'All that I did at Venice was bye-work'. Bye-work in Venice, for Ruskin? Astonishing. 'Venice I regard more and more as a vain temptation', he would add further on (p. 296, II, iii, §57). This is sheer madness, or perversity.

As for the sense of inconclusive achievement, or unachieved success, Ruskin claims that 'very earnestly, I should have bid myself that day keep *out* of the School of St. Roch [*sic*]', so that he should have written '*The Stones of Chamouni* [*sic*], instead of *The Stones of Venice ... but it was not my own proper work ... Its continuity and felicity became thenceforward impossible, and the measure of my immediate success irrevocably lost*' (p. 371-72, II, vii, §140, my emphasis).

A similar statement, referring to his 1845 visit in Venice, is in the 1883 Epilogue of *Modern Painters,* vol. II: 'And very solemnly I wish that I had gone straight home that summer, and never seen Venice,* or Tintoret! ... [*Seen her that is, with man's eyes. My boyhood's first sight of her, when I was fourteen, could not have been brighter, and would not have been forgotten.]' (*CW*, IV, pp. 352-53). In *Praeterita* he is even more aggrieved as he proceeds: 'The events of the ten years 1850-1860, for the most part wasted in useless work ...: 1852. Final work in Venice for *Stones of Venice* ... Six hundred quarto pages of notes for it, fairly and closely written, now useless. Drawings as many—of a sort; useless too' (p. 483, III, i, §10).

This kind of dejection, this sense of waste and loss, gathers momentum towards the end, which closes on a note of disease and loss of consciousness. And it is this kind of distortion of his life achievement that accounts for the discontinuous character of Ruskin's autobiography. It is a willed, preconceived discontinuity, which is almost forced on the narrative by the misconceptions and the vagaries of a once brilliant, now deranged mind, no longer wooing fond memories of a past life, but rather antagonizing them.

3

The next case, that of James, has all to do with the desire and the process of wooing, luring and enticing memory. His is a different kind of
discontinuity, due to the very strength of that desire and procedure.

As we saw, James's narration can be defined as the history of a 'generation', both in a personal sense (being generated as a child and as an
artist), and in the sense of a period that is defined by temporal, environmental, social and community bonds. James evokes his past according
to a compositional pattern of 'accretions', substituting the casualness
of free associations for cause-and-effect sequence, in the way of De
Quincey's *Confessions* (and of Proust). The past recovered as a palimpsest of impressions and experiences is mainly pursued or reflected on
psychological states that make it coexist with the experience of remembering. It is a kind of 'psychology in time' or 'in space', as Proust called
it in *La prisonnière* (as against flat, or level, psychology). In place of
objective representation James substitutes the 'I' in the process of taking in the past through the consciousness of the present.

In his 1905 *Notebook* entries he had written of the 'heavy bag of
remembrance' in which to plunge his hand and his arm 'deep and far',
but where one could meet 'the ineffable ... cold Medusa-like face of
life', recognizing the *dis*continuity of the process of remembering, the
fleeting, at times tormenting, nature of his material: *Basta, basta,* was
his final invocation.[6] In *A Small Boy and Others* the past is pursued and

---

[6]   *The Complete Notebooks,* eds Leon Edel and Lyall H. Powers, New York, Oxford
U. P., 1987, pp. 237-40.—This aspect radically distinguishes *A Small Boy and Others* from James Joyce's *A Portrait of the Artist as a Young Man*, which is motivated
and sustained by an absolute finality and ultimate direction (see ch. 1, note 10). Yet,
to his first biographer Joyce had described the early draft of the *Portrait, Stephen
Hero*, as 'an autobiographical book, a personal history, as it were, of the growth of
a mind, his own mind' (Herbert Gorman, *James Joyce*, London, John Lane the Bod-
ley Head, 1941, p. 133); according to his brother Stanislaus, he had thought of his
character as developing 'from an embryo', as a process of gestation—the gestation

recaptured through a single procedure: letting oneself go along with the flow of images, impressions and experiences in the past—a 'letting go' that James had resisted throughout his life and artistic career, though with some occasional lapses in wishing the contrary (see his July 13, 1881 *Notebook* entry, for instance, already quoted in ch. 1, *Complete Notebooks,* pp. 57-58).

'I lose myself, of a truth, under the whole pressure of the spring of memory', he writes in *A Small Boy and Others*.[7] 'To knock at the door of the past was in a word to see it open for me quite wide', freeing a flow of images, figures, places, and recollections that flooded the mind, so as to create eventually 'a tale of assimilations small and fine'. The small boy is caught and presented as always 'open' to experiences and receptive as a sponge: from the beginning he indulges in *flâneries*, gaping, dawdling, dodging; everything is a spectacle to him. From the very beginning his basic activity is to 'take in', absorb, assimilate, and understand (according to the very first meaning of the term), but also to take in in the sense of internalise, 'incorporate' and digest.

James had often declared an opposition to biography and autobiography: in the Preface to *The Ambassadors* he had condemned 'the terrible *fluidity* of self-revelation'; in a letter to H. G. Wells he had dismissed 'the accurst autobiographic form'. He practiced discretion and hated all forms of personal exposure and exhibition, finding a motivation for this attitude in the deep-seated idea that the writer is in, and only in, his work, not elsewhere ('all we see of the charm-compeller is the back he turns to us as he bends over his work', he wrote at the end of his Preface to *The Tragic Muse*)—an idea that Goethe had already expressed in his autobiography, and that James shared with R. L. Stevenson (who in a letter of 13 March 1884 had written: 'I refuse the offering of my

---

of a soul from foetal to full organism (see Richard Ellmann, *James Joyce*, London, Oxford U. P., 1966, p. 307).

[7] *Henry James's Autobiography*, ed. Frederick W. Dupee, London, Allen, New York, Criterion Books, 1956, pp. 54, 131 (henceforth page references in the text).—Most of this refers back to Chapter 1.

life without my art. I am not but in my art; it is me; I am the body of it merely').[8]

Yet James embarked on his 'autobiography', first by a process of displacement: originally he was to write a 'Family book' based on his brother William's letters, papers, and activities, according to a well-established nineteenth-century pattern. Indulging in the flow of his memories (as he had enjoined himself: 'let my whole conscience and memory play on the past'), however, entailed and determined a gradual removal of William from the scene (James rationalized in a letter to his nephew that 'This whole record of early childhood simply *grew* so as one came to write it that one could but let it take its way').

He, then, Henry, takes the scene, moves among relatives and between Europe and America, a hotel child deliberately deprived of systematic schooling, having his first revelations of books and places, pictures and scenes. The flow of images and impressions recaptured from the past seems to clog the page and to move heavily on: but here the discontinu-ity arises precisely from the very procedure of acting under the spur of memory, from the 'free play of the mind', from the riot or revel of 'the visiting mind'. Memories are uncontrollable, we can only follow a free-association movement of impressions that achieves unity and integrity of sense, but is hazardous and desultory as a text. (As Edmund Wilson wrote of Proust's characters, 'it is only the presentation, and not the development ... which is discontinuous').[9]

There is, of course, finality and construction underneath. The nar-rative drive is clearly towards a conquest of History and of Art. The Civil War is evoked towards the end of the book, while the discovery of, indeed 'the passage' to Style, is beautifully enacted in the Louvre episode, the nightmarish experience or 'immense hallucination' in the

---

8   *The Letters of R. L. Stevenson,* eds Bradford Booth and Ernest Mahew, New Haven, Yale U. P., 1995, IV, pp. 252-53.

9   Edmund Wilson, *Axel's Castle,* London, Fontana Paperbacks, 1976, p. 122, also in *Literary Essays and Review of the 1920s & 1930s,* New York, The Library of America, 2007, p. 744.

Galerie d'Apollon, where James frightens, defeats, and puts to flight a spectral apparition which tried to frighten *him*, that he not only keeps at bay, but routs—turning the tables, as it were, on a ghost which retreats into the dreamy perspective of the Galerie—thus routing the very ghost of the 'apparitional' that haunts the whole book ('To look back at all is to meet the apparitional and to find in its ghostly face the silent stare of an appeal', p. 54). I proposed that here James is conquering his fears, but also mastering Art, preparing himself to be or to become an artist: 'This comes to saying that in those beginnings I felt myself most happily cross that bridge over to Style' (pp. 195-96).

As for construction: we know that, in spite of his unusual 'letting go', James 'composed' and constructed his material, taking 'visionary liberties' with chronology, omitting, transposing and conflating episodes, using strategies of compensation and transposing (in *The Middle Years* he admitted 'sincerities of emphasis and "composition"; perversities, idiosyncrasies, incalculabilities', p. 558) in order to suit his purposes.[10] Here, too, as in Proust or Joyce, free-flowing memories and stream of consciousness possibilities are *shaped* by an autonomous force and an artistic will; they are subjected to a dramatizing, creative process. The Galerie d'Apollon episode which I just mentioned, was moved from where it belonged in the chronological sequence and forcibly inserted where it could enhance dramatic quality and meaning, resonance and relevance: the later experience is almost blended into the narrative as if taking place simultaneously with childhood memories.

Thus we come round full-circle to my two main points about such discontinuous autobiographies of an emergent vocation. Tension arises precisely from the *durée* and accretions of memory and the gaps and disconnections they entail. The enhancing of particular, intermittent moments (what Virginia Woolf would have called 'moments of being') is achieved at the expense—or the exclusion—of others; the story line

---

[10]   On the 'compositional' character of the narration, see ch.1, note 16.

is compromised by the overpowering accretion and expansion of single—however massive—recollections.

Secondly, the autobiographical act is conducted from a position of weakness: *A Small Boy and Others* closes on an illness and a loss of consciousness in Boulogne, the news of a financial crisis in the U. S., and the threatening assault of the aesthetic, historical, and cultural fullness of Europe, of her abundance of signs—the life-long challenge for James. The book itself was written while he was in poor health, suffering from shingles, bouts of depression and possibly a nervous breakdown ('the heritage of woe of those three years', in another letter to his nephew, 19 January 1913). There is now no grandeur or glory in his view of the past, but rather a note of anxiety and failure.

If my reading is correct, James's text inaugurates a kind of discontinuous autobiography—hence its prominence in my title—which is determined by the wooing, luring and enticing of recollections in an almost ghostly, spectral way, in a sort of conjuring trick in which the surprises and vagaries of memory acquire pre-eminence. 'These secrets of the imaginative life', he writes further on, 'referred to actual concretions of existence as well as to the supposititious; the joy of life indeed, drawbacks and all, was just in the constant quick flick of associations, to and fro, and through a hundred open doors, between the two great chambers (if it be not absurd, or even base, to separate them) of direct and indirect experience' (p. 494).

The material *is* unified by the flow of memories, we have their amalgamation in the page, yet the procedure is that of unprompted memory, which carries with it an inherent potentiality for discontinuity. Fusion can coexist with fragmentation and does not disclaim discontinuity. Proust conquers time and achieves his success as a writer at the end of *La Recherche*. James is still uncertain about his future, doubtful of his possible achievement.

4

As I suggested in chapter 1, I am struck by partial similarities with a possible third case, Yeats's *Reveries over Childhood and Youth*, issued in 1915 (though the title-page had 1916: they were published originally as magazine articles). My esteemed colleague and friend Denis Donoghue is not fully convinced, though as far back as 1956, in his Introduction to James's *Autobiography*, F. W. Dupee suggested a possible connection, and in 1960 Roy Pascal found parallelisms between the two texts.[11] So I shall recall the similarities I detect.

Both Yeats and James lack a pre-ordained plan or narrative scheme, and follow the random, fragmentary and inconsequential upsurge of memories, images, recollections. Yeats declares it at the outset, dividing his short book into compressed, isolated, and discontinuous sections (James, on the contrary, dictated his as a *continuum*, but bridged few gaps). He, too, moves from childhood scenes to minute, sometimes confused, family details and cross-genealogies, descriptions of relatives who would determine his future in a complex web of influences, and to his earliest artistic and literary discoveries. Both he and James move from place to place, from one country to another: Yeats from Sligo to Dublin and then to London, James from Albany, to New York, and finally to Europe. Both are encouraged to develop their minds, to educate their 'senses', to cultivate and foster their imagination; they can fulfill the aspiration *to be*, rather than *do*. Yeats forms and exalts himself in the exercise of a *wandering mind*, eager for flights, excuses and evasions form reality; more than once, James insists on his processes of gaping, dawdling, dodging, removing himself from the hubbub of life, standing aside, being an onlooker. Both write of an insisted-upon and sought-for detachment.

For both, day-dreaming, the stimulation and cultivation of sensibility, substitute for direct involvement in life. Their field of action is the sphere

---

[11]   Roy Pascal, *Design and Truth in Autobiography*, Cambridge, Harvard U. P., 1960.

of the ineffectual, of the non-direct or 'second application' (as James calls it in his *Prefaces*). In this perspective, peregrinations and moves result in their liberation from provincialism (though in both cases the question of expatriation and/or 'exile' lurks in the background), and from family ties. Both play crucial games with the interrelation and interpenetration of inner and outer worlds. I noticed obvious differences between Yeats's physical activism and James's passivity; the former revels in sports, loves and visions, which the latter denies himself; one develops into a romantic poet, the other into a sober novelist of manners. But in both their autobiographical texts there is a programmed urge towards an artistic vocation; both embody the discovery and the history of a developing imagination and artistic consciousness; both register a process of growth and self-discovery that reflects the discovery of the world of art.

Yeats's early autobiography, too, is desultory, intermittent and dis-continuous in its telling: the story line is deliberately broken. As an author in mid-career, he writes from a relatively safe level of recognition, but 'without sequence'. Revelling in psychic evocations, he is concerned with the 'apparitional', with visions, in the proper sense of the word, and séances. He writes admittedly from 'unprompted memory', sometimes in the present tense—as if the past were part of his ongoing experience. In the Preface to *Reveries* he claims 'I ... describe what comes oftenest into my memory', and in his sequel *Estrangement* (passages from the Diary of 1909) he notes: 'Every note must come as casual thought'. As he writes, he too is haunted by a sense of insecurity and uncertainty, and his final line is almost chilling in its sense of despondency: 'All life weighed in the scales of my own life seems to me a preparation for something that never happens' (p. 71). This is echoed in the first draft of his subsequent *Memoirs* where he writes of Maud Gonne: 'She was complete; I was not', likening himself to 'a lump of meerschaum not yet made into a pipe' (p. 63), and where the final line reads 'I said, "No, I'm too exhausted; I can do no more"' (p. 134).

That Yeats's is a discontinuous autobiography like James's is also borne out by the later additions that make up his 1936 *Autobiography*

('The Trembling of the Veil', 'Dramatis Personae', down to 'Estrange-ment' and 'The Death of Synge', which are taken almost verbatim from his 1909 Diaries): they are disconnected sections, often as short as half a page or a paragraph. Here, as in the case of James's sequel (*Notes of a Son and Brother*), Yeats moves to tell more of the 'others' than of himself, though he is still very present in the picture and the recaptur-ing process.

My reading is supported by the fact, to which I can devote only a passing note, that if you compare its first two additions with Yeats's first draft of them, edited by Denis Donoghue in 1972 with the title *Memoirs*, these early Memoirs appear much more fluent and coherent in their nar-rative line, much more unified in their telling, than the 1936 excerpts.[12] I place great value on this fact. As we know of Joyce, who constructed his stream of consciousness sections through montage and juxtaposition of pre-prepared passages, Yeats seems to be involved in a deliberate process of cutting and pasting, of separating, isolating, and juxtaposing moments that were originally part of a much more unified flow.

This provides a third kind of motivation for Yeats's discontinuous autobiography: not so much the wooing and luring of memory, as what appears to be a conscious application of Modernist principles and tech-niques of juxtaposition and montage. One is reminded of T. S. Eliot's 'These fragments I have shored against my ruins...'; the constructing mode resembles that of Pound's *Hugh Selwyn Mauberley*. Although, admittedly, Yeats concludes his autobiographies from the vantage point of his achieved Nobel Prize ('The Bounty of Sweden': another obvious difference from James), he relies for his text on forms of fragmentation and discontinuity to the very end.

---

[12]   *Memoirs. Autobiography—First Draft—Journals*, ed. Denis Donoghue, London, Macmillan, 1972; *The Autobiography of W. B. Yeats* [1936], Garden City (NY), Doubleday Anchor Books, 1958. My first quotation is from this volume; in *Auto-biographies*, London, Macmillan, 1955, and following editions, its last line reads differently: 'for all thoughts are connected with emotion and place without se-quence'.

5

I wish to conclude my apercu with a short coda: commandeering memory at work in an autobiography.

Speak, Memory, Vladimir Nabokov enjoins in the very title of his discontinuous autobiography (this was the original English title; the American was *Conclusive Evidence*: almost the reverse). Here discontinuity is willed partly as a choice, mostly as a game. Although Nabokov claims it is a 'systematically correlated assemblage of personal memories' (p. 361),[13] it was composed in instalments and in no chronological order, and subject to 'multiple metamorphosis'. It is also discontinuous in language: chapter 5 was the first to be written, originally in French, in 1936; the others were written in English in 1947-51, then translated into Russian, with corrections, basic changes and conspicuous additions, and with the omission of chapter 11, then recomposed in English with the insertion of those additions and changes. Almost a mess, which rather pleases Nabokov: 'This re-Englishing of a Russian re-version of what had been an English re-telling of Russian memories in the first place, proves to be a diabolical task' (p. 364: the final title reads in fact *Speak, Memory. An Autobiography Revisited*).

Stubbornly rejecting Freud (and believing in no laws of environment or heredity), he acknowledges the anomalies of memory, and seems fully aware that his (or any?) autobiography is a tale of mystification. He places it in a space-time or in a kind of timelessness of his own construction: 'I confess I do not believe in time. I like to fold my magic carpet, after use, in such a way as to superimpose one part of the pattern upon another. Let visitors trip. And the highest enjoyment of timelessness—in a landscape selected at random—is when I stand among rare butterflies' (p. 479). He hoards up impressions, and in his evocation of childhood memories, governesses, tutors, readings, trips

---

[13]   *Novels and Memoirs 1941-1951*, New York, The Library of America, 1996 (henceforth page references in the text).

from one country to another, impressions of landscape, etc., he sounds a bit like James. Exile (forced, in his case) gives an eerie quality to his experience: he writes of 'spectral Germans and Frenchmen in whose more or less illusionary cities we, émigrés, happened to dwell' (p. 594; from mother, he specifies, 'I inherited an exquisite simulacrum—the beauty of intangible property, unreal estate', p. 387). Both 'intangible property' and 'unreal estate' seem to me an admirable definition and an apt description of his autobiographical 'creations'.

His, too, becomes the broken-up story of an artistic education, ending with his passage to America for yet another exile, which is clearly presented as a sort of rebirth, and pre-figures the emergence of a new writer in a new language (Russian Nabòkov turning into American Nàbokov).

In spite of his avowals and disclaimers ('A colorful spiral in a small ball of glass, this is how I see my own life', p. 594); and in keeping with his life-long narrative practice, Nabokov's are basically distorted mirror-images of his youth (p. 422, p. 553), shadows perceived on the wrong side of the street (pp. 613-14). He openly plays a game of reversals ('Old books are wrong. The world was made on a Sunday', p. 617; 'un-real estate'; 'Let visitors trip'), ultimately of muddlement and mystification, which he seems to enjoy immensely.

I will *not* say that with Nabokov we reach the post-modern phase. I will rather say, in conclusion, that he enacts and dramatizes fully those 'perversities' and discontinuities of the autobiographical art that James, too, had timidly envisaged as inherent in the process of writing the self. In the only poetic moment right at the end, when he is about to sail for his life to America—another forced exile—Nabokov actually writes: 'if I were careless enough to break the hush of pure memory that (except, perhaps, for some chance tinnitus due to the presence of my own tired blood) I have left undisturbed, and humbly listened to, from the beginning' (p. 628). What a cheek! He did nothing of the sort: in *Speak, Memory* he harried and commandeered memory, 'faking' and turning it to all kinds of fictional use.

In his first novel in English, *The Real Life of Sebastian Knight* (1941), he had already noted and warned that 'real stories' of young writers are 'shaped by the teller, reshaped by the listener, concealed from both by the dead man of the tale' (*Novels and Memoirs,* p. 40). In his later novel *Ada, or Ardor* (1962) he had written of 'that *third sight* (individual, magically detailed imagination) … without which memory … is, let us face it, a stereotype or a tear-sheet'.[14]

He used this kind of *third sight,* i.e. *invented* memory, profusely in the contrived 'sequel' to *Speak, Memory, Look at the Harlequins!* (1974), where he indulged in a total riot of the autobiographical imagination, to the point of parody. He calls the book a memoir, in fact 'this oblique autobiography—oblique, because dealing mainly not with pedestrian history but with the mirages of romantic and literary matters' (p. 628). This fragmented 'sequel', therefore, presents an extreme case, an embroidered autobiography in which Nabokov repairs omissions, invents (or 'fakes') things, people, places to suit *narrative* purposes, where he is himself in most recognizable traits, and not himself (he has three or four wives, no passion for butterflies); where *reversals* of memory and reality are more important than reality itself. It veers heavily towards fiction, and was published as such—a hybrid between autobiography and autobiographical novel, conducted with rampant Nabokovian distortions.

At this stage, as the saying goes: Don't trust the teller. But don't trust the tale, either.

---

[14]   *Novels 1969-1974*, New York, The Library of America, 1996, p. 201 (hereafter page references in the text). See also Sergio Perosa, 'Nabokov's Uncanny Portraits, Mirror Images, and the Value of Humor', in *Набоков / Nabokov. Un'eredità letteraria,* eds A. Cagidemetrio and D. Rizzi, Venezia, Cafoscarina, 2006, pp. 9-36.

A NOTE ON MEMORY

1   The difference between evoking and possessing memory is essential. It is made clear if we consider the way in which for centuries the
process of remembering was subject to compulsive and complicated
'arts of memory'. In *The Art of Memory* (Harmondsworth, Penguin,
1978), for instance, Frances Yates has shown that since classical times
an orderly arrangement was deemed essential for remembering; memory had to be *trained* through complex forms of mnemonics of places
and images (pp. 18-20); a *systematising* of random associations was required (p. 29) in order to remember, recollect, or recall what lies buried
in one's memory, mainly through the visual sense (pp. 43, 47).

An *artificial memory,* from Aristotle and Plato through the Renaissance, was to be carefully and painstakingly trained and *constructed* in
intellectual, rather than emotional, ways. *Images* were mostly needed
for remembering, propped by, and well disposed in, complicated 'theatres of memory'. Only with Ramón Lull in the 14th century, and later
on with the Renaissance Platonists, could *ars memoratoria* do away
with visualization, so as to gradually achieve a view *from within*. Only
then would memory become an imaginative act, or be linked with the
process of imagination and imagining. The autobiographies I deal with
veer consistently towards this direction, to the point of establishing the
primacy of the imagination in cognitive—as well as mnemonic—processes: they are emotionally, rather than intellectually, involved in the
process of remembering (see below, section 2).

2   'Unprompted memory' seems cognate, if not identical with, Proust's
'involuntary memory', which he sketched in the short Preface intended
for his *Contre Sainte-Beuve* (Paris, Pléiade, 1971, pp. 211-16; English
translation, *On Art and Literature*, New York, Carrol and Graf, 1984,
pp. 3-8), and which would become the sustaining poetics of *À la recher-*

che du temps perdu. Moments from the past, he writes, are only buried in objects where the intellect has not sought to embody them, and they can be resurrected by the springs of an 'involuntary memory' that opens sudden vistas in the past. They are recaptured and resurrected by mere chance ('Leur résurrection a tenu, comme toutes les résurrections, à un simple hazard', p. 212), by casual sense perceptions which have nothing to do with *intelligence* and are indeed opposed to it. (These involve the sense of odour, touch, taste or sound, but *not*—in marked contrast with what we just saw in section 1—that of sight: only the first four sense perceptions can open, determine or create a visual image of the past.

The cases mentioned in the Preface, showing that the past cannot be 'evoked' by conscious processes, but takes form through 'involuntary memory', are those of the smell and taste of a toast soaked in a cup of tea, of the feeling of *'pavés inégaux'* in a garden, of the noise of a spoon dropped on his plate. In the *Recherche* the first would become the famous episode of *la pétite madeleine* in chapter 1 of the first volume (*Du côté de chez Swann,* Paris, Pléiade, 1954, I, pp. 43-48), the second would lead to the crucial recollection of Venice, the third becomes instrumental in the final revelation of *'le temps retrouvé'* in the last chapter [III, pp. 866-68]: but similar episodes are found throughout. The fact that 'involuntary memory' becomes the sustaining poetics for the whole construction of this autobiographical novel, distinguishes it from the 'unprompted memories' of James and Yeats: yet it belongs to the same 'system'. In Proust, too, recapturing and resurrecting the past acquires an eerie and 'spectral' connotation: in the Preface to *Contre Sainte-Beuve* he wrote of those 'fantômes d'un passé cher' which, like the shades meeting Aeneas in the underworld, 'me tendaient des bras impuissants ... et semblaient dire: "Ressuscite-moi"'; ghostly encounters and atmospheres pervade various episodes of the *Recherche*.

About the Author

Sergio Perosa is Professor Emeritus, Ca' Foscari University, Venice, where he was Professor of English and Anglo-American Literature (1968-2003) and served as Chair, Department of Anglo-American and Latin-American Studies (1997-2002), Dean of the Faculty of Modern Languages (1987-1990), Chair of the English Department (1966-83), Director, "Dottorato di Ricerca in Anglistica" (1985-2003), and in various other capacities. He also taught as Instructor and Associate Professor at Ca' Foscari (1958-1968) and the University of Trieste (1961-1966), as Visiting Professor of English, Princeton University, 1974-5; New York University, 1978 (Berg Professor in English and American Literature), 1984, 1991, 1993, 1996, 1999, 2001. He gave lectures at the Rome, Paris and Salzburg Seminars in American Literature, in most European and American Universities, and presented papers in over fifty international conferences around the world.

He was Fulbright Fellow, Princeton University 1957-8; Lyly Fellow, Indiana University School of Letters, 1958; Salzburg Seminar Fellow 1961; Harvard International Seminar Fellow, 1964; American Council of Learned Societies Fellow, Princeton University, 1970-71, Remarque Institute Fellow, New York University, 1998, 2000. He was President (1979-83), Ateneo Veneto; President (1979-81), Italian Association of American Studies (AISNA); member of the Board (1976-1988), Vice-President (1980-1984) and President (1984-88), European Association for American Studies (EAAS); President (1979-81), Italian Society for Australian Studies (SISA). Current member of these Institutions, and of International Association of University Professors of English (IAUPE); Association of Literary Scholars and Critics (ALSC); International Comparative Literature Association (ICLA); Istituto Veneto di Scienze, Lettere ed Arti; Accademia Olimpica; Accademia dei Concordi; Societé Européenne de Culture; P.E.N. Italiano (honorary; member of the Board), F. M. Ford Society (honorary), various scientific committees, etc.

He is or was a member of the awarding committees: Premio Letterario Internazionale Grinzane Cavour, Turin (1982-2004); Premio Internazionale Antico Fattore Chianti Ruffino, Florence (1986-2000); Premio Letterario Giovanni Comisso, Treviso (1996– ; chair 2009-12); Premio All'Amelia, Venezia-Mestre (1973–); Premio Torta per il Restauro, Venezia (1979-2009); Newstadt International Prize for Literature, Norman, OK (1992). Regular contributor for English Literature, "Il Corriere della Sera", from 1969.

General editor, "Annali di Ca' Foscari" (1970-80, Editorial Board, 1970-2003), "Rivista di Studi Anglo-Americani" (1981-1991, Editorial Board, 1981–); Editorial Board, "l'Erasmo" (2004-2006). Co-editor, "Tutto Shakespeare" (A Bilingual Edition), Milano, Garzanti (1993-2000).

PUBLICATIONS

Book-length Studies

L'arte di F.S.Fitzgerald, Roma, Edizioni di Storia e Letteratura, 1961; *The Art of F.S. Fitzgerald*, Ann Arbor, Michigan U.P., 1965; *Storia e Antologia della letteratura inglese*, Milano, Fabbri, 1970, rpt. 1985, 2 vols.; *Henry James and The Experimental Novel*, Charlottesville, Virginia U.P., 1978, rpt. New York, New York U. P., 1983; *L'Euro-America di Henry James*, Venezia, Neri Pozza, 1979; *Vie della narrativa americana*, Torino, Einaudi, 1980; *Il precario equilibrio. Momenti della tradizione letteraria inglese*, Torino, Stampatori, 1980; *Dimore Adam*, Novara, De Agostini, 1981; *Storia del teatro americano*, Milano, Bompiani, 1982, rpt. 1999; *Teorie inglesi del romanzo 1700-1900*, Milano, Bompiani, 1983, rpt. 1999; *American Theories of the Novel, 1793-1903*, New York, New York U. P., 1983 and 1985; *Teorie americane del romanzo, 1800-1900*, Milano, Bompiani, 1986; *Le isole Aran. Figure letterarie inglesi*, Venezia, Marsilio, 1987; *Bagliori dal Commonwealth*, Roma, Bulzoni, 1991; *L'isola la donna il ritratto*, Torino, Bollati Boringhieri, 1996, enlarged edition, Milano, Bompiani, 2013; *From Islands to Portraits*, Amsterdam, IOS Press,

2000; *Il Veneto di Shakespeare*, Roma, Bulzoni, 2002; *L'albero della cuccagna. Classici e post-coloniali di lingua inglese*, Vicenza, Accademia Olimpica, vol 1, 2004, vol. 2, 2009; *Transitabilità. Arti, paesi, scrittori*, Palermo, Sellerio, 2005; *Henry James e Shakespeare*, Roma, Bulzoni, 2011; *Studies in Henry Jaames*, Venezia, Cafoscarina, 2013.

Critical Editions, with introductions and notes

William Shakespeare, *Antony and Cleopatra*, Bari, Adriatica, 1968; Washington Irving, *Sketches and Tales*, Milano, Mursia, 1963; Virginia Woolf, *Romanzi e altro*, Milano, Mondadori, 1978; *Da Frost a Lowell. Poesia americana del '900*, Milano, Nuova Accademia, 1979; Henry James, *Romanzi brevi*, Milano, Mondadori, vol I, 1985, vol. II, 1990; Henry James, *Un bambino e gli altri*, Vicenza, Neri Pozza, 1993; W. D. Howells, *L'ombra di un sogno*, Venezia, Marsilio, 2002.

Translations, with introductions and notes

Herman Melville, *L'uomo di fiducia*, Venezia, Neri Pozza, 1961, Milano, Feltrinelli, 1984, Roma, edizioni e/o, 2014; Henry James, *La fonte sacra*, Venezia, Neri Pozza, 1963, Torino, Einaudi, 1984; John Berryman, *Omaggio a Mistress Bradstreet*, Torino, Einaudi, 1969; R. P. Warren, *Racconto del tempo e altre poesie*, Torino, Einaudi, 1971; John Berryman, *Canti Onirici e altre poesie*, Torino, Einaudi, 1978.
William Shakespeare: *Giulio Cesare*, in *I drammi classici*; *Il Mercante di Venezia*, in *Le commedie romantiche*; *I due gentiluomini di Verona*, in *Le commedie eufuistiche*, Milano, Mondadori, 1978, 1983, 1990; *Antonio e Cleopatra, Otello, La bisbetica domata, Misura per misura*, Milano, Garzanti, 1985, 1990, 1992, 1999; *Drammi romani (Giulio Cesare, Antonio e Cleopatra, Coriolano)*, Venezia, Marsilio, 2000; *Giulietta e Romeo*, versione rimata (Preprint), 2015.

Edited by

Henry James e Venezia, Firenze, Olschki, 1987; *Hemingway e Venezia*, Firenze, Olschki, 1988; *Browning e Venezia*, Firenze, Olschki, 1991; *Venezia e le lingue e letterature straniere*, Roma, Bulzoni, 1991; *Le traduzioni italiane di Herman Melville e Gertrude Stein; Le traduzioni italiane di William Faulkner; Le traduzioni italiane di Henry James,* Venezia, Istituto Veneto di Scienze, Lettere e Arti, 1997, 1998, 2000; *Madness in Great Ones [Hamlet]* (with Loretta Simoni), Vicenza, I Quaderni del Teatro Olimpico, 2000; *Ruskin e Venezia: La bellezza in declino*, Firenze, Olschki, 2001; *Off with his Head! [Shakespeare's Villains]* (with Loretta Simoni), Vicenza, I Quaderni del Teatro Olimpico, 2002; *Tom Stoppard e la costa dell'utopia*, in *Annali di Ca' Foscari*, XLVIII, 1-2, 2009.

Critical prefaces to

Emily Dickinson, *Poesie*, Milano, Nuova Accademia, 1961; Jack London, *Martin Eden*, Milano, Mursia, 1966; C.S. Lewis, *L'allegoria d'amore*, Torino, Einaudi 1969; Fr. Rolfe, Baron Corvo, *Don Renato*, Milano, Longanesi, 1971; Henry James, *Il riflettore*, Torino, Einaudi, 1976; William Blake, *Poesie*, Roma, Newton Compton, 1976; Virginia Woolf, *Mrs. Dalloway*, Milano, Mondadori, 1979; F. S. Fitzgerald, *Taccuini*, Torino, Einaudi, 1980; Henry Fielding, *Jonathan Wild*, Milano, Feltrinelli, 1981; Henry James, *Che cosa sapeva Maisie*, Milano, Feltrinelli, 1981; Henry James, *Vita Londinese*, Torino, Einaudi, 1983; Miles Franklin, *La mia brillante carriera*, Torino, S.E.I., 1984; E. A. Poe, *Racconti*, Milano, Mondadori, 1985, 3 vols; Henry James, *Il carteggio Aspern*, Venezia, Marsilio, 1991; William Shakespeare, *I Sonetti*, Milano, Il Corriere della Sera, 2004; Henry James, *La protesta*, Roma, Fazi, 2006; George Orwell, *Nel ventre della balena e altri saggi*, Milano, Corriere della Sera, 2011; Derek Wakcott, *Nelle vene del mare*, Milano, Corriere della Sera, 2012; Herman Melville, *Bartleby lo scrivano*, Milano, BUR, 2013.

Commencement Speeches/Pamphlets

Shakespeare e Venezia [1986], Università Ca' Foscari di Venezia, 1991.
Tradurre Shakespeare per il nuovo millennio, Università Ca' Foscari di Venezia,1999.
Questo povero Shakespeare..., Istituto Veneto di Scienze, Lettere ed Arti, 2013.

Articles in Encyclopedias/Dictionaries

Dizionario letterario delle Opere, Appendix I-II, Milano, Bompiani, 1964-66; *Grande Enciclopedia De Agostini*, Novara, De Agostini, 1972-78 (Section Editor for English and American Literature); *Grande Dizionario Enciclopedico*, Torino, Utet, 1981; *Dizionario dei personaggi*, Torino, Utet, 2003.

Essays/Chapters in

Il Simbolismo nella letteratura americana, Firenze 1965; *Stephen Crane: A Collection of Critical Essays*, Englewood Cliffs, NJ 1967; *Italia e Stati Uniti all'epoca del Risorgimento e della guerra civile*, Firenze 1969; *F. S. Fitzgerald: A Collection of Criticism*, New York 1973; *Atti del Convegno di studi sul teatro elisabettiano*, Vicenza 1973;*Tolstoj oggi*, Firenze 1980; *Ars Majeutica*, Vicenza 1985; *Pound a Venezia*, Firenze 1985; *La fortuna di Virgilio*, Napoli 1987; *The Legacy of R. P. Blackmur*, New York 1987; *Shakespeare a Verona e nel Veneto*, Verona 1987; *Henry James e Venezia* Firenze 1987; *Science and Imagination in XVIIIth Century British Culture*, Milan 1987; *Gli Shakers*, Venezia 1987; *Leon Edel and Literary Art*, Ann Arbor, MI 1988; *Cross-Cultural Studies (1945-1985)*, Ljubljana 1988; *Hemingway e Venezia*, Firenze 1988; *American Studies in Spain*, Valencia 1988; *Gli universi del fantastico*, Firenze, 1988; *Creazione e Mal-essere*, Milano 1989; *Ritratto di Northrop Frye*, Roma 1989; *The Sweetest Impression of Life. The James Family and Italy*, New York U.P. 1990; *Die Englische und Amerikanische Kurzgeschichte*, Darmstadt 1990; *Annuario della Fondazione Schlesinger*, Lugano 1990; *G. D'Annunzio e la cultura inglese e americana*, Chieti 1990; *Problema e problemi della storia letteraria*, Roma 1990; *Browning e Venezia*, Firenze 1991; *Venezia e le lingue e letterature straniere*, Roma 1991; *Dostoevskij e la crisi dell'uomo*, Firenze

1991; *Henry James. Critical Assessments*, ed. Graham Clarke, The Banks 1991, vol. III; *Victorianism in the United States*, Amsterdam 1992; *Bologna, la cultura italiana e le letterature straniere moderne*, Ravenna 1992; *Il romanzo tra i due secoli (1880-1918)*, Roma 1993; *Imagination and the Creative Impulse in the New Literatures in English*, Amsterdam 1993; *L'Immaginario americano e Colombo*, Roma 1993; *Gli americani e l'Italia*, Milano 1993; *Struttura e sperimentazione in F.M. Ford*, Firenze 1994; *Semeia. Itinerari per Marcello Pagnini*, Bologna 1994; *Canada e Italia verso il Duemila: Metropoli a confronto*, Bari 1994; *Images of Central Europe in Travelogues and Fiction by North American Writers*, Tübingen 1995; *La Traduzione. Materiali (II)*, Roma, 1995; *Storia della civiltà letteraria inglese*, Torino 1996; *America ieri e oggi*, Bari 1997; *La pittura in Europa. La pittura inglese*, Milano 1998; *Red Badges of Courage. Wars and Conflicts in American Literature*, Roma 1999; *Attraversare gli oceani. Da Giovanni Caboto al Canada multiculturale*, Venezia 1999; *Venetian Views, Venetian Blinds. English Fantasies of Venice*, Amsterdam 1999; *Billy Budd di Benjamin Britten*, Venezia 2000; *William Faulkner in Venice*, Venezia 2000; *The Paths of Multiculturalism. Travel Writings and Postcolonialism*, Lisboa 2000; *Before Peggy Guggenheim. Americam Women Art Collectors*, Venezia 2001; *Ruskin e Venezia: La bellezza in declino*, Firenze 2001; *Innovation and Continuity in English Studies*, Frankfurt 2001; *La nascita del concetto moderno di traduzione*, Roma 2001; *Italy and Canadian Culture*, Udine 2001; *Il ritratto dell'artista nel romanzo tra '700 e '900*, Roma 2002; *Ford Madox Ford and 'The Republic of Letters'*, Bologna 2002; *Lezioni di metodo*, Vicenza 2002; *The Reception of Virginia Woolf in Europe*, London 2002; *La porta d'Oriente: Viaggi e poesia*, Lisboa 2002; *Le metamorfosi del ritratto*, Firenze 2002; *La trama nel romanzo del '900*, Roma 2002; *Venezia nella sua storia: morti e rinascite*, Venezia 2003; *William Harvey e la scoperta della circolazione sanguigna*, Venezia 2004; *Libertà di espressione e diritti umani per gli scrittori nel mondo*, Pen Club italiano 2005; *An Academic and Friendly Masala*, Venezia 2005; *Libertà d'espressione, potere e terrorismo*, Pen Club italiano, 2006; *The Reception of Henry James in Europe*, London 2006; *Quale America? Soglie e culture di un continente*, Venezia 2007; *Gondola Signore Gondola. Venice in 20th Century American Poetry*, Venezia 2007; *Il sogno delle Americhe*. Padova 2007; *L'Oriente. Storia di una figura nelle arti occidentali (1700-2000)*, Roma 2007; *Nabokov. Un'eredità letteraria*, Venezia 2007. *Peccato che sia una sgualdrina*, Vicenza 2008; *The*

Protean Forms of Life Writing. Auto/Biographies in English, 1680-2000, Napoli 2008; *Byron e l'Europa / L'Europa di Byron*, Verona 2008; *Le passioni in scena*, Roma 2008; *Civilizing America*, Heidelberg 2009; *A partire da Venezia: eredità, transiti, orizzonti* (CDRom), Venezia, 2009; *Comparaciones en vertical*, Venezia 2009; *Drops of Light Coalescing*, Udine 2010; *Ernest Hemingway and the Geography of Memory*, Kent (OH), 2010; *Contro Palladio*, Mariano del Friuli (GO), 2010; *L'eroe e l'ostacolo. Forme dell'avventura nella narrativa occidentale*, Roma 2010; *Venezia. Immagine, futuro, realtà e problemi*, Venezia 2011; *Indigeno e foresto*, Vicenza 2011; *English Past and Present*, Frankfurt am Mail, 2012; *Confluenze intertestuali*, Napoli 2012; *Henry James and the Poetics of Duplicity*, Cambridge 2013; *La critica letteraria e il 'Corriere della Sera'*, Milano, 2013.

Essays and Reviews in

Le lingue straniere, Letterature moderne, Convivium, Aut-Aut, Il Verri, Studi Americani, Annali di Ca' Foscari, Mosaic, AS: AIN, John Berryman Studies, Libri nuovi, La Fiera Letteraria, Ateneo Veneto, Twentieth Century Literature, Revue de Littérature Comparée, Studies in American Fiction, The Cambridge Quarterly, Anglistica pisana, South Central Review, Letterature d'America, The Hudson Review, Modern Fiction Studies, Comparatistica, EtruriaOggi, RAS Journal, Africa America Asia Australia, American Studies in Europe, Rivista di Studi Canadesi, L'analisi linguistica e letteraria, Quaderni di Insula, I Quaderni del Teatro Olimpico, Memoria di Shakespeare, Atti dell'Istituto Veneto di Scienze, Lettere ed Arti, Studi comparatistici, The Henry James Review, Finnegans, l'Erasmo, New York Times Book Review.

Articles in newspapers

Il Corriere della Sera, 1969-2012: 540 items.
Il Giornale di Vicenza, 1952-2012: 80 items.
Il Resto del Carlino 1966-1969: 31 items.
Il Gazzettino, La Nuova Venezia, L'Indice, Panorama, London Sunday Times, etc: 30 items